CURRENT TOPICS IN

DEVELOPMENTAL BIOLOGY

VOLUME 19

PALATE DEVELOPMENT: NORMAL AND ABNORMAL CELLULAR AND MOLECULAR ASPECTS

CONTRIBUTORS

FRED G. BIDDLE

JOSEPH J. BONNER

LINDA L. BRINKLEY

MARK W. J. FERGUSON

MICHELE P. GARBARINO

ALLEN S. GOLDMAN

ROBERT M. GREENE

ROBERT I. GROVE

LAWRENCE S. HONIG

CHUNG S. KIM

JOYCE MORRIS-WIMAN

ROBERT M. PRATT

RAVINDRA M. SHAH

HAROLD C. SLAVKIN

MICHEL J. J. VEKEMANS

ELIZABETH L. WEE

ERNEST F. ZIMMERMAN

CURRENT TOPICS IN
DEVELOPMENTAL BIOLOGY

EDITED BY

A. A. MOSCONA

CUMMINGS LIFE SCIENCE CENTER
THE UNIVERSITY OF CHICAGO
CHICAGO, ILLINOIS

ALBERTO MONROY

STAZIONE ZOOLOGICA
NAPLES, ITALY

VOLUME 19

PALATE DEVELOPMENT:
NORMAL AND ·ABNORMAL CELLULAR
AND MOLECULAR ASPECTS

VOLUME EDITOR

ERNEST F. ZIMMERMAN

CHILDREN'S HOSPITAL RESEARCH FOUNDATION
CINCINNATI, OHIO

1984

ACADEMIC PRESS, INC.

(Harcourt Brace Jovanovich, Publishers)

Orlando   San Diego   New York   London
Toronto   Montreal   Sydney   Tokyo

ACADEMIC PRESS, INC.
Orlando, Florida 32887

United Kingdom Edition published by
ACADEMIC PRESS, INC. (LONDON) LTD.
24/28 Oval Road, London NW1 7DX

LIBRARY OF CONGRESS CATALOG CARD NUMBER: 66-28604
ISBN 0-12-153119-8

PRINTED IN THE UNITED STATES OF AMERICA

84 85 86 87   9 8 7 6 5 4 3 2 1

CONTENTS

CHAPTER 1. Morphogenesis of a Complex Organ: Vertebrate
Palate Development
HAROLD C. SLAVKIN

CHAPTER 2. Role of Extracellular Matrices in Palatal Shelf Closure
LINDA L. BRINKLEY AND JOYCE MORRIS-WIMAN

CHAPTER 3. Role of Neurotransmitters in Palate Development
ERNEST F. ZIMMERMAN AND ELIZABETH L. WEE

CHAPTER 4.   Role of Cyclic AMP, Prostaglandins, and
              Catecholamines during Normal Palate Development
              ROBERT M. GREENE AND MICHELE P. GARBARINO

CHAPTER 5.   Role of Glucocorticoids and Epidermal Growth Factor
              in Normal and Abnormal Palatal Development
              ROBERT M. PRATT, CHUNG S. KIM,
              AND ROBERT I. GROVE

CHAPTER 6.   Morphological, Cellular, and Biochemical Aspects of
              Differentiation of Normal and Teratogen-Treated
              Palate in Hamster and Chick Embryos
              RAVINDRA M. SHAH

CHAPTER 7. Epithelial–Mesenchymal Interactions during
Vertebrate Palatogenesis
MARK W. J. FERGUSON AND LAWRENCE S. HONIG

CHAPTER 8. Genetics of Palate Development
MICHEL J. J. VEKEMANS AND FRED G. BIDDLE

CHAPTER 9. The *H-2* Genetic Complex, Dexamethasone-Induced
Cleft Palate, and Other Craniofacial Anomalies
JOSEPH J. BONNER

CONTRIBUTORS

Numbers in parentheses indicate the pages on which the authors' contributions begin.

FRED G. BIDDLE, *Departments of Pediatrics and Medical Biochemistry, Alberta Children's Hospital Research Centre, University of Calgary, Calgary, Alberta T2T 5C7, Canada* (165)

JOSEPH J. BONNER, *Dental Research Institute, Center for the Health Sciences, University of California, Los Angeles, California 90024* (193)

LINDA L. BRINKLEY, *Department of Anatomy and Cell Biology, University of Michigan Medical School, Ann Arbor, Michigan 48109* (17)

MARK W. J. FERGUSON,* *Department of Anatomy, Medical Biology Centre, The Queen's University of Belfast, Belfast BT9 7BL, Northern Ireland* (137)

MICHELE P. GARBARINO, *Department of Anatomy, Daniel Baugh Institute, Thomas Jefferson University, Philadelphia, Pennsylvania 19107* (65)

ALLEN S. GOLDMAN, *Section of Teratology, Division of Child Development and Rehabilitation, The Children's Hospital of Philadelphia, and Department of Pediatrics, University of Pennsylvania School of Medicine, Philadelphia, Pennsylvania 19104* (217)

ROBERT M. GREENE, *Department of Anatomy, Daniel Baugh Institute, Thomas Jefferson University, Philadelphia, Pennsylvania 19107* (65)

ROBERT I. GROVE, *Laboratory of Reproductive and Developmental Toxicology, National Institute of Environmental Health Sciences, National Institutes of Health, Research Triangle Park, North Carolina 27709* (81)

*Present address: Department of Basic Dental Science, University of Manchester Dental School, Manchester M15 6FH, England.

LAWRENCE S. HONIG,* *Laboratory for Developmental Biology, Andrus Gerontology Center, University of Southern California, Los Angeles, California 90089* (137)

CHUNG S. KIM, *Laboratory of Reproductive and Developmental Toxicology, National Institute of Environmental Health Sciences, National Institutes of Health, Research Triangle Park, North Carolina 27709* (81)

JOYCE MORRIS-WIMAN, *Department of Anatomy and Cell Biology, University of Michigan Medical School, Ann Arbor, Michigan 48109* (17)

ROBERT M. PRATT, *Laboratory of Reproductive and Developmental Toxicology, National Institute of Environmental Health Sciences, National Institutes of Health, Research Triangle Park, North Carolina 27709* (81)

RAVINDRA M. SHAH, *Department of Oral Biology, Faculty of Dentistry, The University of British Columbia, Vancouver, British Columbia V6T 1Z7, Canada* (103)

HAROLD C. SLAVKIN, *Laboratory for Developmental Biology and Department of Basic Sciences, School of Dentistry, University of Southern California, Los Angeles, California 90089* (1)

MICHEL J. J. VEKEMANS, *McGill University-Montreal Children's Hospital Research Institute, Centre for Human Genetics, and Departments of Pathology, Pediatrics, and Biology, McGill University, Montreal, Quebec H3H 1P3, Canada* (165)

ELIZABETH L. WEE, *Division of Cell Biology, Children's Hospital Research Foundation, Cincinnati, Ohio 45229* (37)

ERNEST F. ZIMMERMAN, *Division of Cell Biology, Children's Hospital Research Foundation, Cincinnati, Ohio 45229* (37)

*Present address: Department of Anatomy and Cell Biology, University of Miami School of Medicine, Miami, Florida 33101.

PREFACE

Much of the impetus for studying development of the palate is derived from observations that its perturbation by environmental agents produces the congenital malformation, cleft palate. In order to understand how such agents (termed teratogens) produce the birth defect, much effort has been expended in understanding the developmental mechanisms involved in palatogenesis. The objectives of this volume of *Current Topics in Developmental Biology* are to describe both current research in secondary palate development during the time of growth, reorientation, and fusion of the palate and research on the mechanisms of some selected teratogens that cause cleft palate.

In some ways, it is not surprising that teratogens easily produce cleft palate—at least in experimental animals. As indicated by Slavkin in his detailed conspectus (Chapter 1), the palate is an example of a complex morphogenetic field. Thus, teratogens that perturb palate morphogenesis would produce the morphological defect. The expression of this defect may be exacerbated by the dramatic reorientation process that occurs during development; any delay could render the elevating shelves incapable of touching, and clefting could therefore occur. Furthermore, there is a time-dependent process of "epithelial fusion," in which the cell surface epithelium located at the medial aspects of the two reoriented shelves secrete adhesive glycoconjugates and the epithelial cells subsequently undergo "programmed cell death." A delay in reorientation may thereby render the medial aspects of the shelves incapable of normal fusion. As the developing head enlarges, the opposing shelves may pull apart, and a cleft ensues. Such a combined scenario would predispose the developing palate to a cleft. In addition, neural crest-derived tissue such as the developing palate could be more sensitive to teratogens.

Chapter 2 by Brinkley and Morris-Wiman describes the role of extracellular matrix components in palate morphogenesis and the role that epithelium may play in directing the intrinsic force to reorient the shelf upward. Chapters 3–7 cover modulators of palate development:

Zimmerman and Wee (Chapter 3) describe neurotransmitters that may be involved in palate reorientation and development, and Greene and Garbarino (Chapter 4) discuss prostaglandins and catecholamines as potential effectors. Pratt, Kim, and Grove (Chapter 5) then discuss glucocorticoids and epidermal growth factor as hormones that may be necessary for normal palate development; they introduce the argument that raising levels of normal hormones such as glucocorticoids could thus produce teratogenic responses. The role of mesenchyme in regulating palate epithelial differentiation is considered by Ferguson and Honig (Chapter 7), as well as by Shah (Chapter 6). Glucocorticoid-induced cleft palate remains the focus of much research. Vekemans and Biddle (Chapter 8) present the genetics of palate development, employing glucocorticoid-induced cleft palate in inbred mice as the model system with which to explore this problem. Bonner (Chapter 9) then follows with a discussion of the genes associated with the major histocompatibility complex (*H-2*) that influence susceptibility to glucocorticoid-induced cleft palate in the mouse. Goldman (Chapter 10) surveys biochemical mechanisms involved in glucocorticoid teratogenesis: arachidonic acid release, with subsequent prostaglandin synthesis, is the purported site of teratogenic lesion. Interestingly, evidence is presented that phenytoin may exert a similar response through the glucocorticoid receptor.

Ernest F. Zimmerman

CURRENT TOPICS IN

DEVELOPMENTAL BIOLOGY

VOLUME 19

PALATE DEVELOPMENT: NORMAL AND ABNORMAL CELLULAR AND MOLECULAR ASPECTS

CHAPTER 1

MORPHOGENESIS OF A COMPLEX ORGAN: VERTEBRATE PALATE DEVELOPMENT

Harold C. Slavkin

LABORATORY FOR DEVELOPMENTAL BIOLOGY
AND DEPARTMENT OF BASIC SCIENCES
SCHOOL OF DENTISTRY, UNIVERSITY OF SOUTHERN CALIFORNIA
LOS ANGELES, CALIFORNIA

I. Introduction

The developing secondary palate is an attractive system for morphogenetic studies. Whereas much less complex than development of the whole embryo, palate morphogenesis provides examples of fundamental problems found within developmental biology. During early stages of development, for example, epithelial–mesenchymal interactions between oral ectoderm and adjacent cranial neural crest-derived ectomesenchyme result in the determination of bilateral palate morphogenetic fields. Determination of polarity in the secondary palate is observed along the anteroposterior axis. Interactions between cells,

1

tissues, and the extracellular matrix milieu result in the induction, determination, and expression of a number of phenotypes, including ectodermally derived nasal, oral, and medial edge palatal epithelia, and ectomesenchyme-derived chondrogenesis, osteogenesis, and fibrogenesis. The detection of glucocorticoid receptors within palatal ectomesenchyme cells suggests possibilities for hormone regulation of cell differentiation. Programmed cell death of medial edge epithelia during mammalian palate fusion is a fascinating developmental problem. Phylogenetic differences among Reptilia, Aves, and Mammalia offer significant developmental questions for the craniofacial developmental biologists. Finally, because normal palate shape and differentiated patterns are well defined, deviations produced by "experiments of nature" or experimental investigations are readily recognized and scored, thereby indicating that palate morphogenesis is an excellent system for investigations of form and pattern in development. Moreover, control of palate form and pattern appears to be particularly sensitive to genetic and/or environmental disturbances, resulting in the high frequency of congenital palatal abnormalities which provide research in this field with important biomedical significance.

In this chapter, the author attempts to indicate several issues of interest to developmental biologists. The rapid and prolific activities within craniofacial developmental biology are too extensive to be cited here in any detail. Therefore, the intent is to envisage the panorama of research, so appropriately highlighted in the following chapters, and to indicate a few problems which now seem accessible to investigation and important toward an understanding of craniofacial developmental biology.

II. The Secondary Palate as a Morphogenetic Field

During embryogenesis, a region within the vertebrate organism within which development of the parts proceeds in relation to their position in the whole embryo, and therefore with a capacity for regulation if the size of the field is reduced or increased, is termed a *morphogenetic field* (see original discussions by Aniken, 1929; Child, 1941; Driesch, 1891; Harrison, 1898; Spemann, 1938). Whereas morphogenetic fields have been identified and analyzed during limb, feather, skin, hair, and tooth morphogenesis (for example, see Bryant, 1978; Fallon *et al.*, 1983; Lumsden, 1979; Osborn, 1978; Saunders, 1977; Summerbell *et al.*, 1973; Wolpert, 1969), little information is available regarding the determination of the presumptive region from which secondary palatal processes normally develop. When, where, and how the palatal morphogenetic field develops are questions remaining to be addressed.

III. Determination of Polarity in the Palate

During embryogenesis, polarities are exhibited by a number of structures within the developing secondary palate. The form and pattern of palatal bone development, for example, clearly reflects polarity. What tissue(s) provide the morphogenetic signals for palatal osteogenesis? Is there a gradient of postitional information within ectodermally derived ectomesenchyme-derived phenotypes? Does this putative gradient of positional information result in the determination and differentiation of the various structures (i.e., cells, tissues, extracellular matrices) found within the developing secondary palate? Direct experimental information is not yet available to pursue these intriguing developmental questions.

Palatal morphogenesis involves precise positioning of cells and their extracellular products in three-dimensional space. During early palatogenesis, the epithelia consist of cells arranged in a nearly planar two-dimensional order. The epithelial cells are ionically and metabolically coupled through lateral specialized intercellular junctions. The apical cell poles contain cell surface specializations oriented toward the free surface, whereas the basal cell pole contains the nucleus and a continuous basal lamina. In juxtaposition to the basal lamina are various subclones or aggregates of palatal ectomesenchyme. A major feature, therefore, of palatal morphogenesis should be a series of stepwise processes in which cells become oriented and produce oriented extracellular matrix constituents. Immunodetection of intracellular intermediate filament gene products (e.g., actin, filamin, vinmentin, symenin, tubulin, keratins), as well as extracellular matrix constituents (i.e., proteoglycans, osteonectin, chondronectin, fibronectin, osteocalcin, various types of collagens), might provide a methodology to detect and analyze the changing polarized patterns during palatogenesis.

IV. Morphogenesis of the Secondary Palate: Cellular and Tissue Interactions

A number of descriptive embryological studies are now available which provide macroscopic and microscopic observations of vertebrate secondary palate morphogenesis (for example, see Fraser, 1961, 1970; Koch and Smiley, 1981; Melnick and Shields, 1982; Patten, 1961;

Pourtois, 1972; Slavkin, 1979; Stark, 1961; Trasler and Fraser, 1977). It is testimony to the fascination of secondary palate morphogenesis that so many excellent scientists have become interested in craniofacial developmental biology, but also testimony to its complexity that so much fundamental information, especially at the cellular and molecular levels, remains to be discovered and that none of the hypotheses regarding palate morphogenetic control mechanisms have as yet been established with certainty.

A. EPITHELIAL PHENOTYPES

As the secondary palate primordia develop, at least three ectodermally derived phenotypes can be distinguished on the basis of their characteristic cytological features: (1) nasal epithelia with specialized apical cilia, (2) oral epithelia with progressive stages of stratification and keratinization, and (3) medial edge palatal epithelia which participate in the fusion of the two mammalian palatal processes along the midline prior to their "programmed cell death." A continuous basal lamina separates these three types of epithelia from the adjacent palatal ectomesenchymal cells and their extracellular matrix constituents. Detailed analyses of the similarities and differences in these epithelial biochemical phenotypes have not as yet been reported.

B. ECTOMESENCHYME PHENOTYPES

During palatogenesis, a number of cranial neural crest-derived ectomesenchyme phenotypes appear. Whereas the sequence of ectomesenchyme cell differentiation into a number of cell types has been described (e.g., chondrogenesis, osteogenesis, fibrogenesis), specific determinative events have not been identified. Prior to overt cytodifferentiation of specific cell types (e.g., chondrocytes, osteocytes, fibrocytes), palatal ectomesenchyme cells appear to form specialized intercellular junctions (i.e., gap junctions), appear to contain oriented contractile elements, contain glucocorticoid receptor-binding proteins, and seem to be responsive to neurotropic substances (see Pratt and Salomon, 1980; Zimmerman et al., 1981). The essential control of initial palatal morphogenesis would appear to reside in intrinsic properties of cranial neural crest cells (see Johnston and Listgarten, 1972; Le Douarin, 1980; Noden, 1975, 1982), their ectomesenchyme progeny, and the extracellular microenvironment.

V. Epithelial–Mesenchymal Interactions

Following the primary induction processes associated with neurulation during early embryogenesis, a number of secondary inductive processes have been described which are often associated with complex organ formation. During craniofacial development, ectodermally derived epithelial and cranial neural crest-derived ectomesenchymal tissues interact and produce a number of intriguing morphogenetic processes such as mandibular and maxillary morphogenesis, salivary gland development, tooth organogenesis, and secondary palate morphogenesis (see recent discussions by Brownell *et al.*, 1981; Ferguson, 1981; Ferguson *et al.*, 1984a,b; Grobstein, 1967; Hall, 1980, 1982; Hata and Slavkin, 1978; Hay, 1981; Kollar, 1983; Ruch *et al.*, 1982; Slavkin, 1974, 1978; Slavkin *et al.*, 1977; Thesleff and Hurmerinta, 1981).

Secondary embryonic inductions or epithelial–mesenchymal interactions are defined as tissue interactions which result in profound changes in one or both of the tissue interactants. These changes do not occur in the absence of epithelial–mesenchymal interactions. A major problem in developmental biology remains regarding (1) the tissue source for instructive or inductive information, (2) the physicochemical properties of the instructive signal(s), (3) the mode of inductive information transfer between dissimilar tissue types, (4) the process by which a responding tissue receives inductive information, and (5) how the responding tissue becomes irreversibly determined for a specific phenotype as a direct consequence of these heterotypic tissue interactions.

A. Intercellular Transfer of Developmental Information in Homologous and Heterologous Tissue Recombinants Using Serumless, Chemically Defined Media in Organ Culture

It is well established that a number of organ primordia can be successfully cultured *in vitro* and demonstrate both cytodifferentiation and morphogenesis comparable to *in situ* developmental patterns. These epidermal organs can be dissociated into epithelial and mesenchymal tissues, which do not express histogenesis when cultured as tissue isolates; however, when these tissues are recombined they proceed to differentiate and express the morphogenetic patterns characteristic for the particular organ rudiment.

Whereas microenvironments have been identified which are permissive for the expression of cytodifferentiation and morphogenesis *in vitro*, these studies have relied upon supplementation using fetal calf sera, embryonic chick extracts, and horse sera. In the last few years, however, methods have been described which resulted in cytodifferentiation as well as morphogenesis using serumless, chemically defined media (see discussion Slavkin *et al.*, 1982b).

Recently, our laboratory showed that a serumless, chemically defined medium was permissive for the initiation, differentiation, and morphogenesis of tooth organs (Yamada *et al.*, 1980a,b). Theiler stage 25 mouse embryos provide mandibular first molar tooth organs which are at the cap stage of odontogenesis (Theiler, 1972). Using a modified Trowell method, tooth organs were placed on Millipore filter disks which were then placed upon stainless steel grids over 700 μl medium within Grobstein Falcon dishes. The explants on each filter disk were then covered with 1% Bactoagar to minimize ectopic keratinization. Care was taken to ensure high humidity in the Grobstein dishes. The serumless and chemically defined medium, permissive for both dentinogenesis and amelogenesis under these experimental conditions, consisted of Eagle's Minimum Essential Medium (MEM) supplemented with 2.05 mM L-glutamine, 0.66 mM L-glycine, 0.56 mM vitamin C, and 15 mM HEPES buffer, pH 7.4 at 37.5°C with optimal humidity. The BGJ medium modified by Fitton-Jackson is also permissive. The culture medium level is adjusted at the initiation of the culture to wet the filter disk and agar overlay. The medium was changed every 2 days. During each such period the culture pH dropped from 7.3 to about 7.1.

The critical point is that cap stage tooth organs are intrinsically determined to develop into teeth which contain highly differentiated cell types (i.e., odontoblasts and ameloblasts) and which also contain highly differentiated extracellular matrices (i.e., dentine and enamel matrices). Exogenous humoral factors, for example, derived from the vasculature or nervous system, are not required. What are absolutely required are reciprocal, close-range, tissue interactions between epithelial and adjacent ectomesenchymal tissues. Steroid or polypeptide hormones are not required for either dentinogenesis or amelogenesis. In addition to the results obtained for culturing various mammalian cap stage tooth organs, we have also successfully cultured embryonic limb buds, mandibular processes, and palatal processes from reptilian, avian, and mammalian species using serumless, chemically defined media (Ferguson *et al.*, 1984a,b; Slavkin *et al.*, 1982a,b; see discussion by Ferguson and Honig, this volume). Instructive metabolic signals appear to be transferred between ectodermally derived epithelia and adjacent mesenchyme. The chemical nature of these signals and the mechanisms for transfer of this developmental information are not known despite nearly eight decades of research (see Maderson, 1983; Needham, 1966; and Spemann, 1938).

B. PALATAL ECTOMESENCHYME TISSUE IS THE SOURCE FOR INDUCTIVE INFORMATION

Instructive or embryonic inductive interactions are exemplified by investigations of the vertebrate integumentary derivatives. Studies of epidermal derivatives have demonstrated that the epithelial biochemical and structural phenotype is dependent upon ectomesenchyme-derived instructive signals (see recent reviews by Dhouailly and Sengel, 1983; Sengel and Dhouailly, 1977). Epithelial–mesenchymal tissue recombinations between skin epidermal tissues representing three classes of vertebrates—Reptilia, Aves, and Mammalia—have provided evidence that the specific quality of reptilian scales, avian feathers, and mammalian hair is determined by the epidermal genotype repertoire, whereas the regional specification for morphogenesis requires several dermis-derived instructive signals (Dhouailly and Sengel, 1983).

Comparable results have been obtained for three classes of vertebrate secondary palate development using *in vitro* methods and serumless, chemically defined medium. Heterospecific epithelial–mesenchymal tissue recombinations between palatal tissues from alligator, chick or quail, and mouse embryos demonstrated that the histological specificity and function of the medial edge epithelial tissue were induced by regional ectomesenchyme specificity (Ferguson *et al.*, 1984b).

In the American alligator (*Alligator mississippiensis*), during fusion of the lateral palatal processes, medial edge epithelial cells do not demonstrate programmed cell death but rather illustrate a loss of epithelial cell polarity and the subsequent formation of mesenchyme–like cells (Ferguson, 1981; Ferguson *et al.*, 1984b). In contrast, chick or quail medial edge epithelia differentiate into a keratinized epidermis covering the avian lateral palatal processes, which normally do not fuse (Koch and Smiley, 1981; Shah and Crawford, 1980). The mouse medial edge epithelial cells fuse along the midline during palatal fusion and subsequently express programmed cell death (Greene and Pratt, 1976; Portois, 1972; Waterman *et al.*, 1973). In reciprocal epithelial–mesenchymal heterospecific recombinations *in vitro,* the expressed epithelial phenotype was complementary to the regional specificity of the ectomesenchyme; chick epithelia when combined with either alligator or mouse palatal ectomesenchyme differentiated into medial edge epithelia complementary to either the alligator or mouse phenotypes and participated in palatal shelf fusion *in vitro* (Ferguson *et al.*, 1984b).

VI. Hormonal Control of Developmental Processes

Several groups of steroids in animals have been found to function as long-range intercellular instructive signals which mediate a few examples of epithelial–mesenchymal interactions. These steroids include the female hormones (estrogens and progestins), the male sex hormones (androgens), and the glucocorticoids. Examples of developing epithelial–mesenchymal interacting systems regulated by these steroids include the chick oviduct, mammary gland, prostate gland, vaginal mucosa, hydrocortisone induction of glutamine synthetase in the embryonic neural retina, and induction of type II epithelial cells with production of pulmonary surfactant during lung morphogenesis (see discussion by Chan and O'Malley, 1976; Goldman, 1973; O'Malley *et al.*, 1977; Sarkar and Moscona, 1977; Sugimoto *et al.*, 1976).

A. MOLECULAR BASIS OF STEROID ACTION ON GENE EXPRESSION

Remarkable progress has recently been made toward understanding how a specific steroid induces differential gene expression in a responsive epithelial tissue. Estrogen causes oviduct epithelium to proliferate and differentiate into three morphologically different cell types: (1) tubular gland cells, (2) ciliated cells, and (3) goblet cells (Tsai and O'Malley, 1977). In addition to the induction of these morphological phenotypes, estrogen induces the biosynthesis of ovalbumin, ovomucoid, conalbumin, lysozyme, and several other gene products. Immunofluorescent antibody microscopy of oviduct sections reveals that all of these proteins accumulate in the same tubular gland cells. Protein synthesis and secretion are critically dependent upon the estrogen stimulus. In estrogen-induced tubular gland cells, for example, both ovalbumin genes present in the diploid genome produce 12 molecules of processed ovalbumin mRNA per minute, each of which can be translated up to 50,000 times, so that ovalbumin can represent nearly 60% of the total protein synthesized in the estrogen-induced oviduct epithelial tubular gland cells (see review by Luckner, 1982).

How does the estrogen inducer mediate *de novo* ovalbumin transcription? Exogenous steroids penetrate the plasma membranes of any eucaryotic cell by means of simple diffusion but in target cells bind to specific, high-affinity receptor proteins (e.g., ~10,000 molecules per cell) (Gorski and Gannon, 1976; Williams, 1974). These steroid receptor proteins bind steroids tightly with dissociation constants of 10^{-10} M. Note that the avidity of the steroid for the receptor is a function of developmental stages, chronological age, and sex, so that a range of values from 10^{-9} to 10^{-11} M should be considered.

Intracellular cytoplasmic steroid–receptor complexes form, and some of these appear to be translocated to the nucleus. The estradiol–receptor complexes, for example, attach to acceptor proteins (e.g., nonhistone chromosomal proteins) which are constitutents of chromatin.

The level of nuclear-bound estrogen receptors approximates saturation within 20 minutes (O'Malley *et al.*, 1977). The responsiveness of the tubular gland epithelial cells to the inductive effects of exogenous estrogen stimuli may be connected with an alteration of the DNA methylation pattern (Mandel and Chambon, 1979); distinct sites may be undermethylated in those tissues competent to respond to steroid-induced differential gene expression. Undermethylation of distinct sites representing the ovalbumin gene domain, for example, apparently reflects the "state of determination" for subsequent transcription of ovalbumin mRNAs. There is no pre-ovalbumin (i.e., the translated ovalbumin polypeptide appears to contain a "signal peptide sequence" in the center of the total amino acid sequence) (Lingappa *et al.*, 1979). Translation of ovalbumin requires 8.5 minutes (Tsai and O'Malley, 1977). Subsequently, the protein is packaged in vesicles or secretory granules, which are then translocated via microtubules/microfilaments and fuse with the plasma membrane for secretion by exocytosis. Therefore, ovalbumin biosynthesis is almost completely regulated by steroid hormones at the level of transcription.

B. MOLECULAR BASIS OF STEROID-INDUCED CRANIOFACIAL MALFORMATIONS

The paradigm for steroid-induced differential gene expression in the estrogen-regulated oviduct system provides an example of positive gene regulation. Of course, clinical evidence for postnatal individuals shows a number of negative regulations of metabolism under glucocorticoid influence, such as reduced DNA, RNA, and protein synthesis (see review by Stevenson, 1977). Further, an interesting steroid dose-dependent response has been demonstrated during embryonic pancreas morphogenesis using concentrations of dexamethasone (Dex) ranging from 10^{-5} to 10^{-3} M (Rall *et al.*, 1977). Increased concentrations of Dex reduced or inhibited gene expression whereas decreased Dex concentrations (10^{-11} to 10^{-13} M) significantly stimulated pancreatic acinar cell protein synthesis (Rall *et al.*, 1977). From these few examples it becomes readily apparent that the localization, distribution, concentration, and competence or responsiveness of the target cell type must be considered when analyzing steroid-induced clefting. Further, it must be acknowledged that a number of different steroid and steroid-like molecules can compete for the same receptor binding proteins. Abnormal competitive binding in specific cell types, including the medial edge epithelia, could result in cell level responses ranging from cell death to overt changes in phenotype in which epithelia become mesenchyme-like cells.

C. Genetic Susceptibility to Steroid-Induced Congenital
   Craniofacial Malformations

Over three decades ago a mouse animal model was identified which
indicated genetic differences between two murine strains in glucocorticoid-induced cleft palate (Fraser and Fainstat, 1951). Possible genetic differences between the highly susceptible A/J strain and the more
resistant C57BL/6J strain might include rates of cell division, numbers and kinetics of cranial neural crest cells differentiating into craniofacial phenotypes, cell size, rates of cellular and extracellular matrix growth, patterns of cell aggregation, cell adhesion, ability of
hyaluronate to bind water, rates of extracellular matrix constituent
turnover, maternally derived nutrients such as glucose for overall
growth, patterns of vascularization, and neurogenesis (see Fraser,
1961, 1970; Pourtois, 1972; Slavkin, 1979). One promising lead to this
question came from evidence which showed that the major histocompatibility complex (H-2 in mouse) haplotype appeared to confer relative susceptibility or resistance to steroid-induced cleft palate; H-2^a or
H-2^k murine strains being susceptible and H-2^b strains being resistant
(Bonner and Slavkin, 1975). Moreover, the maternal haplotype was
found to be a major determinant of the frequency of cleft palate produced following glucocorticoid administration between 11 and 14 days
gestation (Biddle and Fraser, 1977; Bonner and Slavkin, 1975; Bonner
and Tyan, 1983; Melnick et al., 1981; Slavkin, 1980).

What is the nature of H-2-regulated susceptibility? Which phenotypes of the total phenotypes are regulated by H-2 genes? What
genes in addition to H-2 might be involved? Are there temporal and
spatial issues related to the expression of H-2 genes during embryonic
and fetal development? At what level of the biological hierarchy do
glucocorticoids influence cleft palate formation? Are the steroid effects
directly upon maternal metabolic activities, or do they act directly
upon the embryonic activities?

Since in target tissues steroids form specific steroid–receptor complexes which can interact with the genome, resulting in activation of
differential transcription and the appearance of a unique biochemical
phenotype, relative susceptibility to glucocorticoid-induced cleft palate
may be mediated by differences in either maternal or embryonic
glucocorticoid receptor proteins. This hypothesis has been tested by
several investigators who demonstrated that glucocorticoid receptor
proteins are present in palatal processes as early as 11 days gestation,
and the susceptible mouse strain palatal ectomesenchyme cells contain
approximately twice the amount of saturable dexamethasone receptors

as do the more resistant strain cells (i.e., A/J versus C57BL/6J) (Goldman *et al.*, 1977; Pratt and Salomon, 1980; Salomon and Pratt, 1976; Salomon *et al.*, 1978). These investigators suggest that genes within the *H-2* locus or adjacent to this locus appear to encode for the glucocorticoid receptor-binding proteins. Perhaps secondary palate morphogenesis, especially the ectomesenchyme–epithelial interactions, may be mediated by long-range humoral influences (i.e., corticoids) analogous to steroid influences upon mammary gland mesenchyme (Kratochwil and Schwartz, 1976) and upon salivary and urogenital mesenchymes (see recent review by Cunha *et al.*, 1983). However, if, when, and how hormones and hormone-like substances regulate normal and abnormal secondary palate morphogenesis remain provocative and as yet unanswered questions. These topics are further discussed by Pratt *et al.*, Vekemans and Biddle, Bonner, and Goldman in subsequent chapters of this volume.

VII. Prospectus

Vertebrate palate development is a paradigm for understanding the morphogenesis of a complex organ, and consequently, during the last decade there has been a keen interest in craniofacial genetics and developmental biology (see summary in Slavkin, 1983). What follows is an overview, introducing the author's bias, of the status and research direction regarding several developmental problems in secondary palate morphogenesis.

First, the problem of normal secondary palatogenesis can readily be studied *in vivo* as well as *in vitro* using such disparate species as alligator, chick, mouse, rat, or hamster. These studies have clearly indicated that the developmental program for palatal morphogenesis, including the differentiation of epithelial and ectomesenchymal phenotypes, is intrinsic to the embryonic palatal tissues. Long-range humoral factors do not appear to be absolute requirements for the induction, determination, and expression of various phenotypes associated with palatogenesis. The available evidence strongly suggests that ectomesenchyme cells induce adjacent ectodermally derived epithelia to become nasal, oral, and medial edge epithelial phenotypes. The results suggest regional ectomesenchymal specificity. However, the responsive epithelia differentiate biochemically only within their genomic repertoire. The chemical nature of the ectomesenchyme-derived instructive signals is not known. The mode of transmission of these inductive signals is not known. The molecular nature of epithelial responsiveness or competence to receive these inductive signals is not

known. How epithelial tissues receive ectomesenchyme-derived signals and how this putative information is translated into "second messenger" processes which can directly effect differential gene expression
are also not known.

Second, and somewhat paradoxical, are the results showing a genetic basis for steroid-induced cleft palate formation in murine strains.
The evidence implicating the *H-2* locus or related genes (i.e., the *T*
locus) demonstrates a significant association of specific alleles with
frequency of cleft palate formation. The prenatal maternal influence
seems to be a major variable in understanding the role of *H-2* genes
and glucocorticoid-induced cleft palate in mice. In contrast, the evidence implicating steroids in the processes of medial edge epithelial
differentiation, lateral palatal shelf fusion, and subsequent programmed cell death of the medial edge epithelia seems highly equiv-
ocal to this student of craniofacial biology. With the recent advent of
techniques which permit investigations of alligator, chick, quail, and
mouse palatal tissues *in vitro* with serumless, chemically defined medium, it should become feasible to test experimentally several hypotheses regarding the role of glucocorticoids on epithelial–mesenchymal
interactions. Of course, this is not to diminish the significance of the
role of glucocorticoids and the physiology of pregnancy *in vivo*. In regard to this problem, in particular, a number of intriguing studies are
beginning to indicate critical associations between glucocorticoids,
prostaglandins, and intermediary metabolism during embryonic
stages of mammalian pregnancy.

Third, and very interesting, are the efforts to understand how palatal shelves undergo overt morphogenesis and reorient their respective three-dimensional pattern. The newly acquired evidence suggesting neurotropic influences on contractile elements during specific
stages of embryonic and fetal palatogenesis is very promising. The
results showing critical associations between hyaluronate and the
binding of water to affect the size and shape of embryonic processes are
very significant (see discussion by Brinkley and Morris-Wiman, this
volume). However, the biosynthesis of hyaluronic acid, the mechanisms for intracellular transport and secretion, and the modes of localized extracellular degradation in palatal processes are not as yet
known.

Fourth, a number of investigators are attempting to determine the
genes which regulate development in higher organisms. It is clear that
the process of differentiation represents a sequence of events in which
cells of identical genotype develop into phenotypically distinct entities
which reflect a characteristic pattern of gene activity (e.g., estrogen-

induced ovalbumin biosynthesis in tubular gland cells of the chick oviduct). Therefore, differentiation represents a reduction in biochemical options concomitant with overt expression of, in some cases, a few unique macromolecules (e.g., preproerythroblasts differentiating into erythroblasts and the biosynthesis of hemoglobin). In contrast, extremely large segments of DNA have been identified which appear to contain gene clusters which regulate higher levels of biological organization, such as the bithorax gene complex which controls bithorax development in *Drosophila melanogaster*. This approach should be very useful toward understanding the genetic controls for craniofacial development. Significant information may be obtained from critical analysis of coordinated cell differentiation among diverse but complementary cell populations associated with palatal morphogenesis. Temporal and positional information, as well as identification of regulatory and structural genes within the craniofacial "library," appear to be imperative subjects for future study. In a somewhat different tangent, progress continues to be made in the cloning of the genes of the mouse major histocompatibility complex (*H-2* locus). Understanding the genetic organization and function of the *H-2* locus should be useful in understanding the mechanisms influencing relative susceptibility and/or resistance to steroid-induced cleft palate formation in mice.

The recent advent of specific monoclonal antibodies directed against an expanding library of antigens, recent progress and applications derived from recombinant DNA techniques, advances in cell, tissue, and organ culture methods, and the intense interest in developmental biology and genetics suggest significant progress in the years to come. However, despite my enthusiasm for the recent developments in scientific "high technology," I am reminded of the statement,

> Organic form—the architecture and texture of organisms—is better known than understood. (Paul Weiss)

ACKNOWLEDGMENTS

I wish to especially acknowledge my colleagues, Joseph Bonner, Pablo Bringas, Tina Jaskoll, Lawrence Honig, Mark Ferguson, and Michael Melnick, with whom so much was learned about normal and abnormal craniofacial development. This information, in part, was acquired through support provided by the National Institutes of Health Grants DE-02848 and DE-07006.

REFERENCES

Aniken, A. W. (1929). *Wilhelm Roux Arch. Entwicklungsmech. Org.* **114**, 549–577.
Biddle, F. G., and Fraser, F. C. (1977). *Genetics* **85**, 289–302.
Bonner, J. J., and Slavkin, H. C. (1975). *Immunogenetics* **2**, 213–218.
Bonner, J. J., and Tyan, M. L. (1983). *Genetics* **103**, 263–270.

Brownell, A. G., Bessem, C., and Slavkin, H. C. (1981). *Proc. Natl. Acad. Sci. U.S.A.* **78**, 3711–3715.

Bryant, P. J. (1978). *Birth Defects: Orig. Art. Ser.* **14**, 529–545.

Chan, L., and O'Malley, B. W. (1976). *New Engl. J. Med.* **294**, 1322–1328.

Child, C. M. (1941). "Patterns and Problems of Development." Univ. of Chicago Press, Chicago.

Cunha, G. R., Shannon, J. M., Taguchi, O., Fujii, H., and Meloy, B. A. (1983). *In* "Epithelial–Mesenchymal Interactions in Development" (R. H. Sawyer and J. F. Fallon, eds.), pp. 51–74. Praeger, New York.

Dhouailly, D., and Sengel, P. (1983). *In* "Epithelial–Mesenchymal Interactions in Development" (R. H. Sawyer and J. F. Fallon, eds.), pp. 147–162. Praeger, New York.

Driesch, H. (1891). *Z. Wiss. Zool.* **53**, 160–181.

Fallon, J. F., Rowe, D. A., Frederick, J. M., and Simandl, B. K. (1983). *In* "Epithelial–Mesenchymal Interactions in Development" (R. H. Sawyer and J. F. Fallon, eds.), pp. 3–25. Praeger, New York.

Ferguson, M. W. J. (1981). *J. Craniofac. Genet. Dev. Biol.* **1**, 123–144.

Ferguson, M. W. J., Honig, L. S., Bringas, P., and Slavkin, H. C. (1984a). *In Vitro,* in press.

Ferguson, M. W. J., Honig, L. S., and Slavkin, H. C. (1984b). *Anat. Rec.,* in press.

Fraser, F. C. (1961). *In* "Congenital Anomalies of the Face and Associated Structures" (S. Pruzansky, ed.), pp. 11–45. Thomas, Springfield.

Fraser, F. C. (1970). *Am. J. Hum. Genet.* **22**, 336–352.

Fraser, F. C., and Fainstat, T. D. (1951). *Pediatrics* **8**, 527–533.

Goldman, A. S. (1973). *In* "Hormones and Embryonic Development" (G. Raspe, ed.), pp. 17–40. Pergamon, Oxford.

Goldman, A. S., Katsumata, M., Yaffe, S. J., and Gasser, D. L. (1977). *Nature (London)* **265**, 643–645.

Gorski, J., and Gannon, F. (1976). *Annu. Rev. Physiol.* **38**, 425–450.

Greene, R. M., and Pratt, R. M. (1976). *J. Embryol. Exp. Morphol.* **36**, 225–245.

Grobstein, C. (1967). *Natl. Cancer Inst. Monogr.* **26**, 279–294.

Hall, B. K. (1980). *J. Embryol. Exp. Morphol.* **58**, 251–260.

Hall, B. K. (1982). *J. Craniofac. Genet. Dev. Biol.* **2**, 309–322.

Harrison, R. G. (1898). *Arch. Entwicklungs mech. org.* **7**, 430–485.

Hata, R. I., and Slavkin, H. C. (1978). *Proc. Natl. Acad. Sci. U.S.A.* **75**, 2790–2794.

Hay, E. D. (1981). *In* "Cell Biology of Extracellular Matrix" (E. D. Hay, ed.), pp. 379–409. Plenum, New York.

Johnston, M. C., and Listgarten, M. (1972). *In* "Developmental Aspects of Oral Biology" (H. C. Slavkin and L. A. Bavetta, eds.), pp. 55–80. Academic Press, New York.

Koch, W. E., and Smiley, G. R. (1981). *Arch. Oral Biol.* **26**, 181–187.

Kollar, E. J. (1983). *In* "Epithelial–Mesenchymal Interactions in Development" (R. H. Sawyer and J. F. Fallon, eds.), pp. 27–50. Praeger, New York.

Kratochwil, K., and Schwartz, P. (1976). *Proc. Natl. Acad. Sci. U.S.A.* **73**, 4041–4044.

LeDouarin, N. (1980). *Curr. Top. Dev. Biol.* **16**, 31–85.

Lingappa, V. R., Lingappa, J. R., and Blobel, G. (1979). *Nature (London)* **281**, 117–121.

Luckner, M. (1982). *In* "Cell Differentiation" (L. Nover, M. Luckner, and B. Pathier, eds.), pp. 305–323. Springer-Verlag, Berlin and New York.

Lumsden, A. G. S. (1979). *J. Biol. Buccale* **7**, 77–103.

Madersen, P. (1983). *In* "Epithelial–Mesenchymal Interactions in Development" (R. H. Sawyer and J. F. Fallon, eds.), pp. 215–242. Praeger, New York.

Mandel, J. L., and Chambon, P. (1979). *Nucleic Acids Res.* **7**, 2081–2103.

Melnick, M., and Shields, E. D. (1982). *In* "Clinical Dysmorphology of Oral-Facial Structures" (M. Melnick, E. D. Shields, and N. J. Burzynski, eds.), pp. 360–372. Wright, Boston.

Melnick, M., Jaskoll, T., and Slavkin, H. C. (1981). *Immunogenetics* **13**, 443–449.

Needham, J. (1966). "Biochemistry and Morphogenesis." Cambridge Univ. Press, London and New York.

Noden, D. W. (1975). *Dev. Biol.* **42**, 106–130.

Noden, D. W. (1982). *In* "Factors and Mechanisms Influencing Bone Growth" (A. D. Dixon and B. G. Sarnat, eds.), pp. 167–204. Liss, New York.

O'Malley, B. W., Towle, H. C., and Schwartz, R. J. (1977). *Annu. Rev. Genet.* **11**, 239–275.

Osborn, J. W. (1978). *In* "Development, Function and Evolution of Teeth" (P. M. Butler and K. A. Joysey, eds.), pp. 171–201. Academic Press, New York.

Patten, B. M. (1961). *In* "Congential Anomalies of the Face and Associated Structures" (S. Pruzansky, ed.), pp. 11–45. Thomas, Springfield.

Pourtois, M. (1972). *In* "Developmental Aspects of Oral Biology" (H. C. Slavkin and L. A. Bavetta, eds.), pp. 81–108. Academic Press, New York.

Pratt, R. M., and Salomon, D. S. (1980). *In* "Etiology of Cleft Lip and Cleft Palate" (D. Bixler, M. Melnick, and E. D. Shields, eds.), pp. 149–167. Liss, New York.

Rall, L., Pictet, R., Githens, S., and Rutter, W. (1977). *J. Cell Biol.* **75**, 398–409.

Ruch, J. V., Lesot, H., Karcher-Djuricic, V., Meyer, J. M., and Olive, M. (1982). *Differentiation* **21**, 7–12.

Salomon, D. S., and Pratt, R. M. (1976). *Nature (London)* **264**, 174–177.

Salomon, D. S., Zubairi, Y., and Thompson, E. B. (1978). *J. Steroid Biol. Chem.* **9**, 95–107.

Sarkar, P. K., and Moscona, A. A. (1977). *Differentiation* **7**, 75–82.

Saunders, J. W., Jr. (1977). *In* "Vertebrate Limb and Somite Morphogenesis" (D. A. Ede, J. R. Hinchliffe, and M. Balls, eds.), pp. 1–24. Cambridge Univ. Press, London and New York.

Sengel, P., and Dhovailly, D. (1977). *In* "Cell Interactions in Differentiation" (M. Karkinen-Jääskeloinen, L. Saxen, and L. Weiss, eds.), pp. 153–170. Academic Press, New York.

Shah, R. M., and Crawford, B. J. (1980). *Invest. Cell. Pathol.* **3**, 319–328.

Slavkin, H. C. (1974). *Oral Sci. Rev.* **4**, 1–36.

Slavkin, H. C. (1978). *J. Biol. Buccale* **6**, 189–204.

Slavkin, H. C. (1979). "Craniofacial Developmental Biology." Lea & Febiger, Philadelphia.

Slavkin, H. C. (1980). *In* "Etiology of Cleft Lip and Cleft Palate" (M. Melnick, D. Bixler, and E. D. Shields, eds.), pp. 121–147. Liss, New York.

Slavkin, H. C. (1983). *J. Dent. Ed.* **47**, 231–238.

Slavkin, H. C., Trump. G. N., Brownell, A. G., and Sorgente, N. (1977). *In* "Cell and Tissue Interactions" (J. W. Lash and M. M. Burger, eds.), pp. 29–46. Raven, New York.

Slavkin, H. C., Bringas, P., Cummings, E. C., and Grodin M. S. (1982a). *Calcif. Tissue Int.* **34**, 111–112.

Slavkin, H. C., Honig, L. S., and Bringas, P. (1982b). *In* "Factors and Mechanisms Influencing Bone Growth" (A. D. Dixon and B. G. Sarnat, eds.), pp. 217–228. Liss, New York.

Spemann, H. (1938). "Embryonic Development and Induction." Yale Univ. Press, New Haven, Connecticut.

Stark, R. B. (1961). In "Congenital Anomalies of the Face and Associated Structures" (S. Pruzansky, ed.), pp. 11–45. Thomas, Springfield, Illinois.

Stevenson, R. D. (1977). Lancet Jan. 29, 225–226.

Sugimoto, M., Kojima, A., and Endo, H. (1976). Dev. Growth Differ. 18, 319–327.

Summerbell, D., Lewis, J. H., and Wolpert, L. (1973). Nature (London) 244, 492–496.

Theiler, K. (1972). "The House Mouse." Springer-Verlag, Berlin and New York.

Thesleff, I., and Hurmerinta, K. (1981). Differentiation 18, 75–88.

Trosler, D. G., and Fraser, F. C. (1977). Handb. Teratol. 2, 271–292.

Tsai, M. J., and O'Malley, B. W. (1977) In "Cell Differentiation in Microorganisms, Plants and Animals" (L. Nover and K. Mothes, eds.), pp. 109–125. North-Holland Publ., Amsterdam.

Waterman, R. E., Ross, C. M., and Meller, S. M. (1973). Anat. Rec. 176, 361–376.

Williams, D. L. (1974). Life Sci. 15, 583–597.

Wolpert, L. (1969). J. Theor. Biol. 25, 1–47.

Yamada, M., Bringas, P., Grodin, M., MacDougall, M., and Slavkin, H. C. (1980a). J. Biol. Buccale 8, 127–139.

Yamada, M., Bringas, P., Grodin, M., MacDougall, M., and Slavkin, H. C. (1980b). Calcif. Tissue Int. 31, 161–171.

Zimmerman, E. F., Wee, E. L., Phillips, N., and Roberts, N. (1981). J. Embryol. Exp. Morphol. 64, 233–250.

CHAPTER 2

THE ROLE OF EXTRACELLULAR MATRICES IN PALATAL SHELF CLOSURE

Linda L. Brinkley and Joyce Morris-Wiman

DEPARTMENT OF ANATOMY AND CELL BIOLOGY
UNIVERSITY OF MICHIGAN MEDICAL SCHOOL
ANN ARBOR, MICHIGAN

I. Introduction

The palatal shelves themselves play a direct and active role in their reorientation from a vertical position on either side of the tongue to a horizontal one above it. One of the oldest proposed mechanisms for the motive force underlying palatal shelf movement is a rapid increase in shelf volume due to increased cellular volume in the "connective tissue" (Lazzaro, 1940). Later, Walker and Fraser (1956) studied the staining properties of the shelf connective tissue and suggested that either hyaluronic acid acted as a water barrier thus providing "tissue turgor" or an elastic fiber network residing in the shelves produced their movement. The latter suggestion was discarded when no such network could be demonstrated (Stark and Ehrman, 1958; Loevy, 1962; Frommer, 1968; Frommer and Monroe, 1969). Subsequently histochemical and autoradiographic evidence suggested that the acid mucopolysaccharides (glycosaminoglycans or GAGs), principally those

17

CURRENT TOPICS IN
DEVELOPMENTAL BIOLOGY, VOL. 19

that were sulfated, were present in the palatal shelves at the time of shelf reorientation (Larsson *et al.,* 1959; Walker, 1961; Larsson, 1962). Biochemical data later confirmed that glycosaminoglycans (GAGs) were indeed present and synthesized before and during shelf reorientation; however, the major GAG component was hyaluronate (65%), while sulfated GAGs accounted for only about 35% (Pratt *et al.,* 1973).

It is now possible to refine and extend Lazzaro's original suggestion regarding the role of extracellular matrix in palatal shelf reorientation, but to do so one must look at the nature and behavior of the extracellular materials of the palatal shelves *in situ*. The palatal shelves are composed of a core of mesenchymal cells covered by epithelium. Extracellular matrix is found between the cells of the mesenchymal compartment and is also organized as a basal lamina intervening between the mesenchyme and the overlying epithelium. Despite similar basic components, embryonic mouse palatal shelves, our experimental model, have distinct regional differences in both composition and behavior. There are four anatomically distinct regions along the shelf's rostral–caudal axis: anterior, mid, and posterior presumptive hard palate and presumptive soft palate. The anterior and mid regions together comprise approximately one-quarter to one-third of the shelf length while the remainder is divided equally between the posterior and soft regions (Brinkley and Vickerman, 1979). The anterior region is small, less than half the cross-sectional area of the posterior, has a mesenchymal compartment which is densely packed with cells, and moves in an all-or-none manner to reach the horizontal plane. In contrast, the remainder of the shelf, encompassing presumptive mid and posterior hard palate and soft palate, is larger with a lower mesenchymal cell density. In addition, this region undergoes a more fluid remodeling around the tongue to achieve palatal shelf closure.

The epithelial perimeter of the shelves also has behaviorally distinct segments. The epithelium of the medial edge adheres to the opposing shelf and dies, fusing the shelves to one another. Both the presumptive nasal and oral surfaces have local segments of the epithelium that greatly increase in cell density concomitant with shelf reorientation. Neighboring segments do not show such changes. The former segments have been designated active and the latter inactive (Brinkley, 1980, 1984). Such local changes suggest that the mechanism(s) which produce these alterations may also be local, perhaps related to the underlying basal lamina and subjacent mesenchyme.

Those posterior shelf regions that undergo remodeling and are susceptible to alterations of their GAGs (see Section II,B below) seemed to be the most appropriate model with which to explore the role(s) of extracellular matrices in palatal shelf reorientation. Thus all studies presented here have focused on these regions in CD-1 mouse embryos.

II. The Mesenchymal Compartment

A. COMPONENTS AND PROPERTIES OF THE EXTRACELLULAR MATRIX

Extracellular matrix surrounding embryonic mesenchyme is generally composed of sulfated and unsulfated GAGs, collagens, and other glycoproteins such as fibronectin (Hay, 1981; Hawkes and Wang, 1982). All three components have also been identified in palatal shelves. Just prior to shelf reorientation about 60–65% of the extracellular GAGs are hyaluronate (HA) and the remainder are chondroitin sulfates (CS) (Pratt et al., 1973). Both collagen (Pratt and King, 1972; Hassell, and Orkin, 1976) and fibronectin (Silver et al., 1981) are also present at this time.

HA molecules occupy large domains and at physiological concentrations their domains may overlap. The entangled molecules form a dense meshwork (Laurent, 1970). HA may also interact with sulfated proteoglycans and collagen to form gel–fiber networks. These networks exert an osmotic pressure which is in large part produced by the HA. HA has nonideal osmotic behavior, that is, osmotic pressure does not increase directly with HA concentration, but rather more rapidly. A small increase in HA concentration will result in a disproportionately large increase in osmotic pressure. Gel–fiber networks exhibit a swelling pressure which is composed of an osmotic contribution from the macromolecular chains of the GAG gel and an elastic contribution from the contractile collagen fiber network. The osmotic conditions created by the HA molecules tend to bring water into the gel and sequester it, whereas the collagen fibers tend to force it out. In equilibrium these forces balance and no pressure from swelling results. If external mechanical or osmotic forces are applied to the gel, swelling pressure will increase. As fluid is lost, the relative concentration of HA will increase, producing a disproportionately large rise in osmotic force. In contrast, a dilution of the HA concentration causes a relatively small loss of osmotic pressure (see Comper and Laurent, 1978, for an extensive discussion of these properties).

B. ALTERATION OF GLYCOSAMINOGLYCANS BY CHLORCYCLIZINE

Studies of the effects of disruptive agents can often clarify basic mechanisms. Altering the GAG components of the palatal shelves could provide insight into their role in shelf reorientation. Chlor-cyclizine (CHLOR) is an antihistaminic benzhydrylpiperazine com-pound. It has been shown to cause HA and CS to be degraded into smaller molecular weight pieces with lower charge densities, while having little or no effect on their synthesis (Wilk *et al.*, 1978). When the compound is administered by gavage to pregnant mice, all of their offspring will have cleft palate and reduced mandibles (King, 1963; King *et al.*, 1965). The CHLOR effects on the palatal shelves are dis-tinct and regional. The anterior one-quarter is minimally affected and retains the ability to reorient. In contrast, the remainder of the shelf is reduced in cross-sectional area, increased in mesenchymal cell density, and unable to reorient *in vivo* or *in vitro* (Brinkley, 1980; Brinkley and Vickerman, 1982). Apparently native HA and CS molecules are re-quired for the posterior three-quarters of the shelf to reorient. In the studies reported below CHLOR treatment was employed in combina-tion with other manipulations to further elucidate the role of GAGs in shelf reorientation.

C. OSMOTIC MANIPULATIONS OF PALATAL SHELF REORIENTATION

One way GAGs could aid in shelf reorientation is via their osmotic contribution to a gel–fiber network. Since the swelling pressure of such a network can be altered by external osmotic forces, the effects of osmotic manipulations on movement of the palatal shelves were exam-ined. Mouse embryos that were about 24 hours prior to shelf reorienta-tion were obtained. Brain and tongue were removed but the mandible left in place (Brinkley *et al.*, 1975) to reduce the volume of tissue and to remove any physical barriers to shelf movement. The specimens were then incubated for 1 hour in salt solutions which were either hypo-osmotic (100 mOsm), isosmotic (290 mOsm), or hyperosmotic (900 mOsm) to amniotic fluid. The salt solutions contained $CaCl_2$, KCl, $MgSO_4$, NaCl, $NaHCO_3$, NaH_2PO_4, and dextrose. Hypoosmolality was achieved by adding less NaCl, hyperosmolality by increasing NaCl. The hyperosmotic conditions used were above those shown to relax isolated smooth muscle (500 mOsm) (Small and Squire, 1972) and so presumably precluded contractile activity of the mesenchymal cells.

Hyperosmotic conditions provoked posterior shelf remodeling dur-ing the incubation period although isosmotic conditions did not. Fur-ther, with hyperosmotic treatment the mesenchymal cells underlying the superior nasal region of the shelf assumed an elongate morphology with their long axes perpendicular to the overlying epithelium. This was not observed in the isosmotic controls. Since active mesenchymal cell contractility was excluded by the incubation conditions, it seems likely the morphology of these cells reflects a passive response to a change in the surrounding extracellular milieu (Brinkley, 1980).

When osmotic manipulations were carried out on CHLOR-treated specimens, only minimal remodeling was observed after exposure to hyperosmotic conditions and no mesenchymal cell orientation comparable to that seen in similarly exposed normal specimens was observed (Brinkley, 1980). The reduction in size of the HA molecules in the palatal shelves of embryos whose mothers received CHLOR would also reduce their ability both to enmesh and form a gel–fiber network and to sequester water molecules. Thus, theoretically less swelling pressure could be generated.

D. DISTRIBUTION OF COLLAGEN AND HYALURONATE

For a gel–fiber network to form both the GAG components and collagen must be present. The only published study of collagen distribution in the palatal shelves (Hassell and Orkin, 1976) reported that collagen fibers had a highly localized distribution, accumulating predominantly subjacent to the basal lamina of the epithelium on the future oral surface of the shelf and orienting primarily in a rostral–caudal direction. However, for a gel–fiber network to form and be a major morphogenetic force, a more ubiquitous distribution of a collagen would be required. An ultrastructural survey of the glutaraldehyde–tannic acid fixed (Singley and Solursh, 1980) posterior shelf region of shelves which were approximately 18 hours prior to reorientation reveals that this is indeed the case. Frontal sections of nasal active and inactive, medial and oral active and inactive segments of the epithelial–mesenchymal interface as well as the central mesenchymal region were examined (Fig. 1). Collagen was observed in all planes of section in all areas examined with no one orientation predominating.

Because of the importance of HA to the formation and function of a gel–fiber matrix, we sought to identify its pattern of distribution. This has been accomplished using Alcian Blue staining and specific enzymatic digestion coupled with computer-assisted image analysis. Palatal shelves were fixed with phosphate-buffered formalin containing tannic acid and serial paraffin sections of the posterior region cut. Alternating sections were either digested for 3–4 hours at 37°C with 100 TRU/ml of *Streptomyces* hyaluronidase in 0.1 M sodium acetate buffer, pH 5.0, to specifically remove the HA, or incubated in buffer alone as a control. All sections were subsequently stained with 1% Alcian Blue in 3% acetic acid, pH 2.5 with 0.025 M MgCl$_2$, to stain all GAGs (Derby, 1978). Photomicrographs of the stained sections were

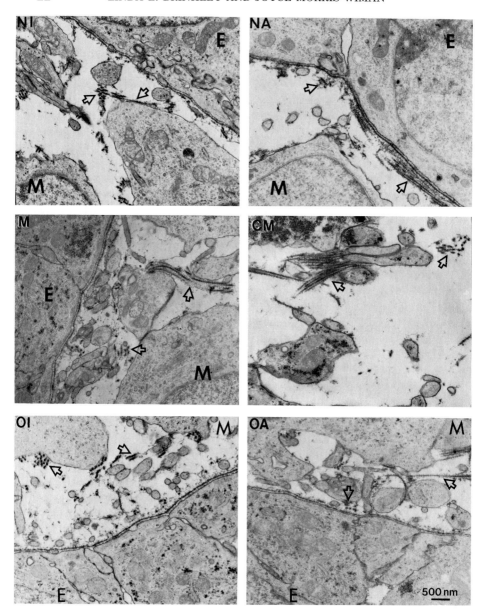

FIG. 1. Distribution of collagen in the posterior region of shelves which were approximately 18 hours prior to reorientation. Five regions of the epithelial (E)–mesenchymal
(M) interface, nasal active (NA), nasal inactive (NI), oral inactive (OI), and oral active
(OA) as well as the core mesenchyme (CM) were examined. Collagen (open arrows) was
observed in both longitudinal and transverse planes of section in all regions.

taken using a 603 ± 10 nm narrow bandpass filter to enhance the staining pattern. The negatives were then digitized using an Optronics rotating drum flying spot scanner. The image was recorded as a matrix of brightness values 512 × 482 picture elements in size. Algorithms which register the images of the control and enzyme-digested sections were run on each pair of images (Knoll and Delp, 1983). Analysis of the pattern of distribution of the HA removed by specific enzyme digestion was then accomplished by means of difference pictures (Knoll *et al.,* 1984). All image processing was done on a VAX-11/780 computer. A brief description of the method follows. The grey levels of each individual digitized image are internally standardized to control for any variability of film or developing. Images of adjacent stained and digested/stained sections are registered with respect to one another and the brightness values of one image are subtracted from the other. The resultant difference picture reveals the location of material removed by the specific enzyme digestion, producing a map of the distribution of HA.

Using these algorithms we are mapping the distribution of GAGs during development of the palate. We have begun by examining the distribution of HA at two time periods during the last 18 hours of palatal development and immediately after shelf reorientation and adhesion. Figure 2 illustrates computer-generated difference pictures showing the patterns of distribution of HA in frontal sections of the posterior (Fig. 2A–C) and soft (Fig. 2D–F) palatal shelf regions at each of the three times. The stages shown are approximately 18 hours (A and D) and 8 hours (B and E) prior to shelf reorientation and adhesion and just after the event is completed (C and F). The location of HA is indicated by the black stippling in the shelf. Eighteen hours prior to shelf reorientation, HA is observed to be densely distributed throughout both posterior and soft shelf regions, except for a strip of peripheral mesenchyme around the medial edge and along the entire oral surface in the posterior (A) and at the mid to lateral-oral periphery in the soft region (D). By 8 hours prior to complete shelf closure (B and E), both shelf regions have expanded noticeably in the medial and dorsoventral directions, although the posterior has expanded and remodeled more than the soft. The pattern of HA distribution now is dispersed in the central portion of both shelf regions while remaining more condensed in the lateral-oral area adjoining the tooth germ. The peripheral medial and oral mesenchyme of the posterior shelf still appears to be relatively free of HA (B). HA distribution becomes even more disperse in the soft region (E), particularly in the oral third of the shelf. After complete shelf reorientation and adhesion, the shelf is elongated in the

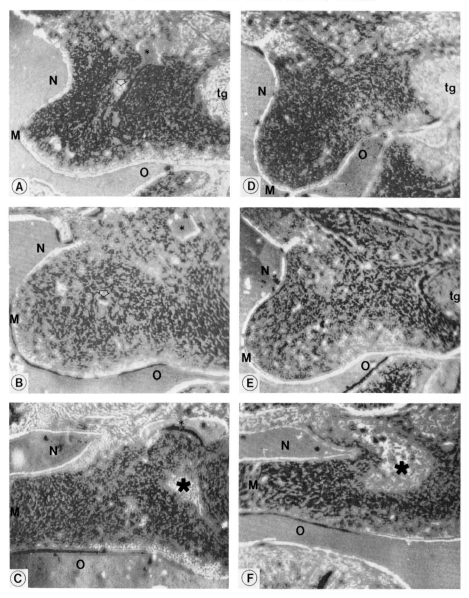

FIG. 2. Computer-assisted visualization of the distribution of hyaluronate (HA) in the posterior (A–C) and soft (D–F) palatal shelf regions. Three different stages are shown: 18 hours (A and D) and 8 hours (B and E) prior to reorientation and soon after reorientation and adhesion have occurred (C and F). The presence of HA is indicated by the black stippling. Distribution of HA is much more disperse at 8 hours prior to elevation (B and E), after shelf expansion has taken place, than at the earlier stage (A and D). Abbreviations and symbols used are N, nasal side, M, medial edge, and O, oral side of shelf; tg, tooth germ; open arrow, blood vessel; *, blood sinus; large asterisk, osteogenic regions.

medial direction and compressed along the dorsoventral axis. It is therefore difficult to determine just how the more intense pattern seen in the core of the shelves is related to the more disperse one seen previously. However, the lack of HA in the peripheral mesenchyme is still apparent.

These patterns, particularly in the soft region, suggest that both posterior and soft shelf regions undergo significant dispersion and/or removal of HA during the shelf expansion accompanying shelf reorientation. Given the nature of a GAG gel–fiber network, areas of high HA concentration would be expected to be ones with the greatest potential for exerting a swelling pressure by expansion of the network. It is possible that regions observed to undergo HA dispersion prior to shelf reorientation (B and E) could be the regions in which this is occurring. The apparent increase in HA accumulation seen in both shelf regions after reorientation and adhesion could reflect synthesis during that period, compression of the region containing HA resulting in a more dense pattern, or both. These alternatives are currently being investigated.

The results of CHLOR treatment of the palatal shelves of embryos and osmotic manipulations of both normal and CHLOR-pretreated specimens lend support to the hypothesis that swelling pressure emanating from a gel–fiber matrix plays a role in shelf remodeling. Hyperosmotic conditions cause water to move out of the palatal shelves. Initially it would be drawn out of the epithelial cells and immediately subjacent mesenchymal compartment, causing these areas to shrink first. Water from the interior of the mesenchymal compartment might be more slowly drawn out and transiently sequestered, especially in the region of highest HA accumulation, the core of the shelf. The combination of external compression of the mesenchymal compartment by initial epithelial shrinkage and transient sequestration of water molecules in the gel–fiber network could result in an acute increase in internal swelling pressure. Although this sequence of events offers an explanation for the generation of an internal shelf force and its manipulation by short-term hyperosmotic exposure, shelf force alone is insufficient to explain shelf reorientation. An internal force, if undirected, could produce generalized shelf expansion, but without a means to channel it, no recognizable shelf remodeling would result. In order to define a path for shelf remodeling it is logical to look to the boundary of the remodeling shelf—the epithelium, its underlying basal lamina, and the subjacent mesenchyme.

III. The Epithelial–Mesenchymal Interface

A. IDENTIFICATION OF EPITHELIAL SEGMENTS WHICH ARE
ACTIVE OR INACTIVE DURING SHELF REMODELING

A first step in determining whether or not the shelf's epithelial perimeter plays a role in reorientation is to observe whether or not alterations in the spatial distribution of epithelial cells occur concomitantly with shelf reorientation. Camera lucida tracings were made of transverse sections of the posterior shelf. The epithelial perimeter was then divided into six equal segments and the number of cells per micron was counted for each segment during the course of both *in vivo* and *in vitro* shelf reorientation. Mitotic indices were monitored by incubating specimens in the presence of [³H]thymidine and identifying the labeled cells by autoradiography. The superior nasal and mid-oral portions of the posterior shelf perimeter showed significant increases

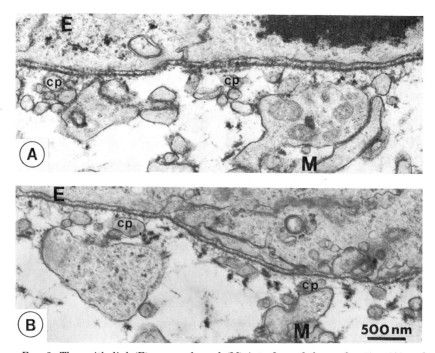

FIG. 3. The epithelial (E)–mesenchymal (M) interface of the oral active (A) and inactive (B) regions of the shelf perimeter of normal embryos. The active region is characterized by larger mesenchymal cell processes (cp) than those seen in inactive regions.

in cell density not attributable to cell division. Their neighboring segments showed no such increases. The former regions have been designated as morphogenetically active, the latter inactive (Brinkley, 1980, 1984). The highly localized nature of these changes suggest they may be the result of local events. If the basal lamina underlying these actively changing segments was removed or remodeled in some way, the overlying basal epithelial cells might be expected to adhere more strongly to their neighboring cells, increasing cell layering and cell density as previously observed. These observations and speculations on the possible mechanisms of reorientation have led to further examination of the epithelial–mesenchymal interface of these regions in both normal and CHLOR-treated specimens during transmission electron microscopy.

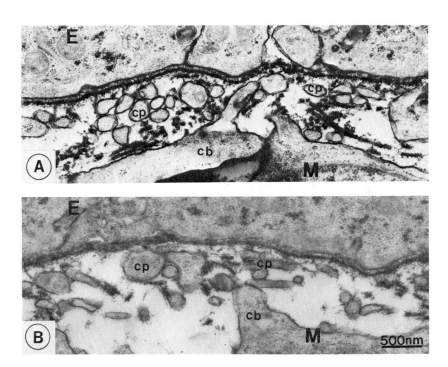

FIG. 4. The epithelial (E)–mesenchymal (M) interface of the oral active (A) and inactive (B) regions of the shelf perimeter of CHLOR-treated embryos. The active region has a significantly greater number of smaller cell processes (cp) than either the inactive region of CHLOR embryos (B) or the active or inactive regions of normal embryos (Fig. 3); cb, cell bodies.

B. Ultrastructural Characterization of Epithelial–
   Mesenchymal Relationships in Active and
   Inactive Oral Epithelial Segments

Shelves of embryos which were about 18 hours prior to shelf re-orientation were obtained, fixed in glutaraldehyde–tannic acid, and embedded in Epon. Sections of the oral active and neighboring inactive segments of the epithelial perimeter of the posterior shelf region were made. Electron micrographs were taken of the epithelial–mesenchymal interface of 8–10 consecutive basally located epithelial cells in both oral active and inactive segments. Four specimens each were examined. Figure 3 illustrates typical areas.

A 500-nm zone of mesenchyme beneath the basal lamina was delineated on each photomontage and the following parameters were measured: percentage of the area covered by mesenchymal cell processes and bodies, number of cell processes per 10^6 nm^2, mean cross-sectional area of the cell processes, number of cell processes per linear nanometer of basal lamina, and mean distance of the cell processes from the lamina densa. The results are shown in Table I. Mesenchymal cell processes near oral active regions were significantly larger than those in inactive regions. In addition, oral active regions had a greater proportion of the sub-basal lamina mesenchyme covered by cell processes and cell bodies. Comparable regions of CHLOR-treated embryos were also examined (Fig. 4; Table I). The oral active regions of CHLOR specimens had a significantly greater number of smaller cell processes per 10^6 nm^2 than did their normal counterparts. There was also a greater number of cell processes per nanometer of basal lamina and these processes were significantly further from the basal lamina in CHLOR-treated embryos as compared to controls. In contrast, the oral inactive segment of CHLOR-treated embryos differed from the normal only in the fact that the cell processes were at a greater distance from the basal lamina than were those of the normal oral inactive region. These findings indicate that the oral active epithelial segment of the posterior shelf is different from its inactive neighbor. CHLOR treatment appears generally to alter the region of the epithelial–mesenchymal interface to keep mesenchymal cell processes at a greater distance in both active and inactive regions. In addition, the active region seems to be more specifically affected so that the mesenchymal cells produce more and smaller cell processes. It seems likely the active segments of the epithelial perimeter may have higher rates of GAG turnover, as they appear to be more sensitive to the effects of CHLOR.

TABLE I

RELATIONSHIP OF MESENCHYMAL CELLS TO THE BASAL LAMINA OF THE ORAL EPITHELIUM[a]

Condition and region	Normal		CHLOR	
	Oral active	Oral inactive	Oral active	Oral inactive
% Area covered by				
cell processes	27%	23%	29%	27%
cell bodies	8%	6%	2%	2%
Number of cell processes per 10^6 nm^2	5.0	5.6	8.3[c,d]	5.5
Cross-sectional area of cell processes (means ± SD)	49,496 ± 84,404[c] (n = 470)	41,826 ± 58,964 (n = 470)	34,840 ± 50,596[c,d] (n = 462)	46,637 ± 60,249 (n = 345)
Number of cell processes per linear nanometer basal lamina	0.0024	0.0026	0.0044[c,d]	0.0029
Distance of cell processes[b] from basal lamina (mean ± SD)	131 ± 111 (n = 419)	125 ± 96 (n = 200)	147 ± 108[d] (n = 332)	150 ± 107[d] (n = 286)

[a]Measurements were made in a 500-nm-wide zone beneath the basal lamina. One shelf from each of four individuals was examined for each combination of condition and region.

[b]Only the distance of those processes with a clear path to the basal lamina was measured.

[c]Different from the other region of the same condition by analysis of variance, $p < 0.01$.

[d]Different from the same region of the alternate condition by analysis of variance, $p < 0.01$.

C. Characterization of the Basal Lamina of the Oral Active Segments Using Resinless Sections

The use of polyethylene glycol (PEG), a water-soluble medium, as an embedding medium for electron microscopy (Wolosewick, 1980) now makes possible the use of specific enzyme digestion as a means of characterizing cellular and extracellular components at the ultrastructural level. Recently, we have begun investigating the nature of the basal lamina of the oral active segment using this technique. Glutaraldehyde–tannic acid fixed normal and CHLOR-treated palates were embedded in high molecular weight PEG (MW 3350, Baker) according to the protocol of Wolosewick (1980) and thin sectioned. Following removal of the PEG with 95% ethanol and rehydration, sections were digested for 2.5 hours with one of the following enzymes: collagenase at 270 U/ml in Tris-buffered Ca^{2+} solution, pH 7.4; chondroitinase ABC at 1 U/ml in Tris–HCl buffer, pH 8.0; or *Streptomyces* hyaluronidase at 100 TRU/ml in sodium acetate buffer, pH 5.0. Control sections were incubated in the appropriate buffers. Sections were then dehydrated, critical point dried, and examined using transmission electron microscopy.

Sections of the epithelial–mesenchymal interface of normal oral active epithelial segments previously treated as described above are shown in Fig. 5. This method does not produce the usual view of the basal lamina seen in traditional plastic sections. In resinless sections the epithelial–mesenchymal interface (Fig. 5A) is characterized by a dense interfacial feltwork about 100–120 nm wide. Two other components are also associated with this feltwork and visible on its mesenchymal side. There is an indistinct amorphous background material which is moderately electron dense and appears as if done by a watercolorist's "wash" technique. Fine strands of material averaging 9–12 nm in diameter are also seen to emerge on the mesenchymal side of the interfacial feltwork. When sections of the normal oral active epithelial–mesenchymal interface were digested with chondroitinase ABC (Fig. 5B), the interfacial area takes on a distinctly different appearance. The interfacial region now appears as a three-part structure: a dense band on the epithelial side ranging from 40 to 65 nm in thickness; a lighter midregion averaging 25 nm in width which is traversed by now-resolvable 5–7 nm strands; and a third thinner dark band approximately 30 nm in width on the mesenchymal side. A large number of 9–12 nm strands are visible on the undersurface on this band. The entire three-part structure ranges from 95 to 120 nm in width with most of the variation attributable to variation in thickness of the dark band on the epithelial side. One possibility is that this band may be composed of the epithelial cell membrane and adjacent cytoplasm. The remaining light middle and lower dark bands may correspond to the lamina lucida and lamina densa observed by routine TEM. Besides revealing this three-part structure at the epithelial–mesenchymal interface, chondroitinase digestion also removed to a large degree the amorphous background material observed in undigested sections. However the 9–12 nm strands associated with the mesenchymal side of the putative lamina densa were untouched.

Digestion with *Streptomyces* hyaluronidase to specifically remove HA (Ohya and Kaneko, 1970) presents quite a different picture (Fig. 5C). The interfacial feltwork is quite reduced, while the 9–12 nm strands are left intact. However, a considerable expansion of the amorphous background material is observed. Collagenase digestion (Fig. 5D) removes both the interfacial feltwork and most of the amorphous background material; however, the 9–12 nm strands again remain untouched.

These findings suggest that collagen and HA may interact in the interfacial feltwork in such a way that removal of one may remove the majority of the other. The CS appear to be more discretely localized to the middle of the feltwork and less well integrated into it. These molecules may be more easily removed for this reason. These results are consistent with those of others who have shown that CS are produced by embryonic epithelia from several sources (Trelstad *et al.*, 1974; Hay and Meier, 1974; Gordon and Bernfield, 1980).

Comparison of the oral active epithelial–mesenchymal interface of normal individuals (Fig. 6A) with that of CHLOR-pretreated specimens offers further insight into the nature of this region. Tissue from CHLOR-treated embryos (Fig. 6B) also shows a three-part interfacial structure similar to that seen in normal individuals after chondroitinase digestion (Fig. 5B). The three-part structure of CHLOR specimens is, however, clearer and more distinct as well as thinner, approximately 70 nm, perhaps because of a reduction in the thickness of both dark bands. The 5–7 nm strands seen crossing the middle light region are still present, as are the 9–12 nm strands seen emerging into the mesenchyme. Reducing the molecular weight and charge densities of HA and the CS seems to prevent the formation of both the dense interfacial feltwork observed at the normal interface and the amorphous background material. Although glutaraldehyde–tannic acid fixation is known to retain native GAGs in the tissue, it is not known whether the smaller molecular weight HA and CS pieces resulting from CHLOR treatment are precipitated by this fixation. Therefore it

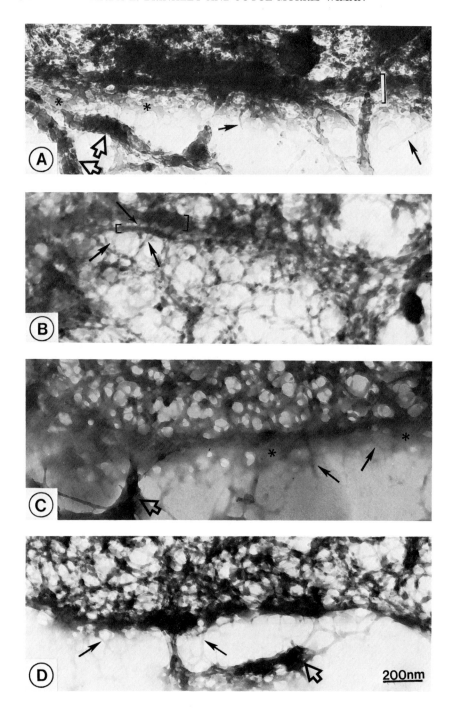

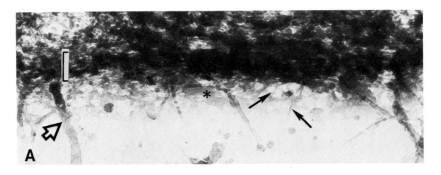

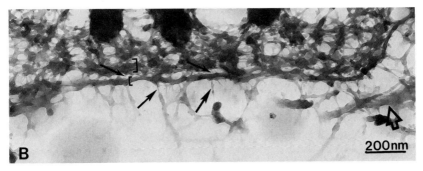

FIG. 6. Appearance of the epithelial–mesenchymal interface of the oral active region of the shelf perimeter of normal (A) compared to CHLOR-treated (B) embryos in polyethylene glycol sections. The symbols are as described for Fig. 5. CHLOR treatment (B) reveals a three-part structure at the interface. Although similar to that seen after chondroitinase digestion of normal tissue (Fig. 5B), it is smaller, ~70 nm in width, and more distinct. The 5–7 nm strands are still observable in the light middle region (small arrows) as well as the 9–12 nm strands on the mesenchymal side (open arrow).

FIG. 5. Enzymatic characterization of the epithelial–mesenchymal interface of the oral active region of the normal shelf perimeter using polyethylene glycol sections. Undigested sections (A) show a 100–120 nm interfacial feltwork (bracket) at the interface. Amorphous background material (*) and 9–12 nm strands emerging on the mesenchymal side can also be seen (small arrows). After digestion with chondroitinase (B) the network now appears as a three-part structure: a dense band of 40–65 nm width (large bracket) on the epithelial side, a lighter midregion traversed by 5–7 nm filaments (small arrows), and a thinner dark band, approximately 30 nm wide (small bracket) on the mesenchymal side. The 9–12 nm mesenchymal side filaments (large arrows) are still visible. *Streptomyces* hyaluronidase digestion (C) reduces the interfacial feltwork but appears to cause an expansion of the amorphous background material (*). The 9–12 nm strands (small arrows) are still visible. Collagenase digestion (D) removes essentially all but the strands (small arrows). Cell processes (open arrows) are also visible.

remains a possibility that those molecules were not retained and were extracted during tissue processing. If this were the case Fig. 6B would represent the profile of the interface seen when both HA and CS were removed.

It is tempting to speculate on the nature of the 5–7 nm strands resolvable with chondroitinase digestions as well as the 9–12 nm ones associated with the mesenchymal side of the lower dark band. The 5–7 nm strands are collagenase digestible and therefore either are composed of that molecule itself or are a composite of collagen and other molecules so closely associated with the apparently considerable collagen of the interfacial feltwork that when it is digested (Fig. 5D) they too are removed. In contrast, at least some of the 9–12 nm strands must be composed of something other than HA, CS, or collagen because they resist digestion by the appropriate degradative enzymes. It is possible that they in whole or part contain fibronectin (Singer, 1979; Yamada et al., 1982). Alternatively, they may be composed at least in part of one or a mixture of these components organized in such a way as to preclude digestion by the methods used.

IV. Summary and Speculations

Studies by Bernfield and others on the role of the basal lamina in embryonic salivary gland morphogenesis have resulted in a proposed model for epithelial morphogenesis in which the mesenchyme remodels the basal lamina, which in turn dictates the morphology of the overlying epithelium (Bernfield and Banerjee, 1982). GAGs within the basal lamina are apparently involved in some way with the folding of epithelial sheets (Gordon and Bernfield, 1980). Our results thus far offer intriguing hints that these events may in part be a factor in shelf reorientation in localized segments of the palatal shelf perimeter. More definitive studies to characterize these regions are presently underway.

Extracellular matrices both within the mesenchymal compartment, probably existing as a GAG–collagen gel–fiber matrix, and at the epithelial–mesenchymal interface, organized as a basal lamina, appear to play vital roles in palatal shelf reorientation. One hypothesis that explains their possible roles is that at least posterior palatal shelf remodeling results in large part from expansion of an HA-rich gel–fiber network within the mesenchymal compartment. This expansion is aided and directed by local increases in epithelial cell density that reduce shelf perimeter and thereby apply compressive forces to the gel and buttress those regions so as to define the path of least resistance primarily in the medial direction. Results of CHLOR perturbation of GAG metabolism, computer-assisted visualization of HA distribution within the shelf, and preliminary ultrastructural characterization of the oral active region of the epithelial–mesenchymal interface support this hypothesis. A great deal of work remains to test this hypothesis fully; however, in light of the evidence available to date it still remains a viable and attractive one.

ACKNOWLEDGMENTS

This work was supported by NIH-NIDR Grants DE02774 and 5-K04-DE00104 to LLB. The Optronics scanner used for portions of this work is part of the Neuroscience Image Processing System of the University of Michigan which is supported in part by NIH-NINCDS Grant 1-P01-NS-15655 and United Cerebral Palsy Foundation Grant R-291.

REFERENCES

Bernfield, M., and Banerjee, S. D. (1982). *Dev. Biol.* **90**, 291–305.
Brinkley, L. L. (1980). *In* "Current Research Trends in Prenatal Craniofacial Development" (R. M. Pratt, Jr. and R. L. Christiansen, eds.), pp. 203–220. Elsevier, Amsterdam.
Brinkley, L. L. (1984). *Dev. Biol.* **102**, 216–227.
Brinkley, L. L., and Vickerman, M. M. (1979). *J. Embryol. Exp. Morphol.* **54**, 229–240.
Brinkley, L. L., and Vickerman, M. M. (1982). *J. Embryol. Exp. Morphol.* **69**, 193–213.
Brinkley, L., Basehoar, G., Branch, A., and Avery, J. (1975). *J. Embryol. Exp. Morphol.* **34**, 485–495.
Comper, W. D., and Laurent, T. C. (1978). *Physiol. Rev.* **58**, 255–315.
Derby, M. A. (1978). *Dev. Biol.* **66**, 321–336.
Frommer, J. (1968). *Anat. Rec.* **60**, 471.
Frommer, J., and Monroe, C. W. (1969). *J. Dent. Res.* **48**, 155–156.
Gordon, J. R., and Bernfield, M. R. (1980). *Dev. Biol.* **74**, 118–135.
Hassell, J. R., and Orkin, R. W. (1976). *Dev. Biol.* **49**, 80–88.
Hawkes, S., and Wang, J. L., eds. (1982). "Extracellular Matrix." Academic Press, New York.
Hay, E. D., ed. (1981). "Cell Biology of Extracellular Matrix." Plenum, New York.
Hay, E. D., and Meier, S. (1974). *J. Cell Biol.* **62**, 815–830.
King. C. T. G. (1963). *Science* **141**, 353–355.
King, C. T. G., Weaver, S. A., and Narrod, S. A. (1965). *J. Pharmacol. Exp. Ther.* **147**, 391–398.
Knoll, T. F., and Delp, E. J. (1983). *IEEE Trans. Pattern Anal. Machine Intelligence* (submitted).
Knoll, T. F., Brinkley, L. L., and Delo, E. J. (1984). *J. Histochem. Cytochem.* (submitted).
Larsson, K. S. (1962). *Acta Odontol. Scand.* **20** (Suppl.), 31.
Larsson, K. S., Böstrom, H., and Carlsöö, S. (1959). *Exp. Cell Res.* **16**, 379–383.
Laurent, T. C. (1970). *In* "Chemistry and Molecular Biology of the Intercellular Matrix" (E. A. Balazs, ed.), Vol. 2, pp. 703–732. Academic Press, New York.
Lazzaro, C. (1940). *Monit. Zool. Ital.* **51**, 249–273.
Loevy, H. (1962). *Anat. Rec.* **142**, 375–390.

Ohya, T., and Kaneko, Y. (1970). *Biochim. Biophys. Acta* **198,** 607–609.

Pratt, R. M., and King, C. T. G. (1972). *Arch. Oral Biol.* **16,** 1181–1186.

Pratt, R. M., Goggins, J. R., Wilk, A. L., and King, C. T. G. (1973). *Dev. Biol.* **32,** 230–237.

Silver, M. H., Foidart, J.-M., and Pratt, R. M. (1981). *Differentiation* **18,** 141–150.

Singer, I. I. (1979). *Cell* **16,** 675–685.

Singley, C. T., and Solursh, M. (1980). *Histochemistry* **65,** 93–102.

Small, J. V., and Squire, J. M. (1972). *J. Mol. Biol.* **67,** 117–149.

Stark, R. M. B., and Ehrman, N. A. (1958). *Plastic Reconstruct. Surg.* **21,** 177–184.

Trelstad, R. L., Hayashi, K., and Toole, B. P. (1974). *J. Cell Biol.* **62,** 815–830.

Walker, B. E. (1961). *J. Embryol. Exp. Morphol.* **9,** 22–31.

Walker, B. E., and Fraser, C. F. (1956). *J. Embryol. Exp. Morphol.* **4,** 176–189.

Wilk, A. L., King, C. T. G., and Pratt, R. M. (1978). *Teratology* **18,** 199–210.

Wolosewick, J. J. (1980). *J. Cell Biol.* **86,** 675–681.

Yamada, K., Hayashi, M., and Akiyama, S. (1982). *In* "Extracellular Matrix" (S. Hawkes and J. L. Wang, eds.), pp. 25–34. Academic Press, New York.

CHAPTER 3

ROLE OF NEUROTRANSMITTERS IN PALATE DEVELOPMENT

Ernest F. Zimmerman and Elizabeth L. Wee

DIVISION OF CELL BIOLOGY
CHILDREN'S HOSPITAL RESEARCH FOUNDATION
CINCINNATI, OHIO

I. Introduction

A major issue in development is the regulation of the requisite processes of growth, migration, and differentiation. Several elements have been implicated in the regulatory process. In addition to cell surface recognition between similar and dissimilar cell types, information may be imparted to specific cells from the extracellular environment. Biological signals to transduce information to cells may come from small molecular weight substances, of which neurotransmitters and prostaglandins are prime candidates; small to large polypeptides, which include various polypeptide hormones and growth factors; and finally, extracellular matrix components, which also provide mechanical support for cells. In this review, the role of neurotransmitters in a few developmental systems is briefly discussed as an introduction to a discussion of such a role in the palate. If a putative neurotransmitter is not only synthesized and released by nerves but also synthesized in nonneural cells and tissues, then perhaps the agent should be considered as both a neurotransmitter and a hormone. Such may be the case with regard to some of the neurotransmitters located in the palate which are synthesized in and released from nerves but which are also

37

CURRENT TOPICS IN
DEVELOPMENTAL BIOLOGY, VOL. 19

found in embryonic mesenchymal and epithelial cells.

Neurotransmitter mechanisms in adult peripheral and central nervous systems are characterized by localized synthesis of neurotransmitters, specific release mechanisms, and their diffusion for short distances at synapses. Cell surface receptors are usually concentrated in the synaptic clefts and stereospecific binding of neurotransmitters produces transductional events which alter ion fluxes and second messenger systems to produce biologic responses. In most cases an action potential is elicited or modulated. To allow rapid discrimination of incoming signals and thus avoid tolerance, specific uptake mechanisms are employed to internalize the neurotransmitter enroute to its metabolic conversion to an inactive product. When one contemplates the neurotransmitter-mediated nervous system in the adult animal, one is struck by the high degree of complexity and the high concentration of synthetic, receptor, and uptake components localized at specific sites. However, it should not be surprising that developing nonneural as well as neural systems utilize the same neurotransmitter systems during embryogenesis, employing structural and metabolic components similar to, although simpler than, those found in the adult peripheral and central nervous systems; the end result in both cases is the spatial and temporal regulation of biological systems.

II. Neurotransmitters in Development

There is as yet no universal acceptance that neurotransmitters exert epigenetic influences to regulate embryonic and fetal development. Nevertheless, there are an increasing number of reports that neurotransmitters, including acetylcholine and the monoamines, function to regulate morphogenesis, growth, and differentiation in many vertebrate and invertebrate species. A "nontransmitter" role for the monoamines generally has been suggested since they are present during embryogenesis prior to the development of the nervous system. Thus, serotonin and acetylcholine have been proposed to control cell division and cell movements during morphogenesis of the invertebrate sea urchin. During gastrulation, elongated filopodial projections of secondary mesenchymal cells selectively adhere to the ectodermal roof of the blastocele and contract to complete invagination of the archenteron. Serotonin appears to regulate mesenchymal cell movements during this process (Gustafson and Toneby, 1970). Although the biochemical measurement and histochemical localization of serotonin appear to support its role during morphogenesis (Buznikov et al., 1964, 1972), the methylated derivative, 5-methoxytryptamine, may serve as the proximate regulator (Renaud *et al.*, 1983). Furthermore, the presence of serotonin within these cells may occur by differing means, either by *in situ* synthesis or by uptake of extracellular serotonin (Toneby, 1977). Thus, cells that concentrate monoamines may represent sites at which the monoamines may act intracellularly to influence gastrulation during this early phase of embryonic development (Buznikov and Shmuckler, 1981). However, direct evidence for an intracellular function of neurotransmitters, as opposed to a cell surface, receptor-mediated one, has not been obtained in developmental systems.

The role of monoamines in morphogenesis has also been investigated in vertebrate species and much research has focused on the chick embryo. One criterion for neurotransmitter involvement has been its localization during early development. Catecholamines and serotonin have been demonstrated to be present endogenously (Ignarro and Shideman, 1968; Strudel *et al.*, 1977; Wallace, 1982) and to be concentrated in the notocord and developing neural tube (Kirby and Gilmore, 1972; Lawrence and Burden, 1973; Wallace, 1979). Another criterion for the role of neurotransmitter involvement in morphogenesis is the production of congenital anomalies after perturbing neurotransmitter levels. Interference with catecholamine metabolism during early stages of morphogenesis by inhibition of monoamine oxidase or catecholamine synthesis can lead to congenital anomalies (Lawrence and Burden, 1973). These results have been interpreted by the authors to indicate that catecholamines present in the early neural tube and notochord are involved in regulation of early morphogenetic movements in the chick embryo. Similar conclusions about serotonin involvement in morphogenesis have been reached since disturbances in its metabolism produce teratogenic effects in neural tube closure (Palén *et al.*, 1979). These morphogenetic disturbances can be correlated with the appearance of serotonin in the neural tube and notochord spatially and temporally and with the progression of caudal neuropore closure (Wallace, 1982). Nevertheless, there is difficulty accepting the implications of the teratologic data since the concentrations of antagonists employed are high and both neurotransmitter agonists and their precursors show teratogenic effects as well (Emanuelsson and Palén, 1975; Schowing *et al.*, 1977; Palén *et al.*, 1979).

Neural crest cells give rise to a number of neuronal and glial cell types (Weston, 1970; D'Amico-Martel and Noden, 1983). Thus, it would not be surprising for these neural cells to contain neurotransmitters. However, the neurotransmitter phenotypes appear before any obvious neural maturation has begun. For example, the acetylcholine synthetic enzyme choline acetyltransferase has been demonstrated in the mesencephalic neural crest of quail embryos at 1.5 days of incubation (Smith *et al.,* 1979) and in trunk crest cells that are migrating within the sclerotomal area of the somite at 3 days (Fauquet *et al.,* 1981). This cholinergic marker correlates with the presence of acetylcholinesterase in migrating crest cells in the chick embryo (Drews, 1975). Since acetylcholinesterase was found in about 90% of the migrating chick crest cells (Cochard and Coltey, 1983), it is likely that crest precursors to both neuronal and nonneuronal cell types will contain the cholinergic marker. As indicated previously, neurotransmitters may be involved in regulation of morphogenetic movements and cell migrations. Thus, the question arises whether cholinergic traits in neural crest cells represent an early differentiation of presumptive neurons or are related to the process of cell migration, or both. In this respect, it is noteworthy that neural crest cells apparently devoid of acetylcholinesterase activity appear to migrate as well as their enzyme active counterparts (Cochard and Coltey, 1983). In addition, it has been recently shown that cultured crest cells can express a serotonin phenotype (Sieber-Blum, 1983). Therefore much has to be learned about neurotransmitter involvement in neural crest growth, migration, and differentiation.

Another facet of neurotransmitter involvement in neurogenesis is the indication that serotonin may serve as a trophic agent in the development of target cells of serotoninergic neurons. When serotonin synthesis in the embryonic rat brain is inhibited by maternal administration of *p*-chlorophenylalanine (PCPA), the onset of differentiation (time of last division) of certain neuronal populations is delayed (Lauder and Krebs, 1978). Using immunocytochemistry and [^{3}H]thymidine autoradiography, Lauder and associates have recently demonstrated that these populations are derived from regions of the neuroepithelium through which serotoninergic axons are growing during the period of the PCPA effect (Lauder *et al.,* 1982; Wallace and Lauder, 1983). Rapidly dividing neurons were shown to be in close apposition to the migrating serotoninergic axons. It has been hypothesized, therefore, that serotoninergic neurons may exert a trophic influence on the proliferation and differentiation of their neuronal and glial target cells through their interactions with such elements in the developing brain (Lauder *et al.,* 1982).

Evidence is accumulating that the neurotransmitters mediate their effects on growth, morphogenesis, and differentiation through cyclic nucleotide mechanisms (McMahon, 1974). It has been shown that norepinephrine modulates cyclic AMP levels (Oey, 1975), dopamine has a similar effect on cyclic AMP (Penit *et al.,* 1977), and catecholamines regulate cyclic GMP (Schwartz, 1976). Furthermore, regional differences in cyclic AMP levels have been observed in the head process stage of chick embryos (Reporter and Rosenquist, 1972), and *in situ* delivery of cyclic AMP to the chick notochord area of the chick embryo produced axial bending of the notochord (Robertson and Gingle, 1977).

III. Neuropharmacologic Action of Teratogens

Congenital malformations represent a major tragedy to the affected family and subsequent treatment commands much of the resources of society. If the list of chemical agents proven or strongly suspected to be teratogenic in humans is examined, one is struck by a singular correlation. In 6 out of 10 instances, there is a positive correlation between teratogens that cause neural defects (including mental retardation) and those known to possess neuropharmacologic activity in the adult. These agents include the sedative thalidomide (Lenz, 1962); methyl mercury (Matsumoto *et al.*, 1965); alcohol (Jones and Smith, 1975); the anticonvulsants, including phenytoin (Meadow, 1970), trimethadione (Feldman *et al.*, 1977), and valproic acid (Robert and Guibaud, 1982); the benzodiazepine tranquilizers, including diazepam (Safra and Oakley, 1975; Nakane *et al.*, 1980); and excessive phenylalanine arising from maternal phenylketonuria (Lenke and Levy, 1980). In addition, other agents which are teratogenic to the human cause a host of congenital anomalies that are general in nature and cannot be easily construed to involve neural mechanisms. However, hydrocephalus is an important feature associated with the anticoagulant warfarin (Warkany, 1975), while meningomyelocele, hydrocephalus, and cleft palate have been associated with the folic acid antagonist aminopterin when given to pregnant women (Thiersch, 1952). The other generally accepted human teratogens, the hypoglycemics (Campbell, 1961) and androgens (Grumbach and Ducharme, 1960), are not associated with neural defects.

These observations suggest that developing neural tissue may be more sensitive to toxic agents than other types of developing tissue. Examples of developing neural tissue may be neuroepithelium present in the folding neural tube, or migrating neural crest cells, which give rise to a whole host of tissues. Furthermore, it suggests that neuropharmacologic agents may be particularly toxic to developing tissues. Many neuropharmacologic agents function therapeutically due to their ability to bind to neurotransmitter receptors or perturb levels of neurotransmitters at their site of origin. One explanation for these observations is that neurotransmitters function in the regulation of development. As indicated in the previous section, there is increasing evidence for this postulate. Thus, neuropharmacologic agents would disrupt neurotransmitter function, and abnormal development (e.g., teratogenesis) would ensue. This has been our working hypothesis for the last few years. In order to test this hypothesis we have been investigating the role of neurotransmitters in palate development. The palate is a useful model system since many teratogens including the neuropharmacologic agents phenytoin (Dilantin) and diazepam (Valium) cause clefting. Furthermore, palatal tissue, which is part of the craniofacial area, is derived from the neural crest (D'Amico-Martel and Noden, 1983). As described previously, the neurotransmitter acetylcholine appears to be associated with migrating neural crest cells before differentiation to neuronal phenotypes could occur. Therefore it is possible that neurotransmitter regulation of palate development (see Section V) might be a consequence of the palate being derived from the neural crest. This neurotransmitter association could in turn lead to sensitivity to neuropharmacologic agents such as phenytoin and diazepam to produce cleft palate.

IV. Mechanisms of Palate Reorientation

One main feature of palate development is that two shelves grow vertically while surrounding the tongue. At a particular time in development the shelves reorient to a horizontal position and subsequently fuse. The anterior portion forms the hard bony palate and the posterior forms skeletal muscle in the soft palate. It has been proposed that the impetus to reorient is provided by an expression of forces established developmentally within the palate itself (Walker and Fraser, 1956). There is increasing evidence for a direct involvement of extracellular matrix components, the glycosaminoglycans. Significant amounts of glycosaminoglycan synthesis and accumulation, particularly of hyaluronic acid, have been chemically detected in the palate just prior to reorientation (Pratt et al., 1973). It is thought that hyaluronic acid hydrates and expands its molecular domain (Comper and Laurent, 1978) to produce an intrinsic tissue pressure to reorient the palate (Ferguson, 1978; Brinkley and Vickerman, 1982). How this force could be channeled and developmentally controlled to reorient the palate is the subject of intense debate. We have shown that glycosaminoglycans are localized regionally, with much more hyaluronate present in the anterior than the posterior end (Knudsen and Zimmerman, 1982). Thus a nonuniform strain on the palatal cell architecture produced by hyaluronate expansion could influence palate reorientation. Alternatively, the intrinsic force could be derived by contractility of palate mesenchymal and epithelial cells. It is also possible that cellular tension (either active or passive) could counterbalance the hyaluronate-induced swelling pressure and alteration of either or both forces could regulate the reorientation process.

For the last few years our research has addressed the question whether palatal cell contractility itself or its counterbalance of hyaluronate swelling could be responsible for the intrinsic force of palate reorientation. Our first efforts were to study the biochemistry of the contractile proteins in the mouse palate. We showed that actin and myosin were synthesized in the palate at the time just prior to reorientation, day 14.5 of gestation, at a rate approximately equal to that of synthesis in the tongue. Since the tongue is rapidly synthesizing skeletal muscle at this time in development, this result suggested that the palate was capable of synthesizing large amounts of contractile proteins, possibly involved in a contractile mechanism of palate reorientation (Lessard *et al.*, 1974). Morphological studies using myosin ATPase histochemistry, electron microscopy, and immunofluorescence with actin and myosin antibodies have localized contractile systems to three regions: region 1, a skeletal muscle system on the oral side of the far posterior palate; region 2, a nonmuscle contractile system on the tongue side (nasal septum) extending along the top of the shelf from mid palate to the posterior limit; and region 3, another nonmuscle contractile system along the oral epithelium from the mid palate extending into the anterior and posterior ends (Kuhn *et al.*, 1980). Several experiments were carried out to determine whether the putative nonmuscle contractile systems function to reorient the mouse palate. An analysis of cell morphology during palate reorientation indicated that the peripheral mesenchymal cells, including regions 2 and 3, become elongated and are arranged perpendicular to the basement membrane and thereafter round up as the shelf assumes the horizontal position. Epithelium on the tongue side (nasal) also undergoes cell shape changes during reorientation (Babiarz *et al.*, 1979). These studies suggest that contraction of cytoplasmic processes would be directly responsible for palate reorientation or, alternatively, that the cells maintain a tensional force to counterbalance those produced by hyaluronate hydration.

Analogous cellular systems in the hamster mesenchyme have been described and their involvement in palate reorientation has also been postulated (Shah, 1979). Furthermore, comparable cellular systems have been observed in the palate mesenchyme of the rat embryo, whose palate also undergoes reorientation. Interestingly, the corresponding cellular systems are absent in the palate mesenchyme of the alligator embryo, whose palate shelves do not reorient but grow together from horizontal positions (Ferguson, 1981). Thus, the lack of the cellular masses in the alligator mesenchyme is consistent with their hypothetical role in mammalian palate reorientation but does not provide direct proof.

We attempted to test directly whether a contractile component functions in palate reorientation. Heads from day 14.5 mouse embryos were glycerinated to allow the polar ATP molecule, involved in both skeletal muscle and cytoplasmic actomyosin condensation, to diffuse into palatal shelves. It was observed that addition of 5 mM ATP and a 30-minute incubation at 25°C optimally stimulated palate reorientation. Elevation of the anterior end was nearly complete; the palate shelf index was 3.9 with reorientation judged on a basis of 1–5 (1, vertical; 5, horizontal). Although reorientation of the posterior end was significant, movement was limited (Fig. 1). When the shelves were examined histologically, it was observed that the cytoplasmic processes condensed and underwent an apparent contraction. Further, it was shown that cytochalasin B, an agent which disrupts the microfilamentous contractile network of a cell, reversed the effects of ATP on

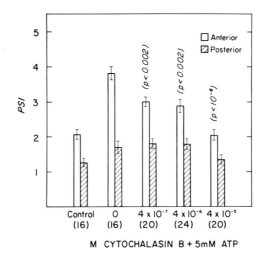

Fig. 1. Palate shelf reorientation in glycerinated head preparation induced by ATP and inhibited by cytochalasin B. PSI is palate shelf index. Number of palates employed are indicated in parentheses for each experimental condition. Bars indicate standard errors of the mean. p values obtained by comparison with ATP + 0.2% ETOH by Student's t test. (Data from Wee and Zimmerman, 1980.)

condensation of cell processes and reorientation of the palate (Fig. 1). These results suggest that contraction of actomyosin-containing microfilaments in nonmuscle contractile cells generates a motive force to reorient the palate (Wee and Zimmerman, 1980). In another series of experiments we were able to show that the migratory behavior of palate mesenchymal cells might be analogous to palate cells interacting with the extracellular matrix to elevate shelves during development. Palate cells migrated out of explants toward each other and exerted strong tractional forces on collagen fibers in hydrated gels, as indicated by the alignment and condensation of the collagen fibers. Another indication of the strong tractional forces that palate mesenchymal cells are capable of comes from the observation that they produced strong wrinkles on polysiloxane films (Venkatasubramanian and Zimmerman, 1983). In summary, these experiments are consistent with a direct role of palatal cell contractility in producing a force to orient the palate or producing a cellular tension to counteract the force of hyaluronate-dependent expansion of the extracellular space.

V. Role of Neurotransmitters in Palate Reorientation

The reorientation process occurs at a precise time in development. Further, any intrinsic force allowing the shelf to reorient from a vertical to a horizontal position has to be modulated in a precise spatial manner. Neurotransmitters may function to achieve this temporal and spatial regulation of palate reorientation. We have devised a useful embryo culture system whereby individual mouse embryos are incubated in vials containing tissue culture medium with human serum. The tongue is dissected and although bleeding occurs, it is minimal. However, the palate shelf can reorient in the space created by removal of the tongue. Thus, the anterior end completely reorients while the morphogenetic process in the posterior is nearly complete. The time course of reorientation is about 4–6 hours, which is similar to that *in vivo*. Employing the embryo culture system has allowed the testing of neurotransmitters on the reorientation process (Table I). Specificity of the agonist could be confirmed by the use of appropriate antagonists. We noted that the anterior and posterior palate behave independently. Acetylcholine agonists stimulate anterior shelf reorientation, and hexamethonium but not atropine inhibits the posterior end. This result implies that the ganglionic blocking agent is exerting its effect on posterior palate cells through the pterygopalatine ganglion. This neural tissue could function directly to regulate these palatal cells or indirectly by exerting a trophic influence on them to contain nicotinic

TABLE I

EFFECT OF NEUROTRANSMITTERS ON PALATE
ELEVATION IN EMBRYO CULTURE

| Neurotransmitters | Palate Reorientation | |
	Anterior	Posterior
Acetylcholine	—[a]	Stimulate
Serotonin	Stimulate	—
GABA	Inhibit	Inhibit
Norepinephrine	—	—
Dopamine	—	—

[a]Little or no effect.

receptors (Wee *et al.*, 1980). Conversely, serotonin stimulated the anterior end of the palate to elevate. The antagonist methysergide reversed the effects of serotonin and inhibited anterior shelf reorientation by itself (Wee *et al.*, 1979). GABA, on the other hand, inhibited shelf movement at both the anterior and posterior ends, although the predominant end varied with the inbred strain used (Wee *et al.*, 1983). Thus, the palate showed a specificity strikingly similar to the nervous system: some neurotransmitters are stimulatory and another, such as GABA, is inhibitory. However, not all neurotransmitters affect palate shelf reorientation in embryo culture. Norepinephrine and dopamine up to 10^{-4} M had no effect on either anterior or posterior palate reorientation.

VI. Serotoninergic Mechanisms in the Palate

Although neurotransmitters could regulate palate movement in embryo culture, these effects could be elicited through the cardiovascular system, vasodilation or vasoconstriction of blood vessels altering O_2 and nutrient delivery to palatal cells. Therefore, we sought the presence of these neurotransmitters in the palate as one criterion of a functioning neurotransmitter mechanism. Serotonin was first analyzed. Palate cells were capable of synthesizing the neurotransmitter from its radioactive precursor, 5-[^{3}H]HTP. Also, an active uptake mechanism for serotonin could be shown in dissected palates. Serotonin was directly measured in dissected palates (Zimmerman *et al.*, 1981) as well as in cultured palate mesenchymal cells (Wee *et al.*, 1981). The content of serotonin derived from dissected palates was 0.40 ± 0.04 ng/mg protein, about eightfold less than in embryonic brain at

TABLE II

Content of Neurotransmitters in Palate
and Brain at Day 14.5 of Development[a]

	Palate	Brain
Serotonin	0.40 ± 0.04	3.09 ± 0.20
GABA	19.2 ± 0.48	653.3 ± 33
Dopamine	1.63 ± 0.25	2.38 ± 0.64

[a]Values presented are means ± SE in nanograms per milligram protein, determined in A/J mouse embryos. Data for serotonin and dopamine from Zimmerman et al. (1981).

that time in development (Table II). The value in palate is considered to be significant; it is estimated that it corresponds to 10^{-7} M. The localization of serotonin in palatal structures was carried out by incorporation of the radioactive serotonin precursor in embryo culture and autoradiography on histologic sections. Grains were observed throughout the palate. Region 3 cells contained grains, as did structures in region 2, epithelium, and internal mesenchyme. Surprisingly, the pterygopalatine nerve and ganglion showed a high concentration of grains (Fig. 2). This result is surprising since the pterygopalatine nerve is sensory, although there may also be a parasympathetic component as well. In addition, we have cultured day 14.5 palate explants and performed immunocytochemistry with an antibody specific for serotonin. It was observed that neurons were strongly stained and in some preparations these serotoninergic neurons emanated from the pterygopalatine ganglion. Mesenchymal cells showed a weaker stain when explants were incubated with 10^{-5} M serotonin. However, little stain was present when cells were not loaded with serotonin (E. Zimmerman, E. Wee, and J. Lauder, unpublished observations). These results confirm our previous experiments (see Fig. 2) and suggest that the palate contains nerves with elevated levels of serotonin and mesenchymal cells with low concentrations of serotonin and a specific uptake mechanism. The function of these serotonin-containing structures in palate reorientation is not known at present.

As indicated previously, palate reorientation may involve direct contractility of palate cells or a modulation of cell tension to counterbalance the force derived from hyaluronate-induced hydration. Since serotonin stimulated palate reorientation, it was of interest to determine whether serotonin could affect cell contractility or tension. Therefore, we tested the effect of serotonin on cell motility as an assay

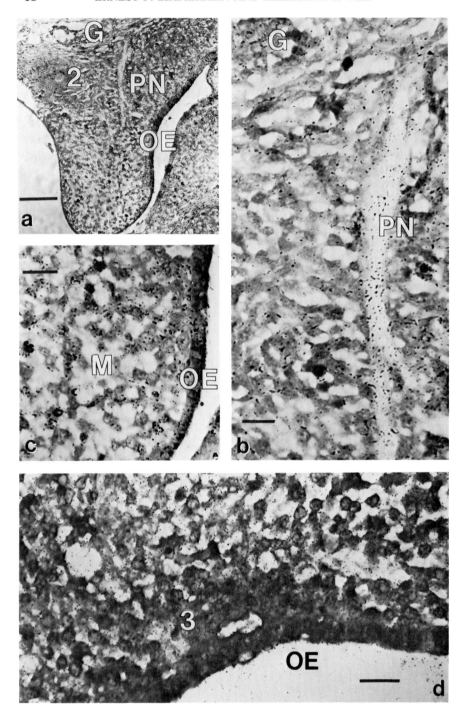

for cell contractility. In one system, the migration of palate mesenchymal cells from two explants toward each other in a hydrated collagen lattice was employed. Palatal cells move along the fibrous tracks, which can be observed by phase microscopy. It was ascertained by scanning electron microscopy that the fibrous tracks were bundles of coalesced collagen fibrils aligned parallel to the moving cell process. Thus, palate mesenchymal cells exerted tractional forces on the extracellular environment composed of hydrated collagen in a matrix. The tractional force thus could transfer cell tension to the whole tissue via the extracellular component (e.g., collagen) to effect palate reorientation (see above). Next, palate shelves were incubated at 37°C for 1 hour with 10^{-5} M serotonin and then explanted in the hydrated collagen lattice. Serotonin markedly stimulated cell migration out of the explant along the fibrous tracks after 2 and 3 days in culture, compared to the appropriate controls. Cell migration was quantitated by counting the number of cells migrating out of the explants after 18 hours. In a dose–response experiment serotonin stimulated cell migration by 100% (Table III). The 5×10^{-6} M and 10^{-5} M serotonin concentrations were optimal, and the stimulation was agonist specific, since the antagonist methysergide blocked the response (Fig. 3). However, it cannot be discerned whether or not the enhanced cell migratory behavior by serotonin causes an increase or a decrease in tensional force; there was no obvious effect on the number or size of the fibrous tracks in a hydrated collagen gel (Venkatasubramanian and Zimmerman, 1983).

The effect of serotonin on cell motility was monitored in another type of assay, based on chemotaxis since palate cells produce a chemotactic response to neural chemoattractants. The chemotactic system

---

FIG. 2. Autoradiography of palate after incorporation of 5-[^{3}H]HTP in embryo culture. Day 14.5 mouse embryos were cultured with 5-[^{3}H]HTP (10^{-4} M) for 3 hours in the presence of a monamine oxidase inhibitor, nialamide (400 μg/2 ml). Embryos were washed and fixed in Karnovsky's fixative. This procedure fixes serotonin or its derivatives in dense core vesicles within cells. After paraffin embedment, serial sections were coated with Kodak NTB2 emulsion, and slides were developed and stained histologically. Presence of grains were criteria of serotonin or its derivatives in palatal cells. (a) Mid-posterior section of palate indicating region 2, pterygopalatine ganglion (G), pterygopalatine nerve (PN), and oral epithelium (OE). Bar, 75 μm. (b) Higher magnification of ganglion and nerve showing grains. Bar, 10 μm. (c) Lower area of oral side of palate shelf with grains in mesenchyme (M) and oral epithelium. Bar, 20 μm. (d) Grains are present throughout region 3 cells. Bar, 20 μm. (Adapted from Zimmerman et al., 1981.)

TABLE III

Effect of Serotonin on Palate Morphogenesis and Metabolic Systems

System	Optimal concentration (M)	Optimal time	% Control
Morphogenetic			
Palate reorientation in embryo culture	$10^{-8} + 10^{-5}$	2 hours	250
Cell motility in hydrated collagen lattice	5×10^{-6} to 10^{-5}	1 hour	200
Cell motility in chemotactic system	10^{-5}	1 hour	192–490
Metabolic			
Protein carboxyl methylation	3×10^{-7} to 3×10^{-6}	45 minutes	200[a]
Cyclic AMP level	10^{-5}	3 hours	19
Cyclic GMP level	10^{-5}	30 seconds	610

[a]In many experiments the optimal concentration of serotonin varied from 3×10^{-7} to 3×10^{-6} M. Stimulation in each experiment was approximately 100% (200% of control).

employed comprised cultured palate mesenchymal cells, the chemotactic substance(s) in neuroblastoma-conditioned medium, and a modified Boyden chamber. Trypsinized cells were pretreated with serotonin, and it was observed that serotonin markedly stimulated cell motility. Serotonin at 10^{-5} M was optimal, with nearly 100% stimulation achieved employing undiluted neuroblastoma-conditioned medium. With the chemotactic preparation diluted 1:100 less cell motility was achieved. Serotonin (10^{-5} M) now stimulated cell motility 4.9-fold (Table III). However, serotonin itself was not chemotactic and stimulation was only achieved if the cells were undergoing migration toward the chemoattractant. Thus, serotonin served to modulate the movement of cells but did not induce movement (Zimmerman et al., 1983).

We next wished to test for the effect of serotonin on biochemical reactions that are associated with cell motility, protein secretion, and differentiation. Protein carboxyl methylation is an ubiquitous metabolic process. In mammals, chemotactic peptides stimulate protein carboxyl methylation (O'Dea et al., 1978) but its role in chemotaxis is still unclear. However, it is also associated with sperm motility (Gagnon et al., 1980). It is increasingly believed that protein carboxyl methylation mediates stimulus–secretion coupling since catecholamines stimulate both protein carboxyl methylation and amylase secretion in parotid glands (Strittmatter et al., 1978). Protein carboxyl methylation also

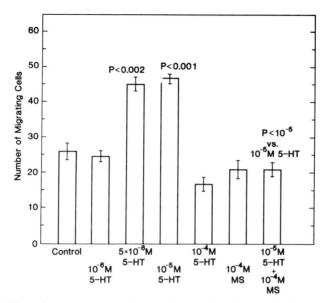

Fig. 3. Effect of serotonin and methysergide on migration of cells from explants in a collagen gel matrix. Explants were incubated with various concentrations of serotonin (5-HT) and/or 10^{-4} M methysergide (MS) for 1 hour at 37°C. Explants set 2 mm apart were cultured in hydrated collagen lattices for 18 hours. Cells that migrated between the explants were counted. Values presented are means of eight explants, and bars represent standard errors of the mean. p values obtained by comparison with control by Student's t test. (Data from Venkatasubramanian and Zimmerman, 1983.)

increases during postnatal development, the time when neurogenesis is occurring (Clark *et al.*, 1982). Cultured palate cells were capable of carrying out protein carboxyl methylation. When palate cells were treated with serotonin, protein carboxyl methylation was stimulated about 100% at concentrations ranging from 3×10^{-7} to 3×10^{-6} M in different experiments (Table III). Thus, enhanced protein carboxyl methylation by serotonin could lead to a stimulation of palate reorientation. One possibility is that increased methylated proteins could produce an increase in cell motility by serotonin, as previously described. Alternatively, a stimulation of protein carboxyl methylation by serotonin could induce a secretion of cellular lysosomal proteins to the extracellular matrix. Specific degradation of extracellular matrix components could possibly stimulate palate reorientation (see below).

Second messengers which regulate a vast array of metabolic reactions by phosphorylation of cellular proteins are modulated by neurotransmitters (Greengard, 1978). Therefore, we analyzed the effect of serotonin on palatal cyclic AMP and cyclic GMP levels in cultured mesenchymal cells and it was shown that cyclic AMP levels were inhibited and cyclic GMP levels were stimulated (Table III). In other biological systems it has been observed that the binding to a specific receptor in a particular target tissue by a neurotransmitter will elicit a specific response to either cyclic AMP or cyclic GMP. Thus, serotonin will stimulate cyclic AMP in most areas of the brain and stimulate cyclic GMP in platelets and monocytes (Goldberg and Haddox, 1977). Cyclic AMP elicits a vast array of responses during differentiation (Greengard, 1978). The other second messenger, cyclic GMP, also elicits a wide array of responses, although its role in the physiological regulation of metabolism is less certain than that of cyclic AMP. In the palate, 10^{-5} M serotonin depressed cyclic AMP levels. Within 10 minutes cyclic AMP was markedly reduced, and by 3 hours cyclic AMP was 19% of the control value (Table III). Since serotonin was inhibitory to cyclic AMP in palate cells, it was expected that cyclic GMP would be stimulated, which was observed. Serotonin at 10^{-5} M stimulated cyclic GMP with a spike of stimulation (6.1-fold) within 30 seconds (Table III). Thereafter cyclic GMP levels fell and tended to plateau after 2 minutes. At 60 minutes, cyclic GMP was still stimulated 2.4-fold. The optimal level of serotonin in stimulating cyclic GMP was 10^{-5} M, equivalent to its optimal effect in stimulating cell motility and inhibiting cyclic AMP. The effects of serotonin on palatal cyclic GMP are in accord with the effects of serotonin and cyclic GMP on chemotaxis of leukocytes. Thus, serotonin stimulated chemotaxis and cyclic GMP (Sandler et al., 1975). A causal relationship is implied since exposure of these cells to cyclic GMP stimulated chemotaxis (Estenden et al., 1973). Another known effect of cyclic GMP is to stimulate secretion of lysosomal enzymes (see Goldberg and Haddox, 1977).

It has been observed that when palate shelves reorient in situ there is a dramatic increase in the extracellular space that has been attributed to the rapid hydration of palatal hyaluronic acid (Diewert and Tait, 1979). This result is consistent with the view that hydration of hyaluronate supplies the motive force to reorient the palate. Toole et al. (1980) have suggested that swelling and subsequent shelf reorientation due to hyaluronate hydration could occur from changes in physical constraints within the palate or, alternatively, by ionic changes on the hyaluronate molecule to allow expansion of its molecular domain. We have incubated palate shelves in culture and observed swelling due to hydration of hyaluronic acid and an increase in the extracellular space between mesenchymal cells (Knudsen and Zimmerman, 1983). As indicated previously, the serotonin antagonist methysergide inhibited the reorientation of the anterior palate in embryo culture (Wee *et al.*, 1979). Furthermore, when the palatal shelves were examined histologically after methysergide treatment of mouse embryos in culture, swelling of the palatal mesenchyme in the area of region 3 was inhibited. As observed in Fig. 4a, palate shelves of control embryos reoriented significantly in culture after 2 hours and appreciable swelling of the extracellular space in the mesenchyme occurred. Cells in the putative nonmuscle contractile system, region 3, which was oriented perpendicular to oral eptithelium (Babiarz *et al.*, 1979), lost their orientation and rounded up. Furthermore, swelling of the extracellular space between these cells also occurred during the reorientation process (Fig. 4c). In contrast, methysergide completely inhibited reorientation of the mid palate (Fig. 4b) and anterior palate (not shown). The morphology of the shelf was abnormal, and although swelling on the upper tongue side of the mesenchyme occurred (Fig. 4b), swelling in the area of region 3 was markedly inhibited and the orientation of these cells was abnormal (Fig. 4d). These results suggest that serotonin may also modulate the hyaluronate-induced swelling in the extracellular space to facilitate palate reorientation.

A model describing the biochemical control of palate reorientation and its modulation by serotonin is presented (Fig. 5). As indicated by Toole *et al.* (1980), the hyaluronate (HA)-dependent swelling which would produce a molecular expansion of the extracellular space (ECS) may be controlled by mechanical constraints such as cell junctions or cell–cell or cell–extracellular matrix (ECM) adhesion. In addition, cell tension could counterbalance the HA-dependent swelling. Neurotransmitters such as serotonin or other hormones bind to their respective palatal cell receptors (R). Serotonin in the palate inhibits adenylate cyclase to depress cAMP levels, stimulates guanylate cyclase (GC) to elevate cGMP levels, and stimulates protein carboxymethylase (PCM) to stimulate protein carboxyl methylation. Serotonin stimulates Ca^{2+} influx in other tissues (Rasmussen, 1975; Kandel and Schwartz, 1982; Siegelbaum *et al.*, 1982). Ca^{2+} binds to calmodulin (CaM), the active complex playing a role in exocytosis (DeLorenzo *et al.*, 1979; Gagliardino *et al.*, 1980; Nishikawa *et al.*, 1980). Calmodulin may serve as a substrate for protein carboxymethylase (Gagnon *et al.*, 1981), the consequence of which may be a stimulation of exocytosis of specific cell products such as glycosaminoglycans (GAG) or degradative enzymes. Release of intracellular or pericellular GAG including HA, chondroitin sulfate (CS), or heparan sulfate (HS) could result in an altered conformation of HA leading to HA hydration. It has been shown that HA may exist in particulate form in the ECM (Schubert and LeCorbiere,

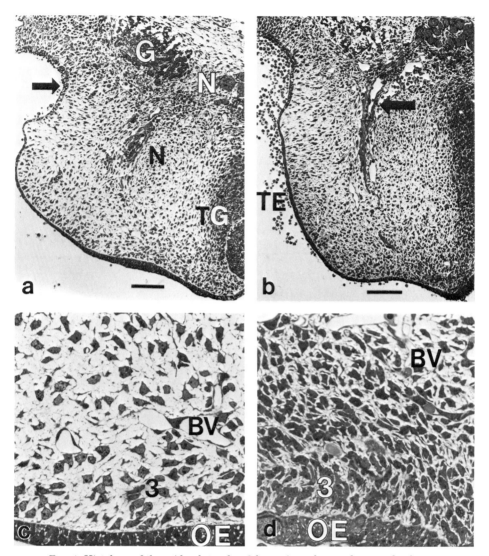

Fig. 4. Histology of the mid palate after 2 hours in embryo culture and subsequent reorientation. (a) Mid palate of control embryo. Horizontalization of oral epithelium is observed with a loss of orientation of region 3 cells (see c). In addition, a bend at the tongue side is formed as shelf reorients horizontally (arrow). G, Pterygopalatine ganglion; N, nerves; TG, tooth germ. Bar, 50 μm. (b) Mid palate of embryo cultured with methysergide (10^{-4} M) for 2 hours reveals abnormal shape of the shelf. Arrow, Major palatine artery; TE, tongue side epithelium. Bar, 50 μm. (c) Higher magnification of region 3 cells in control embryo after 2 hours in culture. Region 3 cells show a loss in orientation along oral epithelium (OE). A marked expansion of the extracellular space compared to noncultured control (not shown) has taken place, which is associated with hyaluronate hydration (Knudsen and Zimmerman, 1983). BV, Blood vessel. (d) Region 3 cells after methysergide treatment appear to have rounded less and to be slightly distorted in shape. Expansion of the extracellular space is markedly inhibited. (Adapted from Wee et al., 1979.)

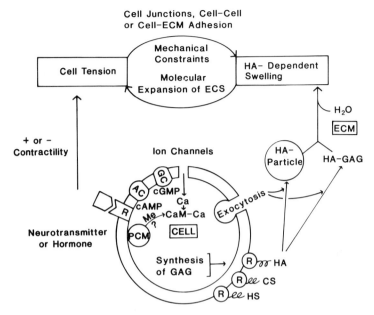

FIG. 5. Model for biochemical control of palate shelf reorientation. Events are described in text.

1982; Schubert *et al.*, 1983). Thus, the release of degradative enzymes could result in a selective degradation of components in the putative HA particle or in the HA–GAG–protein complex in the ECM. The subsequent hydration of HA would produce a HA-dependent swelling of the ECS. This expansion would overcome palatal cell tension and produce an intrinsic shelf force. There is precedence for selective degradation of ECM components. During salivary gland morphogenesis, the mesenchyme has been shown to degrade basal lamina GAG, such as heparan sulfate proteoglycan, that are synthesized by the epithelium (Bernfield, 1981; David and Bernfield, 1981). Also, metastatic tumor cells produce a selective degradation of the endothelial matrix, whereby fibronectin and heparan sulfate are hydrolyzed (Kramer *et al.*, 1982). In summary, serotonin could be regulating hydration of HA in the ECS. Alternatively, serotonin could influence cell contractility by an increase or a decrease in cell tension which would alter the equilibrium of HA-induced forces. In any case, temporal and spatial expression of serotonin or other hormonal activity could produce a vector of force to reorient the palate to a vertical position.

VII. Catecholamines in the Palate

The first report that catecholamines may play a role in palate development was from Waterman *et al.* (1976), who showed that these monoamines but not serotonin stimulated adenylate cyclase. These results implied that catecholamine receptors, which could have a regulatory function, were present in the palate. In our own study of the presence of palatal serotonin, dopamine was also measured. As seen in Table II, the concentration of palatal dopamine was 1.63 ng/mg protein, about fourfold greater than that of serotonin. Surprisingly, palatal dopamine was 68% of that in the brain at the same time in development. The relatively high level of dopamine suggests a functional role in palate development, rather than just serving as a precursor to norepinephrine. Recently, β-adrenergic receptors in palate mesenchymal cells have been monitored employing the labeled β-adrenergic ligand [^{3}H]dihydroalprenolol (Garbarino and Greene, 1984; see discussion by Greene and Garbarino, this volume). Although there appear to be catecholamine systems present in the palate, it is unlikely that they function in palate reorientation. As indicated previously, $10^{-4} M$ norepinephrine or dopamine produced no significant effect on either anterior or posterior palate reorientation in embryo culture (Table I). However, catecholamines may function in palate differentiation. Employing immunocytochemistry, the biosynthetic catecholamine enzyme tyrosine hydroxylase was observed in certain cells of the posterior palate after 3 days of culture. No activity was found in either mid or anterior palate explants (Zimmerman, Lauder, Wee, and Joh, unpublished observations). The posterior end will develop into the soft palate, containing skeletal muscle. In fact, a strong positive reaction for tyrosine hydroxylase was observed in fusing myotubes. Since it has been shown that catecholamines stimulate myogenesis in chick myoblasts *in vitro* (Curtis and Zalin, 1981), it would seem likely that catecholamines could serve to regulate myogenesis in the developing palate.

VIII. GABAergic System in the Palate and Its Relationship to Diazepam Teratogenesis

As indicated previously, GABA inhibits palate shelf reorientation. It is thought that benzodiazepines, such as diazepam, interact with benzodiazepine receptors, which in turn are linked with GABA receptors in a functional complex. The net result in either the central or peripheral nervous systems would be to mimic GABA (Tallman *et al.*,

1980; Richards *et al.*, 1982). Thus, we have investigated whether palatal GABA could function by inhibiting elevation and whether diazepam mimics palatal GABA to produce the malformation. Diazepam produced cleft palate much more markedly in the SWV strain than the A/J (Table IV). Further, we tested the effects of GABA and diazepam on palate reorientation in embryo culture, employing both strains. In the SWV strain we could markedly inhibit palate reorientation in the posterior end. The anterior end was resistant to inhibition. Interestingly, we had to use 10-fold more GABA to inhibit palate reorientation in the A/J strain and the effect was elicited at the anterior end. Picrotoxin, a GABA antagonist, significantly reversed the inhibitory effect of GABA on both strains. As with GABA, the effect was greater in SWV mice. Finally, it was shown that picrotoxin reversed the inhibition produced by diazepam (Table IV). These results suggest that diazepam inhibits shelf reorientation to produce cleft palate by interacting with a functional GABAergic system. Also, genotypic differences exist within the putative GABAergic system in the two murine strains (Wee and Zimmerman, 1983).

In our current research we have been attempting to characterize this putative GABAergic system in the palate. As one criterion of a GABAergic system, its presence in the palate has been sought. Employing gas chromatography/mass spectrometry, GABA content in the day 14.5 A/J palate was observed to be 19.2 ng/mg protein, which compares with 653.3 ng/mg in the embryonic brain (Table II). GABA concentration in both fore and hind limbs was approximately equal to

TABLE IV

COMPARISON OF DIAZEPAM AND GABA EFFECTS
ON PALATE DEVELOPMENT[a]

	A/J	SWV
Cleft palate		
Diazepam	+	+ + +
Inhibition of palate reorientation		
10^{-5} *M* GABA		+ +
10^{-4} *M* GABA	+ +	
10^{-4} *M* Diazepam	+	+ +
Picrotoxin reversal of inhibition		
GABA	+	+
Diazepam	+	+

[a]Increase in number of + symbols indicates greater effect.

that in the palate at this time in development. Interestingly, the palatal GABA concentration was significantly lower at day 14.5, the time just prior to shelf reorientation, compared to day 13.5 and 15.5 of development in the A/J mouse strain. This result is consistent with GABA functioning as an inhibitory modulator in palate development. It is also interesting that GABA levels were significantly higher in SWV than in A/J mice at day 14.5. Again this observation is consistent with the notion that a threshold exists in the palate with regard to GABA. Elevated endogenous levels are close to a threshold and addition of exogenous GABA or diazepam could exceed the GABA threshold, inhibiting shelf movement.

In order to further characterize the GABAergic system in the palate, a GABA uptake mechanism has been sought. It was observed that [³H]GABA is incorporated into palate mesenchymal cells from both SWV and A/J strains in primary culture. Employing increasing concentrations of GABA, its uptake was analyzed by a Lineweaver–Burk plot. The analysis revealed both a high-affinity and a low-affinity mechanism in mesenchymal cells from palates at day 14.5 of gestation of both SWV and A/J strains. The uptake of GABA into SWV cells is seen in Fig. 6, plotting the velocity (V) versus substrate concentration

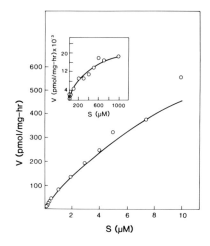

Fig. 6. GABA uptake into primary culture of day 14.5 SWV palate mesenchymal cells as a function of the external GABA concentration. Cells were cultured for 2 days, rinsed in Earle's balanced salt solution, and incubated in this solution with 3 μCi of [³H]GABA and increasing concentrations of nonradioactive GABA for 1 hour at 37°C. Monolayer cells were washed, dissolved in 0.4 N NaOH, and radioactivity and milligrams of protein determined. High-affinity uptake of GABA is plotted as indicated in text. The inset shows low-affinity uptake at higher concentrations of GABA.

(S). The lines drawn represent computer plots generated by the V_{max} and K_m of the high-affinity and low-affinity systems (inset). When V_{max} and K_m values were compared between the SWV and AJ strains, quantitative differences were observed. An analysis of the high-affinity system employing 0.1–10 μM GABA revealed a V_{max} value for SWV of 0.020 nmol/mg·minute, 3.5-fold greater than that of A/J, 0.0057. These values are about 20-fold less than those of glial cells and about 50-fold less than those of neuronal cells (Yu and Hertz, 1982). The K_m of A/J cells was 3.57 μM, which was 4.8-fold less than SWV (17.0 μM). However, this does not indicate the true relative efficiency of the system, as does V_{max}. Analyzing the low-affinity uptake system, employing 10–1500 μM GABA, SWV cells showed a 2.5-fold greater V_{max} than A/J: SWV, 0.435; A/J, 0.177. The K_m of A/J cells (197 μM) was again less than SWV (437 μM). Further indications that the high-affinity uptake mechanism in both strains was active come from the observations of a Na^+ ion dependency, a temperature dependency, and a marked inhibition by the glial uptake inhibitor β-alanine. The neuronal inhibitor diaminobutyric acid was relatively inactive. Finally, high concentrations of K^+ ion (100 mM) caused a specific secretion of [³H]GABA from SWV cells.

In summary, these results suggest the presence of a functioning GABA system in the mouse palate during development. It would appear that the system is more efficient in the SWV than the A/J strain. GABA apparently functions in palate reorientation, although its mechanism of action is unknown. It may also function in growth and differentiation of the palate, although no evidence is as yet available. Diazepam is also more teratogenic in the SWV strain than in the A/J, and its mechanisms may be mediated through a GABAergic system in analogy with its effects on neuronal activity.

IX. Concluding Remarks

It is hypothesized that humans are more susceptible to the teratogenic effects of neuropharmacologic agents than other types of agents. Since many neuropharmacologic agents function through neurotransmitter mechanisms, then neurotransmitters should function to regulate embryonic development. Evidence has been presented that neurotransmitters do indeed function as biological signals in palate development as well as in other developmental systems. It has been shown that palate reorientation is modulated by neurotransmitters with a wide range of diversity, as is also true with the central nervous system. Thus, serotonin and acetylcholine stimulate and GABA inhibits the reorientation process. Spatial diversity is also observed:

serotonin functions at the anterior and acetylcholine at the posterior end; GABA functions more efficiently at either end in different inbred strains. Many criteria of functioning neurotransmitters have been met. Both serotonin and GABA have been measured in the palate and developmental changes were observed. Physiological responses to serotonin have been monitored. Serotonin has been shown to stimulate palate cell motility as well as protein carboxyl methylation and cyclic GMP. The serotonin effects on protein carboxyl methylation and cyclic GMP could function to stimulate palate reorientation by modulating cell contractility, which could either directly reorient the palate or alter cell tension to counterbalance the force of hyaluronate hydration in the extracellular space. Alternatively, serotonin effects on protein carboxyl methylation and cyclic GMP could stimulate protein secretion, the consequence of which might lead to degradation of extracellular matrix components and thus HA hydration, expansion of ECS, and palate reorientation. Catecholamine systems have been observed in the palate, which suggests a role in its development. Further support for the hypothesis that neuropharmacologic agents could be teratogenic by perturbation of neurotransmitter mechanisms comes from studying GABA and diazepam. Evidence has been obtained that diazepam induces cleft palate by mimicking GABA in a functional GABAergic system in palate development. A significant finding is that genetic differences both in diazepam teratogenesis and in a GABAergic system have been observed. Comparing the SWV and A/J strains, the SWV mouse showed (1) a greater sensitivity to diazepam-induced cleft palate, (2) a greater sensitivity to GABA and diazepam inhibition of palate reorientation in embryo culture, (3) a greater concentration of palatal GABA, and (4) a more efficient GABA uptake system. These results are suggestive that diazepam may be more teratogenic in individual mice and humans who possess a more developed GABAergic mechanism. If such a result would obtain in the human, these genotypic differences in GABA would probably not influence the individual to a significant degree in most situations, except for the even greater risk to the embryo in the case of diazepam treatment of the mother.

REFERENCES

Babiarz, B. S., Wee, E. L., and Zimmerman, E. F. (1979). *Teratology* **20**, 249–278.
Bernfield, M. R. (1981). *In* "Morphogenesis and Pattern Formation" (T. G. Connelly, L. L. Brinkley, and B. M. Carlson, eds.), pp. 139–162. Raven, New York.
Brinkley, L. L., and Vickerman, M. M. (1982). *J. Embryol. Exp. Morphol.* **69**, 193–213.
Buznikov, G. A., and Shmukler, Y. U. (1981). *Neurochem. Res.* **6**, 55–68.

Buznikov, G. A., Chudakova, I. V., and Znezdina, N. D. (1964). *J. Embryol. Exp. Morphol.* **20,** 119–128.

Buznikov, G. A., Sakharova, A. V., Manukhin, B. M., and Markova, L. V. (1972). *J. Embryol. Exp. Morphol.* **27,** 339–351.

Campbell, G. D. (1961). *Lancet* **1,** 891–892.

Clark, R. L., Venkatasubramanian, K., and Zimmerman, E. F. (1982). *Dev. Neurosci.* **5,** 465–473.

Cochard, P., and Coltey, P. (1983). *Dev. Biol.* **98,** 221–238.

Comper, W. D., and Laurent, T. C. (1978). *Physiol. Rev.* **58,** 255–315.

Curtis, D. H., and Zalin, R. J. (1981). *Science* **214,** 1355–1357.

D'Amico-Martel, A., and Noden, D. M. (1983). *Am. J. Anat.* **166,** 445–468.

David, G., and Bernfield, M. (1981). *J. Cell Biol.* **91,** 281–286.

DeLorenzo, R. J., Freedman, S. D., Yohe, W. B., and Maurer, S. C. (1979). *Proc. Natl. Acad. Sci. U.S.A.* **76,** 1838–1842.

Diewert, V. M., and Tait, B. (1979). *J. Anat.* **128,** 609–618.

Drews, U. (1975). *Prog. Histochem. Cytochem.* **7,** 1–52.

Emanuelsson, H., and Palén, K. (1975), *Wilhem Roux Ach.* **117,** 1–17.

Estenden, R. D., Hill, H. R., Quie, P. G., Hogan, H., and Goldberg, N. (1973). *Nature (London)* **245,** 458–460.

Fauquet, M., Smith, J., Ziller, C., and LeDouarin, N. M. (1981). *J. Neurosci.* **1,** 478–492.

Feldman, G. L., Weaver, D. D., and Lovrien, E. W. (1977). *Am. J. Dis. Child.* **131,** 1389–1392.

Ferguson, M. W. (1978). *J. Anat.* **125,** 555–577.

Ferguson, M. W. (1981). *Arch. Oral Biol.* **26,** 427–443.

Gagliardino, J. J., Harmson, D. E., Christie, M. R., Gagliardino, E. E., and Ashcroft, S. J. H. (1980). *Biochem. J.* **192,** 919–927.

Gagnon, C., Sherins, R. J., Mann, T., Bardin, C. W., Amelar, R. D., and Dubin, L. (1980). *In* "Testicular Development, Structure and Function" (E. Steinberger and A. Steinberger, eds.), pp. 491–495. Raven, New York.

Gagnon, C., Kelly, S., Manganiello, V., Vaughan, M., Odya, C., and Strittmater, W. J. (1981). *Nature (London)* **291,** 515–516.

Garbarino, M. M., and Greene, R. M. (1984). *Biochem. Biophys. Res. Commun.* **119,** 193–202.

Goldberg, N. D., and Haddox, M. K. (1977). *Annu. Rev. Biochem.* **46,** 823–896.

Greengard, P. (1978). *Science* **199,** 146–152.

Grumbach, M. M., and Ducharme, J.R. (1960). *Fertil. Steril.* **11,** 157 180.

Gustafson, T., and Toneby, M. (1970). *Exp. Cell Res.* **62,** 102–117.

Ignarro, L. J., and Shideman, F. E. (1968). *J. Pharmacol. Exp. Ther.* **159,** 38–48.

Jones, K. L., and Smith, D. W. (1975). *Teratology* **12,** 1–10.

Kandel, E. R., and Schwartz, J. H. (1982). *Science* **218,** 433–443.

Kirby, M. L., and Gilmore, S. A. (1972). *Anat. Rec.* **173,** 469–478.

Knudsen, T. B., and Zimmerman, E. F. (1982). *Anat. Rec.* **202,** 100A.

Knudsen, T. B., and Zimmerman, E. F. (1983). *Anat. Rec.* **205,** 100A.

Kramer, R. H., Vogel, K. G., and Nicholson, G. L. (1982). *J. Biol. Chem.* **257,** 2678–2686.

Kuhn, E. M., Babiarz, B. S., Lessard, J. L., and Zimmerman, E. F. (1980). *Teratology* **21,** 209–233.

Lauder, J. M., and Krebs, H. (1978). *Dev. Neurosci.* **1,** 15–30.

Lauder, J. M., Wallace, J. A., Krebs, H., Petrusz, P., and McCarthy, K. (1982). *Brain Res. Bull.* **9,** 605–625.

Lawrence, I. E., and Burden, H. W. (1973). *Am. J. Anat.* **137,** 199–207.

Lenke, R. R., and Levy, H. L. (1980). *N. Engl. J. Med.* **303,** 1202–1208.

Lenz, W. (1962). *Lancet* **1**, 45.

Lessard, J. L., Wee, E. L., and Zimmerman, E. F. (1974). *Teratology* **9**, 113–126.

Matsumoto, H. G., Koya, G., and Takeuchi, T. (1965). *J. Neuropathol. Exp. Neurol.* **24**, 563–574.

McMahon, D. (1974). *Science* **185**, 1012–1021.

Meadow, S. R. (1970). *Proc. R. Soc. Med.* **63**, 12–13.

Nakane, Y., Okuma, T., Takahashi, R., Sato, Y., Wada, T., Sato, T., Fukushima, Y., Kumashiro, H., Ono, T., Takahashi, T., Aoki, Y., Kazamatsuri, H., Inami, M., Komai, S., Seino, M., Miyakoshi, M., Tanimura, T., Hazama, H., Kawahara, R., Otsuki, S., Hosokawa, K., Inanaga, K., Nakazawa, Y., and Yamamoto, K. (1980). *Epilepsia* **21**, 663–680.

Nishikawa, M., Tanaka, T., and Hidaka, H. (1980). *Nature (London)* **287**, 863–864.

O'Dea, R., Viveros, O., Axelrod, J., Aswanikumar, S., Schiffmann, E., and Corcoran, B. (1978). *Nature (London)* **272**, 462–464.

Oey, J. (1975). *Nature (London)* **257**, 317–319.

Palén, K., Thorneby, L., and Emanuelsson, H. (1979). *Wilhelm Roux Arch.* **187**, 89–103.

Penit, J., Cantau, B., Huot, J., and Jard, S. (1977). *Proc. Natl. Acad. Sci. U.S.A.* **74**, 1575–1579.

Pratt, R. M., Goggins, J. F., Wilk, A. L., and King, C. T. (1973). *Dev. Biol.* **32**, 230–237.

Rasmussen, H. (1975). *In* "Cell Membranes-Biochemistry Cell Biology and Pathology" (G. Weismann and R. Claiborne, eds.), pp. 203–212. HP Publ., New York.

Renaud, F., Parisi, E., Capasso, A., and DePrisco, P. (1983). *Dev. Biol.* **98**, 37–46.

Reporter, M., and Rosenquist, C. G. (1972). *Science* **178**, 628–630.

Richards, J. G., Mohler, H., and Haefely, W. (1982). *Trends Pharmacol. Sci.* **3**, 233–235.

Robert, E., and Guibaud, P. (1982). *Lancet* **2**, 937.

Robertson, A., and Gingle, A. R. (1977). *Science* **197**, 1078–1079.

Safra, M. J., and Oakley, G. P. (1975). *Lancet* **2**, 478–480.

Sandler, J. A., Gallen, J. I., and Vaughan, M. (1975). *J. Cell Biol.* **69**, 480–484.

Schowing, J., Sprumont, P., and Van Toledo, B. (1977). *C. R. Acad. Sci. Paris* **171**, 1163–1166.

Schubert, D., and La Corbiere, M. (1982). *J. Neurosci.* **2**, 82–99.

Schubert, D., La Corbiere, M., Klier, F. G., and Birdwell, C. (1983). *J. Cell Biol.* **96**, 990–998.

Schwartz, J. P. (1976). *J. Cyclic Nucleotide Res.* **2**, 287–296.

Shah, R. M. (1979). *J. Embryol. Exp. Morphol.* **53**, 1–13.

Sieber-Blum, M. (1983). *Dev. Biol.* **99**, 352–359.

Siegelbaum, S. A., Camardo, J. S., and Kandel, E. R. (1982). *Nature (London)* **299**, 413–417.

Smith, J., Fauquet, M., Ziller, C., and Le Douarin, N. M. (1979). *Nature (London)* **282**, 853–855.

Strittmatter, W., Gagnon, C., and Axelrod, J. (1978). *J. Pharmacol. Exp. Ther.* **207**, 419–424.

Strudel, G., Recasens, M., and Mandel, P. (1977). *C. R. Acad. Sci. Paris* **284**, 967–969.

Tallman, J. F., Paul, S. M., Skolnick, P., and Gallagher, D. W. (1980). *Science* **207**, 274–281.

Thiersch, J. B. (1952). *Am. J. Obstet. Gynecol.* **63**, 1298–1304.

Toneby, M. (1977). *Wilhelm Roux's Archives* **181**, 247–259.

Toole, B. P., Underhill, C. B., Mikuni-Takagaki, Y., and Orkin, R. W. (1980). *In* "Current Research Trends in Prenatal Craniofacial Development" (R. M. Pratt and R. L. Christiansen, eds.), pp. 263–275. Elsevier, Amsterdam.

Venkatasubramanian, K., and Zimmerman, E. F. (1983). *J. Craniofac. Genet. Dev. Biol.* **3,** 143–157.

Walker, B. E., and Fraser, F. C. (1956). *J. Embryol. Exp. Morphol.* **4,** 176–189.

Wallace, J. A. (1979). Ph.D. thesis, University of California, Davis.

Wallace, J. A. (1982). *Am. J. Anat.* **165,** 261–276.

Wallace, J. A., and Lauder, J. M. (1983). *Brain Res. Bull.* **10,** 459–479.

Warkany, J. (1975). *Am. J. Dis. Child.* **129,** 187–288.

Waterman, R. E., Palmer, G. C., Palmer, S. J., and Palmer, S. M. (1976). *Anat. Rec.* **185,** 125–138.

Wee, E. L., and Zimmerman, E. F. (1980). *Teratology* **21,** 15–27.

Wee, E. L., and Zimmerman, E. F. (1983). *Teratology* **28,** 15–22.

Wee, E. L., Babiarz, B. S., Zimmerman, S., and Zimmerman, E. F. (1979). *J. Embryol. Exp. Morphol.* **53,** 75–90.

Wee, E. L., Phillips, N. J., Babiarz, B. S., and Zimmerman, E. F. (1980). *J. Embryol. Exp. Morphol.* **58,** 177–193.

Wee, E. L., Kujawa, M., and Zimmerman, E. F. (1981). *Cell Tissue Res.* **217,** 143–154.

Weston, J. A. (1970). *Adv. Morphog.* **8,** 41–114.

Yu, A. C. H., and Hertz, L. (1982). *J. Neurosci. Res.* **7,** 23–35.

Zimmerman, E. F., Wee, E. L., Phillips, N., and Roberts, N. (1981). *J. Embryol. Exp. Morphol.* **64,** 233–250.

Zimmerman, E. F., Clark, R. L., Ganguli, S., and Venkatasubramanian, K. (1983). *J. Craniofac. Genet. Dev. Biol.* **3,** 371–385.

CHAPTER 4

ROLE OF CYCLIC AMP, PROSTAGLANDINS, AND CATECHOLAMINES DURING NORMAL PALATE DEVELOPMENT

Robert M. Greene and Michele P. Garbarino

DEPARTMENT OF ANATOMY
DANIEL BAUGH INSTITUTE
THOMAS JEFFERSON UNIVERSITY
PHILADELPHIA, PENNSYLVANIA

I. Introduction

The embryonic mammalian secondary palate provides the developmental biologist with an extremely attractive biological system since a wide variety of developmental phenomena easily lend themselves to investigation. Morphogenetic movements (Wee *et al.*, 1976, 1980; Kuhn *et al.*, 1980), epithelial–mesenchymal interaction (Tyler and Koch, 1977a,b; Tyler and Pratt, 1980), cellular adhesion (Greene and Pratt, 1977), and programmed cell death (Pratt and Greene, 1976; Greene and Pratt, 1979a) have all been examined during palatal development.

In addition, the developing orofacial region is of obvious clinical interest. Craniofacial malformations are expressed in a large number of newborn human infants. One baby in approximately every 600 live births will display an orofacial cleft. This translates into over 15,000 new cleft infants born each year in the United States alone (Slavkin, 1979).

Although much is known about the descriptive morphology of normal and abnormal development of the mammalian secondary palate (Greene and Pratt, 1976), biochemical control mechanisms governing differentiative processes during craniofacial ontogenesis have been, until recently, largely unknown. Studies focused on understanding

CURRENT TOPICS IN DEVELOPMENTAL BIOLOGY, VOL. 19

ISBN 0-12-153119-8

how normal embryonic development may be perturbed, with resultant palatal clefts, should be encouraged in view of the disturbingly high incidence of cleft palate among newborn infants.

Recent evidence suggests that hormonally regulated levels of cyclic adenosine 3′,5′-monophosphate (cAMP) influence normal growth and differentiation of the developing orofacial region. In this chapter we discuss some of our current work dealing with the metabolic interrelationships between cyclic AMP, prostaglandins, and catecholamines during craniofacial development and how they may regulate the biochemical events known to be involved in palate formation.

II. Morphology of Secondary Palate Formation

Several reviews are available which deal with the salient features of the developing secondary palate (Walker and Fraser, 1956; Greene and Pratt, 1976; Greene, 1983). Only a brief overview will be presented here to acquaint the reader with the system.

The mammalian palate originates as bilateral outgrowths from the oral aspect of the maxillary processes. These outgrowths consist of mesenchymal cells, embedded in a hyaluronate-rich (Pratt et al., 1973) extracellular matrix enclosed by epithelium. Each palatal process undergoes a series of morphogenetic movements which brings it from a vertical position on either side of the tongue to a horizontal position above the tongue. Palatal extracellular matrix components and nonmuscle contractile systems (see Chapters by Brinkley and Morris-Wiman, and Zimmerman and Wee, this volume) have been most frequently and recently implicated as being responsible for this movement.

Soon after this reorientation, the medial edge epithelia of homologous palatal processes adhere to one another via newly synthesized cell surface glycoconjugates (Pratt and Hassell, 1975; Greene and Pratt, 1977; Meller and Barton, 1978) and desmosomes (Smiley, 1970), forming a midline epithelial seam (Fig. 1). This epithelial band of cells undergoes autolysis (Hayward, 1969; Chaudhry and Shah, 1973), allowing mesenchyme from the two originally separate palatal processes to merge and form the secondary palate. The common oronasal cavity is thus separated into an oral cavity below the palate and a nasal cavity above the palate.

III. Cyclic AMP and Palate Differentiation

Cyclic AMP is known to modulate cellular differentiation in a wide variety of developing tissues (Zalin and Leaver, 1975; Ahrens et al.,

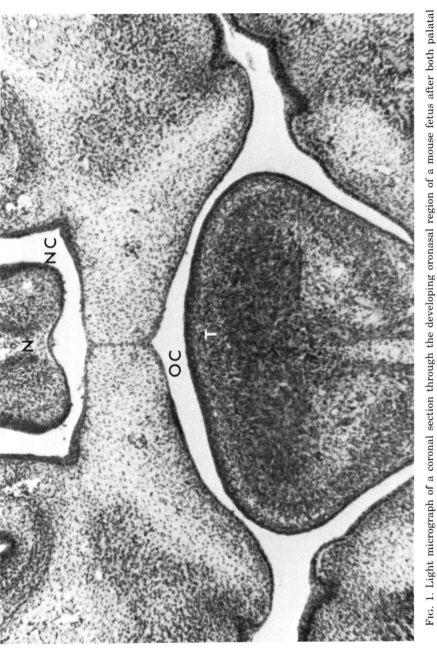

FIG. 1. Light micrograph of a coronal section through the developing oronasal region of a mouse fetus after both palatal processes have reoriented into a position between the tongue (T) and nasal septum (N). Note that the two shelves have merged into a single definitive secondary palate separating the nasal cavity (NC) from the oral cavity (OC). ×50. (From Greene, 1983).

1977; Perry and Oka, 1980; Juliani *et al.*, 1981; Chapman, 1981), including the developing palate (Erickson *et al.*, 1979; Olson and Massaro, 1980; Pratt *et al.*, 1980; Greene *et al.*, 1981a). These latter studies demonstrate a positive correlation between teratogenic agents or mutant genes known to affect palatal development adversely and alterations in palatal cAMP levels.

The gestation period of maximal palatal adenylate cyclase activity (Waterman *et al.*, 1976) has been shown to correlate temporally with the transient elevation of palatal cAMP levels during palatal reorientation and epithelial differentiation (Greene and Pratt, 1979b) (Fig. 2). The precise role which cAMP plays in palatal differentiation is not known, although palatal cAMP may play a key role in controlling the synthesis of cell products identified with palatal differentiation (Pratt and Martin, 1975; Pratt and Greene, 1976; Greene *et al.*, 1982). Palatal differentiation may be defined in terms of glycosaminoglycan (Wilk *et al.*, 1978), collagen (Hassell and Orkin, 1976), cell surface glycoconjugate (Greene and Pratt, 1977), and prostaglandin (Palmer *et al.*, 1980; Chepenik and Greene, 1981) biosynthesis as well as epithelial autolysis (Pratt and Greene, 1976). Elevated levels of intracellular cAMP have been correlated, in other systems, with induction of all these processes. Moreover, elevation of cAMP in the developing palate has been shown to modulate both autolysis (Goldman, 1981) and glycosaminoglycan synthesis (Greene *et al.*, 1982).

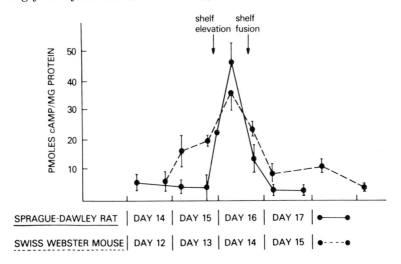

FIG. 2. Specific activity of palatal cAMP is plotted as a function of gestational age. Full line traces Sprague–Dawley rat palatal cAMP/mg protein. Broken line traces Swiss Webster mouse palatal cAMP/mg protein. (From Greene and Pratt, 1979b.)

Palatal extracellular glycosaminoglycans have been frequently cited as playing a critical role in morphogenetic movement of the developing palate (Larsson, 1961; Wilk et al., 1978). We have recently shown that the synthesis of extracellular glycosaminoglycans by murine palatal mesenchymal cells in vitro was stimulated in a dose-dependent manner by treatment with exogenous dibutyryl cAMP, 8-Br cAMP, the phosphodiesterase inhibitor 3-isobutyl-1-methylxanthine, and doses of prostaglandin E_2 (PGE_2) or prostacyclin (PGI_2) that stimulate the synthesis of endogenous cAMP (Greene et al., 1982). Qualitative analysis of palatal glycosaminoglycans indicated a preferential stimulation of hyaluronic acid synthesis. This is an interesting observation in light of the putatively critical role played by hyaluronic acid in palatal shelf movement (Brinkley, 1980).

Interpretation of studies dealing with elevation of endogenous cAMP must be tempered by the fact that the developing palate is a heterogeneous tissue composed of many different cell types. We have found that employing immunohistochemical procedures to detect cAMP is valuable in providing information on cAMP tissue localization and distribution. Using this approach, a differential localization of cAMP in developing rodent palatal tissue was in fact observed (Greene et al., 1980). Staining for cAMP was most intense in palatal medial edge epithelial cytoplasm just prior to and during differentiation of this epithelium. In addition, cAMP was localized along epithelial and mesenchymal plasma membranes. More recently, this technique has been used to demonstrate reduction of palatal epithelial cAMP staining intensity during glucocorticoid-induced cleft palate (Greene et al., 1981a) and reduced staining intensity in the avian medial edge epithelium (Greene et al., 1983). Avian palatal tissue fails to undergo epithelial differentiation characteristic of the mammalian palate and exhibits a median cleft. In this latter study, we have taken advantage of the finding that staining intensity serves as a semiquantitative means to assess cellular cAMP levels (Ortez, 1978). By measuring the relative intensity of immunohistochemical staining for cAMP in single palatal cells with a microphotometer, we quantitatively confirmed that the apparent difference in staining intensity seen when comparing murine and avian palatal medial edge epithelium was significant ($p < 0.01$).

These data may be interpreted as suggesting that normal development of the secondary palate is dependent upon the proper synthesis, both temporally and quantitatively, of epithelial, and quite possibly mesenchymal, cAMP. This interpretation draws support from studies which demonstrate that exogenous dibutyryl cAMP prevents epidermal growth factor–induced inhibition of medial edge epithelial differentiation (Hassell, 1975) and induces precocious epithelial differentiation of immature palatal tissue *in vitro* (Pratt and Martin, 1975).

IV. Prostaglandins in Palatal Tissue

Virtually all aspects of palatal differentiation that have been described *in vivo* occur *in vitro* (Pourtois, 1966; Smiley and Koch, 1972; Pratt *et al.*, 1973; Greene and Pratt, 1977). It has also been shown that palatal mesenchyme modulates epithelial differentiation (Tyler and Koch, 1977a,b; Ferguson, 1981). In view of evidence presented in the preceding section supporting a role for cAMP in development of the palate, it is reasonable to speculate that palatal cAMP levels may be modulated by factors derived locally from mesenchyme.

Prostaglandins constitute a diverse family of locally active lipids, many of which are known to stimulate synthesis of cAMP in a wide variety of mammalian cells (Samuelsson *et al.*, 1978). Since relatively little is known about the biosynthesis and physiological roles of prostaglandins during fetal development (Powell and Solomon, 1978; Chepenik and Smith, 1980), we have begun to pursue the hypothesis that mesenchymal lipid autocoids play a regulatory role in palatal development. Primary cultures of fetal palatal mesenchymal cells were shown to synthesize several prostaglandins, which were identified by thin-layer chromatography (Chepenik and Greene, 1981), high-performance liquid chromatography, and radioimmunoassay (Alam *et al.*, 1982). Serum stimulated the release of several different metabolites of arachidonic acid including prostaglandin E_2, prostaglandin $F_{2\alpha}$, and 6-ketoprostaglandin $F_{1\alpha}$ (the stable breakdown product of prostacyclin, prostaglandin I_2). Indomethacin and 5,8,11,14-eicosatetraenoic acid, both inhibitors of prostaglandin synthesis, prevented stimulated increases in palatal prostanoid synthesis.

These prostaglandins may serve as local modulators of palatal cAMP levels, since we have recently shown that primary monolayer cultures of palatal mesenchyme responded to challenge from PGE_2 and PGI_2 by accumulating cAMP in a dose-dependent manner (Greene *et al.*, 1981b) (Fig. 3). PGI_2 was significantly more effective than PGE_2 in stimulating the synthesis of cAMP, with physiologic concentrations (10^{-11} M) producing significant increases in intracellular cAMP.

A rate-limiting step in prostaglandin synthesis is the mobilization of arachidonic acid from cellular phospholipids by phospholipase A_2 (EC 3.1.1.4) (Lands, 1979). It follows, therefore, that the activity of this enzyme may be critical for normal palatal development. Evidence sup-

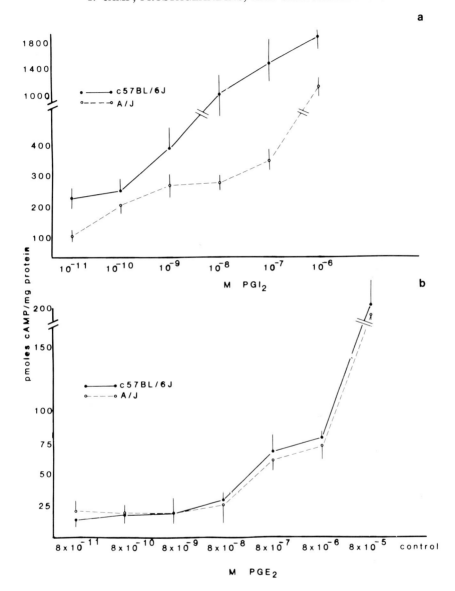

FIG. 3. Effect of increasing concentrations of prostacyclin (PGI$_2$) (a) or prostaglandin E$_2$ (PGE$_2$) (b) on intracellular levels of cAMP in murine palatal mesenchymal cells in monolayer culture. Cells are grown to subconfluency, placed in serum-free medium, and stimulated with either PGI$_2$ for 5 minutes or PGE$_2$ for 15 minutes. Note the greater ability of C57 cells to respond to PGI$_2$. Values represent the mean ± standard error of quadruplicate determinations. (From Greene *et al.*, 1981b.)

porting this hypothesis may be drawn from the observations that glucocorticoids, known to induce an inhibitor of phospholipase A_2 in other cells and tissues (Flower and Blackwell, 1979; Hirata *et al.*, 1980), induce cleft palate in several strains of mouse embryos. Moreover, Tzortzatou *et al.* (1981) have suggested that glucocorticoid induction of cleft palate is accompanied by a reduction in available arachidonic acid in developing fetal oral tissues.

Glucocorticoids more readily induce cleft palate in A/J than in C57BL/6J strain mouse embryos (Walker and Fraser, 1957). When palatal mesenchymal cells from both strains are labeled with [^{14}C]arachidonate *in vitro* and subsequently stimulated with endogenous phospholipase A_2, A/J cells release less radiolabel than C57BL/6J cells (Chepenik and Greene, 1981). We have postulated that this impaired ability to mobilize endogenous arachidonic acid, coupled with a decreased sensitivity to stimulation by prostaglandins (Fig. 3), would render a prostaglandin-dependent process in the palate sensitive to alteration by any agent (e.g., glucocorticoids) or condition which alters arachidonate metabolism.

To investigate whether such agents or conditions alter mobilization of arachidonic acid, conditions under which palatal cells hydrolyze lipids must first be defined. In a recent study, George *et al.* (1983) demonstrated palatal phospholipase activity at acid, neutral, and basic pH. Calcium was found to stimulate phospholipase activity at neutral and basic pH, but it was inhibitory at acid pH. Thus, the extent to which multiple phospholipase A activities regulate, or are in turn regulated, during orofacial development may now be pursued.

V. Catecholamines and Palate Development

Current studies in our laboratory have focused on other possible regulators of cyclic AMP levels during palate morphogenesis. It is well known that the primary biochemical event in β-adrenergic receptor-mediated responses in a variety of tissues is the activation of adenylate cyclase and the subsequent generation of cyclic AMP (Lefkowitz *et al.*, 1982). Moreover, catecholamines have been implicated as modulators of cellular differentiation in many developing tissues (Lawrence and Burden, 1973; Polson *et al.*, 1977; Lipshultz *et al.*, 1981; Curtis and Zalin, 1981; East and Dutton, 1982; Pairault *et al.*, 1982) including the secondary palate (Waterman *et al.*, 1976; Palmer *et al.*, 1980). Catecholamines are able to stimulate palatal adenylate cyclase *in vivo*, with maximum sensitivity to hormonal activation occurring during the period of palatal cellular differentiation (Waterman *et al.*, 1976).

The β-blocking agent propranolol was shown to antagonize nor-epinephrine-sensitive adenylate cyclase, suggesting that developing palatal tissue has the capability to respond to catecholamines by activation of the cyclase via binding to β-adrenergic receptors.

Our studies (Greene *et al.*, 1981b; Greene, 1983) demonstrate that palatal mesenchymal cells *in vitro* are able to respond to challenge from isoproterenol, a potent β-agonist, with a dose-dependent increase in cyclic AMP (Table I). Since the actions of catecholamines are initiated by their interaction with receptors (Lefkowitz *et al.*, 1982), these data suggest the presence of β-adrenergic receptors in the developing secondary palate.

Preliminary investigations have identified and partially characterized a palatal β-adrenergic receptor system (Garbarino and Greene, 1984). Using [³H]dihydroalprenolol ([³H]DHA), a β-adrenergic antagonist with high affinity and specificity for β-adrenergic receptors in a direct binding assay (Lefkowitz, 1975), we have demonstrated that specific binding of the ligand to day 13 palatal tissue is saturable at approximately 5.0 nM (Fig. 4). Since true receptors exist in limited number, these data indicate the presence of a finite number of high-affinity binding sites. Analysis of these data by the method of Scatchard (1949) (inset, Fig. 4) yielded a binding site density (B_{max}) of 16.0 fmol/mg protein and an equilibrium binding constant (K_D) of 1.5 nM.

Propranolol, a β-adrenergic antagonist, was able to compete with [³H]DHA for the finite number of binding sites, as evidenced by a dose-dependent decrease in specifically bound DHA (Fig. 5). The biphasic nature of the curve suggests that propranolol is competing with [³H]DHA for palatal binding sites with different affinities. Indeed,

TABLE I

ISOPROTERENOL STIMULATION OF PALATAL
MESENCHYME *in Vitro*[a]

Treatment	pmoles cAMP/µg DNA ± SD[b]
Control	0.22 ± 0.02
Isoproterenol (1 µM)	2.64 ± 0.15
Isoproterenol (10 µM)	8.5 ± 0.30

[a]Murine palatal mesenchyme was treated with iso-proterenol (15 minutes) and cellular cAMP levels determined by radioimmunoassay.

[b]Values are means ± SD of at least three separate determinations.

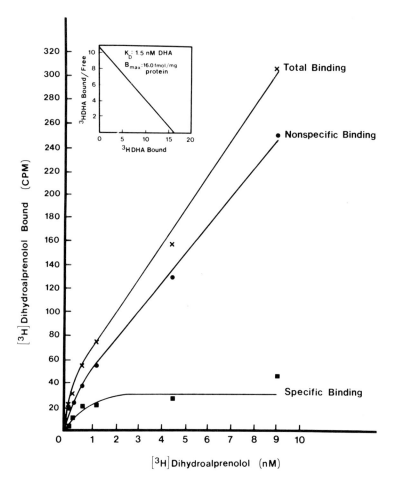

FIG. 4. [³H]DHA saturation binding to day 13 fetal mouse palatal tissue homogenates. Aliquots of homogenate (50 µg protein/100 µl) were incubated with increasing concentrations of [³H]DHA (0–10 nM) in the absence or presence of 0.5 µM (±) propranolol for 10 minutes at 37°C. Bound and free [³H]DHA were separated by vacuum filtration over glass fiber filters. Specific binding was determined from the difference between total binding (in absence of propranolol) and nonspecific binding (in presence of propranolol). Scatchard analysis of saturation binding data yielded a B_{max} (maximum number of [³H]DHA binding sites) of 16.0 fmol/mg protein and a K_D (equilibrium binding constant) of 1.5 nM [³H]DHA.

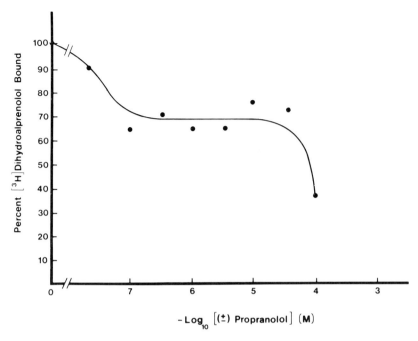

FIG. 5. Competition between [³H]DHA and propranolol (a β-adrenergic antagonist) for binding to day 13 fetal mouse palatal tissue homogenates. Aliquots of homogenate (50 μg protein/100 μl) were incubated with [³H]DHA (6.9 nM) in the absence or presence of increasing concentrations of (±) propranolol for 10 minutes at 37°C. Total binding of [³H]DHA at each concentration of propranolol is expressed as a percent of binding in the absence of competitor.

determination of specifically bound [³H]DHA over a wider range of radioligand concentrations (0–140 nM) resulted in a second region of saturation indicating a second class of moderate-affinity (K_D, 20.8 nM) binding sites (B_{max}, 31.0 fmol/mg protein). The reversibility of [³H]DHA binding was further confirmed by a dissociation kinetic study. Following the establishment of maximal [³H]DHA binding, excess propranolol was shown to compete specifically bound [³H]DHA off receptors, indicating dissociation of the radioligand from its binding sites (Fig. 6).

Binding of hormones to cellular receptors generally results in a biological response. Such cellular responsiveness differentiates receptor–ligand from "acceptor"–ligand interactions. The primary biochemical response of β-adrenergic receptor-mediated responses is the activation of adenylate cyclase and the generation of cAMP (Lefkowitz *et al.*, 1982). In a preliminary study, the responsiveness of fetal palatal

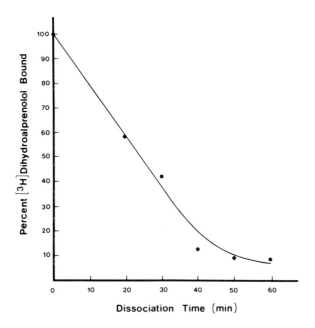

FIG. 6. Reversibility of [³H]DHA binding to day 13 fetal mouse palatal tissue homogenates. Aliquots of homogenates (50 μg/100 μl) were incubated with [³H]DHA (6.9 nM) for 10 minutes at 37°C. At time 0 (time immediately following initial 10 minutes incubation), binding was reversed by the addition of excess propranolol (2.0 μM) and incubation continued at 37°C. At the indicated times, binding was terminated by dilution and filtration of the incubation mixtures. [³H]DHA specifically bound at each time point is expressed as a percent of specific binding at time 0.

tissue to a variety of catecholamines was investigated by measuring accumulation of cAMP. Catecholamine stimulation resulted in a dose-dependent accumulation of cAMP. This response was stereospecific and displayed pharmacologic specificity characteristic of β-adrenergic receptors (isoproterenol >> epinephrine > norepinephrine).

Binding of the radioligand [³H]DHA is thus to true physiological receptors in palatal tissue since binding was shown to be saturable, of high affinity and low capacity, and reversible, and to have pharmacologic and stereospecificity, as well as to result in a biological response, i.e., elevation of cyclic AMP. These data suggest a role for the β-adrenergic receptor-adenylate cyclase system in development of the secondary palate.

VI. Summary

The biochemical regulatory mechanisms controlling palatal differentiation are largely unknown. Published data suggest that hormonally regulated levels of cyclic AMP may be important in normal, as well as abnormal, development of the secondary palate. Palatal cAMP, prostaglandins, and catecholamines appear to be integrally involved in cellular differentiation during normal palatal development.

Studies such as those outlined in this chapter are fundamental to meaningful investigations probing the etiology of abnormal development. Questions dealing with biochemical mechanisms of action of potential cleft palate teratogens, or with genetically based orofacial malformations, must be grounded on a thorough understanding of biochemical events and regulation of these events during normal craniofacial development. Evidence suggests that cyclic AMP levels, possibly regulated by prostaglandin and/or catecholamine receptor occupancy, may play an important role in *normal* growth and differentiation of the developing orofacial region and may serve as metabolic foci for teratogenic perturbation resulting in palatal clefting.

ACKNOWLEDGMENTS

Supported by NIH Grants DE05550 and DE06397. RMG is recipient of NIH Research Career Development Award DE00095. Michele P. Garbarino is supported by a generous predoctoral fellowship from the Percival E. and Ethel Brown Foerderer Foundation.

REFERENCES

Ahrens, P. B., Solursh, M., and Reiter, R. S. (1977). *Dev. Biol.* **60,** 69–82.

Alam, I., Capitanio, A., Smith, J. B., Chepenik, K. P., and Greene, R. M. (1982). *Biochem. Biophys. Acta* **712,** 408–411.

Brinkley, L. (1980). *In* "Current Research Trends in Prenatal Craniofacial Development" (R. M. Pratt and R. L. Christiansen, eds.), pp. 203–220. Elsevier, Amsterdam.

Chapman, L. P. (1981). *Exp. Cell Res.* 135, 415–418.

Chaudhry, A. P., and Shah, R. M. (1973). *J. Morphol.* **139,** 329–350.

Chepenik, K. P., and Greene, R. M. (1981). *Biochem. Biophys. Res. Commun.* **100,** 951–958.

Chepenik, K. P., and Smith, R. M. (1980). *IRCS Med. Sci.* **8,** 783–784.

Curtis, D. H., and Zalin, R. J. (1981). *Science* **214,** 1355–1357.

East, J. M., and Dutton, G. R. (1982). *Dev. Neurosci.* **5,** 117–124.

Erickson, R. P., Butley, M. S., and Sing, C. F. (1979). *J. Immunogenet.* **6,** 253–262.

Ferguson, M. W. J. (1981). *Am. Zool.* **21,** 952–958.

Flower, R. J., and Blackwell, G. J. (1979). *Nature (London)* **278,** 456–459.

Garbarino, M. M., and Greene, R. M. (1984). *Biochem. Biophys. Res. Commun.* **119,** 193–202.

George, M., Chepenik, K. P., and Greene, R. M. (1983). *Biochim. Biophys. Acta* (submitted).

Goldman, A. S. (1981). *Proc. Soc. Exp. Biol. Med.* **166,** 418–424.

Greene, R. M. (1983). *Handb. Exp. Pharmacol.* **65,** 75–92.

Greene, R. M., and Pratt, R. M. (1976). *J. Embryol. Exp. Morphol.* **36,** 225–246.

Greene, R. M., and Pratt, R. M. (1977). *Exp. Cell Res.* **105**, 27–37.

Greene, R. M., and Pratt, R. M. (1979a). *J. Histochem. Cytochem.* **26**, 1109–1114.

Greene, R. M., and Pratt, R. M. (1979b). *J. Histochem. Cytochem.* **27**, 924–931.

Greene, R. M., Shanfeld, J. L., Davidovitch, Z., and Pratt, R. M. (1980). *J. Embryol. Exp. Morphol.* **60**, 271–281.

Greene, R. M., Goldman, A. S., Lloyd, M., Baker, M., Brown, K. S., Shanfeld, J. L., and Davidovitch, Z. (1981a). *J. Craniofac. Genet. Dev. Biol.* **1**, 31–44.

Greene, R. M., Lloyd, M. R., and Nicolaou, K. C. (1981b). *J. Craniofac. Genet. Dev. Biol.* **1**, 261–272.

Greene, R. M., McAndrew, V., and Lloyd, M. R. (1982). *Biochem. Biophys. Res. Commun.* **107**, 232–238.

Greene, R. M., Shah, R. M., Crawford, B., Suen, R., Shanfeld, J. L., and Davidovitch, Z. (1983). *J. Exp. Zool.* **225**, 43–52.

Hassell, J. R. (1975). *Dev. Biol.* **45**, 90–102.

Hassell, J. R., and Orkin, R. W. (1976). *Dev. Biol.* **49**, 80–88.

Hayward, F. (1969). *Arch. Oral Biol.* **14**, 661–673.

Hirata, F., Schiffman, E., Venkatasbrumanian, K., Salomon, D., and Axelrod, J. (1980). *Proc. Natl. Acad. Sci. U.S.A.* **77**, 2533–2536.

Juliani, M. H., Brusca, J., and Klein, C. (1981). *Dev. Biol.* **83**, 114–121.

Kuhn, E. M., Babiarz, B. S., Lessard, J. L., and Zimmerman, E. F. (1980). *Teratology* **21**, 209–223.

Lands, W. E. M. (1979). *Annu. Rev. Physiol.* **41**, 633–652.

Larsson, K. S. (1961). *Acta Morphol. Neerl Scand.* **4**, 349–367.

Lawrence, I. E., and Burden, H. W. (1973). *Am. J. Anat.* **137**, 199–208.

Lefkowitz, R. J. (1975). *Biochem. Pharmacol.* **24**, 1651–1660.

Lefkowitz, R. J., Caron, M. C., Michel, T., and Stadel, J. M. (1982). *Fed. Proc. Fed Am. Soc. Exp. Biol.* **41**, 2664–2670.

Lipshultz, S., Shanfeld, J., and Chacko, S. (1981). *Proc. Natl. Acad. Sci. U.S.A.* **78**, 288–292.

Meller, S., and Barton, L. H. (1978). *Anat. Rec.* **190**, 223–232.

Olson, F. C., and Massaro, E. J. (1980). *Teratology* **22**, 155–166.

Ortez, R. A. (1978). *J. Cyclic Nucleotide Res.* **4**, 233–244.

Pairault, J., Lasnier, F., and Landat, M. H. (1982). *Eur. J. Biochem.* **127**, 351–358.

Palmer, G. C., Palmer, S. J., Waterman, R. E., and Palmer, S. M. (1980). *Pediatr. Pharmacol.* **1**, 45–54.

Perry, J. W., and Oka, T. (1980). *Proc. Natl. Acad. Sci. U.S.A.* **77**, 2093–2097.

Polson, J. B., Goldberg, N. D., and Shideman, F. E. (1977). *J. Pharmacol. Exp. Ther.* **200**, 630–637.

Pourtois, M. (1966). *J. Embryol. Exp. Morphol.* **16**, 171–182.

Powell, W. S., and Solomon, S. (1978). *Adv. Prostaglandin Thrombox. Res.* **4**, 61–74.

Pratt, R. M., and Greene, R. M. (1976). *Dev. Biol.* **54**, 135–145.

Pratt, R. M., and Hassell, J. R. (1975). *Dev. Biol.* **45**, 192–198.

Pratt, R. M., and Martin, G. R. (1975). *Proc. Natl. Acad. Sci. U.S.A.* **72**, 874–877.

Pratt, R. M., Goggins, J. R., Wilk, A. L., and King, C. T. G. (1973). *Dev. Biol.* **32**, 230–237.

Pratt, R. M., Salomon, D. R., Diewert, V. M., Erickson, R. P., Burns, R., and Brown, K. S. (1980). *Teratol. Carcinog. Mutag.* **1**, 15–23.

Samuelsson, B., Goldyne, M., Granstrom, E., Hamberg, M., Hammarstrom, S., and Malmsten, C. (1978). *Annu. Rev. Biochem.* **47**, 997–1029.

Scatchard, G. (1949). *Ann. N.Y. Acad. Sci.* **51**, 660–673.

Slavkin, H. C. (1979). *Ear Nose Throat J.* **58,** 7–20.

Smiley, G. R. (1970). *Arch. Oral Biol.* **15,** 287–296.

Smiley, G. R., and Koch, W. E. (1972). *Anat. Rec.* **173,** 405–416.

Tyler, M. S., and Koch, W. E. (1977a). *J. Embryol. Exp. Morphol.* **38,** 19–36.

Tyler, M. S., and Koch, W. E. (1977b). *J. Embryol. Exp. Morphol.* **38,** 37–48.

Tyler, M. S., and Pratt, R. M. (1980). *J. Embryol. Exp. Morphol.* **58,** 93–106.

Tzortzatou, G. G., Goldman, A. S., and Boutwell, W. C. (1981). *Proc. Soc. Exp. Biol. Med.* **166,** 321–324.

Walker, B. E., and Fraser, F. C. (1956). *J. Embryol. Exp. Morphol.* **4,** 176–189.

Walker, B. E., and Fraser, F. C. (1957). *J. Embryol. Exp. Morphol.* **5,** 201–209.

Waterman, R. E., Palmer, G. C., Palmer, S. J., and Palmer, S. M. (1976). *Anat. Rec.* **185,** 125–138.

Wee, E. L., Wolfson, L. G., and Zimmerman, E. F. (1976). *Dev. Biol.* **48,** 91–103.

Wee, E. L., Phillips, N. J., Babiaz, B., and Zimmerman, E. F. (1980). *J. Embryol. Exp. Morphol.* **58,** 177–193.

Wilk, A. L., King, C. T. G., and Pratt, R. M. (1978). *Teratology* **18,** 199–210.

Zalin, R. J., and Leaver, R. (1975). *FEBS Lett.* **53,** 33–36.

CHAPTER 5

ROLE OF GLUCOCORTICOIDS AND EPIDERMAL GROWTH FACTOR IN NORMAL AND ABNORMAL PALATAL DEVELOPMENT

Robert M. Pratt, Chung S. Kim, and Robert I. Grove

LABORATORY OF REPRODUCTIVE AND DEVELOPMENTAL TOXICOLOGY
NATIONAL INSTITUTE OF ENVIRONMENTAL HEALTH SCIENCES
NATIONAL INSTITUTES OF HEALTH
RESEARCH TRIANGLE PARK, NORTH CAROLINA

I. Introduction

It has been over 30 years since Fraser and colleagues discovered that certain inbred strains of mice were sensitive to cleft palate induction by glucocorticoid administration during midgestation. Although a great deal of progress has been made during this time in understanding the etiology of glucocorticoid-induced cleft palate in the rodent, we still have a large number of unanswered questions, especially at the biochemical and molecular level. Much of the progress made during this time has come in understanding the effect of glucocorticoids on the morphological aspects of secondary palatal development. In addition, researchers have found a number of biochemical events to be altered by glucocorticoids, i.e., cellular proliferation and extracellular matrix synthesis. It has become all too apparent that a large number of morphological as well as biochemical events are altered by glucocorticoids. This was to be expected since glucocorticoids cause numerous changes

81

in adult tissues and cells depending on the various conditions utilized such as *in vivo* or *in vitro,* age of the tissue, cell type, and dose of steroid. It has therefore become essential to design experiments in order to identify only those key events which are altered by glucocorticoids and therefore are directly involved in the etiology of cleft palate formation. During the last decade, various groups have found that the glucocorticoid receptors present in the embryo and palatal shelves are essential for glucocorticoids to induce cleft palate. It has also become clear that these receptors are located in the embryo in order to mediate the action of physiological levels of glucocorticoids, which are present in the normal rodent embryo.

During the last 5–10 years, a large number of growth factors have been discovered in a variety of adult tissues and in certain embryonic and fetal tissues. It is now clear that the rodent yolk sac and placenta are not capable of transferring maternal peptide growth factors intact to the embryo. A number of observations by Pratt and co-workers strongly suggest that an embryonic form of epidermal growth factor (EGF) is essential for normal palatal development, especially growth and differentiation of the palatal epithelial cells. EGF and other growth factors are probably important in a number of other embryonic and fetal tissues. It is the intent of this review chapter to analyze critically recent progress in those areas involving glucocorticoid and EGF involvement in normal and abnormal secondary palate development.

II. Glucocorticoids

A. GLUCOCORTICOID-INDUCED CLEFT PALATE

Glucocorticoids are important regulators of carbohydrate, protein, and fat metabolism in adult tissues (Baxter and Forsham, 1972). Glucocorticoids also perform important functions during various stages of embryonic and fetal development (Sugimoto *et al.,* 1976). Glucocorticoids, either alone or with other hormones such as thyroxine, insulin, and growth hormone, control the morphological and biochemical differentiation of a variety of fetal and postnatal tissues. For example, glucocorticoids enhance the maturation of the small intestine and lung (Greengard, 1969) and promote an increase in the synthesis of specific enzymes in the neural retina, liver, and pancreas (Moscona, 1975).

Glucocorticoids administered to several species of experimental animals at midgestation inhibit complete formation of the secondary palate (Fraser and Fainstat, 1951; Walker, 1967; Nanda *et al.,* 1970; Shah and Travill, 1976). Development of the mammalian secondary palate is a complex process which depends upon the presence of various hormones and growth factors (Salomon and Pratt, 1979). The palatal shelves first appear as outgrowths from the maxillary process and subsequently grow in a vertical position alongside the tongue. The shelves undergo a rapid reorientation to the horizontal position above the tongue, which brings the apposing epithelia into contact at the midline. The medial epithelial cells then undergo a programmed cell death with resorption of the basement membrane and cell remnants, and the two shelves fuse into a single tissue, the secondary palate, which separates the oral and nasal cavities (Walker and Fraser, 1957; Greene and Pratt, 1976). Different strains of inbred mice exhibit different degrees of susceptibility to glucocorticoid-induced cleft palate (Fraser and Fainstat, 1951; Kalter, 1954, 1965, 1981). All of the viable offspring of A/J mice treated with cortisone between days 11 and 14 of gestation have cleft palate, whereas C57BL/6J mice treated with the same dose produce 20–25% offspring with cleft palate (Biddle and Fraser, 1976; Kalter, 1954).

A number of mechanisms have been proposed to explain the different responses of various strains of mice to the teratogenic action of glucocorticoids (Greene and Kochhar, 1975; Salomon and Pratt, 1979). Walker and Fraser (1957) showed that during normal development the palatal shelves became horizontal later in development in the A/J than in the C57BL/6J strain. They suggested that A/J mice are more susceptible to cortisone than are C57BL/6J mice because of this difference, which leads in the sensitive strain to a greater delay in elevation beyond the time the shelves could still fuse when they became horizontal (Biddle and Fraser, 1977). A recent study utilizing frozen sections (Diewert and Pratt, 1981) showed that in addition to delaying palatal shelf elevation, cortisone treatment severely reduced the extent of contact between the palatal shelves in A/J mice. Other studies in which shelf contact was assessed in glucocorticoid-treated fetuses reported contact in 27–30% of the fetuses. This limited contact observed between the shelves in the midpalate region was considered adequate for complete palatal fusion, and a failure in the fusion mechanism was proposed. (Greene and Kochhar, 1973; Shah and Travill, 1976). Diewert and Pratt (1981) also observed shelf contact in the mid palate region; however, the shelves remained separated in the anterior and posterior regions. Since contact between the shelves normally occurs first in the middle region, some contact in this region would be expected; the presence of a small area of contact in some cortisone-treated palates cannot be considered equivalent to the extensive contact present in controls.

Studies of the effects of glucocorticoids on the palatal shelf epithelium in organ culture and *in vivo* suggested that there may be significant differences between tissue responses *in vitro* and *in vivo*. Investigations of the *in vivo* effects of triamcinolone on the palatal epithelium in the sensitive CF-1 mouse showed that terminal differentiation events were delayed but not prevented (Kurisu *et al.*, 1977, 1981). These results suggested that glucocorticoids did not affect programmed degenerative changes in the epithelium *in vivo*. However, one study of glucocorticoids *in vitro* reported changes in the medial epithelium; cortisol was reported to prevent medial epithelial breakdown in the sensitive A/J strain, but not in the resistant C57BL/6J strain (Herold and Futran, 1980). Based on the results of previous *in vitro* studies showing palatal fusion in the presence of hydrocortisone (Lahti and Sáxen, 1967; Lahti *et al.*, 1972; Sáxen, 1973), differences in culture conditions appear to have significant effects on the results. Therefore, although the palatal epithelium may be affected by glucocorticoids *in vitro,* these effects need not be similar to the major effect contributing to development of cleft palate *in vivo*.

Other possible explanations of strain differences in response to glucocorticoid-induced cleft palate are metabolism, level of endogenous steroids, and differential distribution of the steroid in maternal and fetal tissues. Additionally, there might be differences in sensitivity of embryonic facial structures toward the steroid. Variations in the endogenous levels of glucocorticoids in sensitive and resistant strains were not correlated with the sensitivity of the strains to steroids; there were no significant differences between A/J and C57BL/6J mice in the concentration of maternal or fetal corticosterone during midgestation (Salomon *et al.*, 1979). Glucocorticoids can cross the rodent placenta without being metabolized. The amount that reaches the embryo is dependent in part on the maternal ability to metabolize glucocorticoids. When administered in pharmacologic doses to pregnant mice, a large fraction of the administered steroid reaches embryos unmetabolized and appears to function as the active teratogenic agent (Zimmerman and Bowen, 1972).

B. Glucocorticoid Receptor Involvement in Normal and Abnormal Secondary Palate Development

Glucocorticoid effects in adult and fetal tissues are mediated through the interaction of the hormone with specific intracellular receptor proteins in the cytoplasmic fraction of target cells. Schmidt and Litwack (1982) proposed a five-step model for activation of the glucocorticoid–receptor complex. The receptor, which is an 87,000-dalton protein (Nordeen *et al.*, 1981), is present in the cytoplasm in a form that is phosphorylated, contains reduced sulfhydryl groups, and is capable of binding glucocorticoid. The unbound receptor may have associated with it a low molecular weight, heat-stable factor (f) which maintains the protein in a conformation favorable for steroid binding and inhibits the subsequent activation. The phosphorylated receptor protein binds glucocorticoid to form an unactivated complex. This complex then undergoes a conformational change (activation) which results in the exposure of positively charged amino acid residues and hence an increased affinity for polyanions like DNA. During the activation step, the receptor or another component becomes dephosphorylated. Likewise, activation also may involve the dissociation of the low molecular weight, heat-stable factor. The activated glucocorticoid–receptor complex then translocates to the nucleus, where it binds to chromatin acceptor sites and alters the transcription of specific genes. Presumably, the steroid eventually dissociates from the nuclear receptor protein, and the receptor may then be recycled to the cytoplasm where it can be either degraded or reactivated with the heat-stable factor.

The appearance in specific embryonic tissues of cytoplasmic glucocorticoid receptors at discrete developmental stages has been implicated as one factor that determines the appearance of hormonal responsiveness in these tissues (Ballard *et al.*, 1974). Likewise, the presence of functional nuclear acceptor proteins for the steroid–receptor complex is also required for embryonic target tissues about to undergo hormone-dependent differentiation (Cake and Litwack, 1975; Moscona, 1975).

Most of the available evidence suggests that glucocorticoid teratogenicity is due to a direct action on the embryo. The total binding of labeled glucocorticoid to palatal and other embryonic tissue proteins varies in different strains of mice and correlates with the teratologic responsiveness of the strains to glucocorticoids. Salomon and Pratt (1976, 1978, 1979, 1980) demonstrated that mouse embryonic palatal mesenchyme cells possess high-affinity, specific receptor proteins for glucocorticoids. The synthetic glucocorticoids dexamethasone and triamcinolone acetonide have a higher affinity for these receptors than the natural glucocorticoid hydrocortisone, and their affinity correlates well with their teratogenicity (Pinsky and DiGeorge, 1965).

Although the glucocorticoid receptors in embryonic mouse palatal shelves have not been isolated and biochemically characterized, various properties of receptors prepared from whole day 13 A/J and C57BL/6J mouse embryos have been studied (Salomon *et al.*, 1979).

Embryonic cytosols from both strains were found to contain high-affinity, limited capacity binding proteins for dexamethasone and triamcinolone acetonide, which bind both natural and synthetic glucocorticoids and can be distinguished from serum corticosteroid-binding globulin (transcortin) by their heat sensitivity, sedimentation, gel filtration properties, and sensitivity to sulfhydryl reagents. These embryonic receptor proteins appear to be indistinguishable from the adult glucocorticoid receptor found in the liver.

Embryonic A/J facial mesenchyme cells, both freshly isolated and in primary culture, possessed two to three times more cytoplasmic receptors than C57BL/6J mesenchyme cells (Salomon and Pratt, 1976; Goldman et al., 1977). Strain differences in the concentration of cytoplasmic receptors for glucocorticoids in the day 14 embryo were generally restricted to the orofacial region (Salomon and Pratt, 1979). Salomon and Pratt (1976), Goldman et al. (1977), and Butley et al. (1978) showed that the levels of cytoplasmic glucocorticoid receptor in embryonic palate and adult liver cytosols were correlated with sensitivity to glucocorticoid-induced cleft palate. In one other case these results were not corroborated. Utilizing whole mouse fetal heads and an unconventional method of cytosol preparation, Hackney (1980) did not find a positive correlation between triamcinolone acetonide binding and cleft palate sensitivity in A/J, C3H, and C57BL/6J mice.

Salomon and Pratt (1979) reported that the concentration of glucocorticoid receptors in day 14 Swiss Webster mouse embryos was higher in the orofacial region than that observed in the liver, brain, or forelimb. The location of these glucocorticoid receptors in the developing embryo has recently been determined using immunocytochemical techniques (Kim and Pratt, 1983). The pattern appears similar to that determined biochemically in that the palate has the highest level with much lower amounts found in brain, liver, and other tissues of the day 13 CD-1 mouse embryo. Within the secondary palate, it was clear that a high percentage (90%) of the mesenchymal cells contained glucocorticoid receptors with dramatically less found in the epithelium (10%), especially in the medial and oral epithelial cells. The biochemical basis for the relatively high level of receptors in the palate is not apparent but presumably indicates that the normal developing secondary palate is dependent on glucocorticoids and their receptors.

Information concerning the level of glucocorticoid receptors present in the developing human palatal shelf would be of great interest. Yoneda and Pratt (1981a) have established a line of human embryonic palatal mesenchymal cells (HEPM) from a prefusion human abortus and found that these cells contained approximately 10-fold higher levels of glucocorticoid receptors than primary cell cultures from mouse palatal shelves. However, it should be pointed out that comparison of established cell lines and primary cell cultures may not be valid. These HEPM cells have proved to be useful for understanding the complex hormonal regulation of palatal growth and differentation.

Yoneda *et al.* (1981) have reported a study in which various fibroblastic cell lines from tissues of persons with cleft lip and/or cleft palate were examined for level of glucocorticoid receptors. Skin punches were obtained from various affected and normal individuals in addition to oral tissue obtained during surgery from the site of lip or palate repair. A significant deficiency in glucocorticoid receptors was noted in the cell lines from clefted individuals. Although some of these tissues are far removed from the developing embryonic primary and secondary palate, the results were interpreted as indicating that a defect in the complex hormonal regulatory mechanism for embryonic growth may have occurred and persisted into various neonatal or adult tissues. Since this was a preliminary study with only a limited number (22) of cell lines, this work must be expanded before definitive conclusions can be drawn.

Experimental modulation of receptor number or activity would provide further evidence of involvement in glucocorticoid-induced cleft palate. Yoneda and Pratt (1982) have reported that the level of vitamin B_6 exerts a large influence on glucocorticoid-induced cleft palate in Swiss Webster mice. When the maternal vitamin B_6 level was increased by administration in the drinking water, cortisone-induced cleft palate decreased, in contrast with the increase in the cleft palate frequency observed when animals were placed on a vitamin B_6-deficient diet. This effect was interpreted as being due to the direct interaction in the palatal shelf of vitamin B_6 with the DNA-binding site of the glucocorticoid receptor (Disorbo and Litwack, 1978), thereby strongly influencing the amount of steroid–receptor complex that enters the nucleus and therefore also the resultant biological response.

C. *H-2* INFLUENCE ON GLUCOCORTICOID-INDUCED CLEFT PALATE

The *H-2* complex in the mouse (HLA in the human) is a gene complex on chromosome 17 containing a variety of genes specifying a number of immune-related functions such as certain transplantation antigens (Demant, 1973). Haplotypes within the *D* and *K* regions of the *H-2* complex influence palate susceptibility to steroid-induced cleft palate. Using congenic strains of mice, Bonner and Slavkin (1975) showed that mice of the H-2^a haplotype, A/J and B10.A, were highly susceptible to steroid-induced cleft palate, whereas animals carrying the H-2^b haplotype, C57BL/6J and C57BL/10ScSn, were resistant.

The H-2 complex is not the sole determinant of cleft palate sensitivity since C3H/HeJ and CBA/J mice have the same H-2 haplotype (H-2^k) but quite different susceptibilities. Biddle and Fraser (1977) calculated that the enhanced sensitivity of A/J mice compared with C57BL/6J mice was due to two or three independent loci. Vekemans et al. (1981) reported that the sensitivity of recombinant inbred strains derived from the cross of strains C57BL/6J and DBA/2J was associated with the phosphoglucomutase-1 locus on chromosome 5 and not H-2 on chromosome 17.

Goldman et al. (1977) demonstrated higher steroid receptor levels in palates from mice carrying H-2^a than those with the H-2^b haplotype and suggested that an H-2 linked gene affects the quantity of a cytosolic glucocorticoid-binding protein. However, Butley et al. (1978) showed that specific glucocorticoid binding is not mediated by the H-2 complex, and Francke and Gehring (1980) reported that the structural gene for the murine glucocorticoid receptor was located on chromosome 18, not on chromosome 17, which contains the H-2 haplotype. Furthermore, differences in dexamethasone binding observed by Katsumata et al. (1981) cannot be explained by different levels of the endogenous heat-stable factor, and the level of the endogenous factor is not regulated by the H-2 complex (Leach et al., 1982).

The genetic factors that control the response of the secondary palatal shelf to agents that influence the intracellular levels of cyclic AMP are not known. Although Meruelo and Edidin (1975) found an association between H-2 haplotype and endogenous levels of cyclic AMP in livers of adult H-2 congenic strains of mice, Erickson et al. (1979) were unable to find a similar correlation in the mouse secondary palate. The endogenous levels of cyclic AMP were higher in the palatal shelves of A/J (H-2^a) and A.by (H-2^b) than C57BL/10J (H-2^b) and B10.A (H-2^a) mice. However, there was no significant difference in cyclic AMP levels in the palate between the two parental strains and their congenic pairs. This suggested that a portion of the H-2-controlled component of susceptibility to steroid-induced cleft palate is mediated through alterations in the metabolism of cyclic AMP. Pratt et al. (1980b) showed that mutant brachymorphic mice (bm/bm), which differ from nonmutant C57BL/6J mice at a major non-H-2 locus, are extremely sensitive to steroid-induced cleft palate. This mutant condition did not alter the levels of glucocorticoid receptors present in the palatal shelf but did result in delayed shelf elevation and increased levels of palatal cyclic AMP. The biochemical basis for the delayed elevation is not known.

Several lines of investigation suggest that cortisone treatment, used to elicit cleft palate induction in the mouse, alters levels of palatal cyclic AMP. Waterman *et al.* (1977) observed in hamsters that the sensitivity of adenyl cyclase for parathyroid hormone and calcitonin was greatly reduced in steroid-treated embryos. Greene *et al.* (1981) observed a decrease in palatal cyclic AMP levels in both A/J and C57BL/6J mice after cortisone treatment.

D. GLUCOCORTICOID EFFECTS ON CULTURED PALATAL MESENCHYME CELLS

The mechanism by which the glucocorticoid dexamethasone (DEX) induces palatal clefting is thought to include the inhibition of palatal mesenchyme cell proliferation. Evidence which supports this hypothesis includes the observation that DEX inhibits cell proliferation both in primary cultures of mouse palatal mesenchyme cells (Salomon and Pratt, 1978) and in a fibroblastic cell line derived from a human embryonic palate (HEPM cells) (Yoneda and Pratt, 1981a,b).

The inhibitory effect of DEX on HEPM cell proliferation in culture can be prevented by adding epidermal growth factor (EGF) simultaneously (Yoneda and Pratt, 1981c) with DEX or reversed by adding EGF to cell cultures treated for the previous 3 days with DEX (R. I. Grove, unpublished observation). Therefore, it is possible to use EGF as a probe for investigating the mechanism by which DEX inhibits HEPM cell proliferation. Assuming that EGF acts to inhibit the primary biochemical event induced by DEX which leads to inhibition of cell proliferation, one of our approaches has been to determine which DEX-induced biochemical alterations are inhibited by EGF.

It is well known that there are various proteins on the cell surface of untransformed cells which influence cell proliferation. These include receptors for various growth factors (Roth and Taylor, 1982) as well as cell surface proteins which appear to be responsible for contact inhibition (Nortraj and Datta, 1978; Lieberman *et al.*, 1981). Possible mechanisms by which DEX might inhibit palatal mesenchyme cell proliferation include a decrease in the number of cell surface receptors for a specific growth factor or an alteration in the quantity of another growth-regulating cell surface protein. Using gel electrophoresis to investigate the effect of DEX on HEPM cell membrane proteins, we found increases in membrane proteins with molecular weights of 31K and 38K and decreases in membrane proteins with molecular weights of 32K, 60K, 64K, 220K, and 300K (R. I. Grove, unpublished observations). EGF completely prevented the DEX-induced alterations in plasma membrane proteins. Although the identities of these membrane proteins affected by DEX are unknown, it is possible that one or more of the altered membrane proteins are related to the mechanism by which DEX decreases HEPM cell proliferation.

Since glycosaminoglycans (GAG) and other glycoconjugates have been implicated in cellular growth control (Dietrich and Armelin 1978) and since glucocorticoids alter the level of these components in certain cells (Hill, 1981), we investigated the effect of DEX and EGF on HEPM cell GAG synthesis. At 10^{-6} M DEX, incorporation of labeled glucosamine into secreted GAG was decreased to 67% of control values, while more physiological levels of DEX (10^{-9} M) also significantly reduced the appearance of labeled GAG in the medium. EGF only partially prevented the DEX effect on GAG synthesis. Furthermore, chondroitin sulfate (mixed isomers) and hyaluronic acid, the major GAG synthesized by the secondary palate (Pratt *et al.*, 1973), could not prevent the decrease in proliferation induced by DEX when added daily to the cell cultures at 5 μg/ml. Taken together these results suggest that the DEX-induced decrease in incorporation of label into secreted GAG is not related to the DEX effect on cell proliferation.

Similar results were obtained when the effects of DEX and EGF were determined for the incorporation of [³H]glucosamine into cell-associated glycoconjugates. EGF was unable to prevent the DEX-induced decrease in synthesis of labeled glycoconjugates. In order to determine whether the DEX-induced decrease in cell-associated glycoconjugates included decreases in the levels of specific membrane glycoproteins, [³H]glucosamine-labeled cell membranes were subjected to sodium dodecyl sulfate–polyacrylamide gel electrophoresis followed by autoradiography. Differences were not observed in the incorporation of label into individual membrane glycoprotein bands from either DEX- or EGF-treated cells.

The breakdown and resynthesis of phosphatidylinositol (PI), an important plasma membrane phospholipid, is thought to play a key role in the mechanism of growth stimulation induced by a wide variety of hormones, growth factors, and other mitogenic agents (Habenicht *et al.*, 1981; Hasegawa-Sasaki and Sasaki, 1981; Grove and Schimmel, 1982). It is postulated that these agents first bind to and activate their plasma membrane receptor. The activated receptor stimulates a phosphatidylinositol-specific phospholipase C which degrades the phospholipid to phosphorylinositol and 1,2-diacylglycerol. Diacylglycerol is then phosphorylated to phosphatidic acid, which is used in the resynthesis of phosphatidylinositol. The activation of this "PI cycle" is thought to result in stimulated calcium entry into the cell and/or an increase in prostaglandin synthesis (Lapetina, 1982). Proliferation may be stimulated by the action of one or both of these "second messengers" within the cell. Therefore, agents which alter normal PI turnover might prevent proliferation induced by growth factors which act by stimulating the PI cycle. Since PI turnover is involved in the mechanism of action of certain growth factors and glucocorticoids are known to alter phospholipid synthesis in fetal lung tissue (Farrell, 1977), an investigation of the effect of glucocorticoids on HEPM cell phosphatidylinositol synthesis and degradation was undertaken.

When confluent HEPM cells which had been treated with dexamethasone (DEX) for varying times were labeled with [³H]inositol, a 2.5-fold increase in label incorporated into HEPM cell lipids occurred by 30 hours (Grove et al., 1983a). The effect of DEX on phosphatidylcholine synthesis was investigated since DEX stimulates the synthesis of this phospholipid in embryonic lung tissue (Farrell, 1977), and since a generalized increase in the turnover of all phospholipids might explain the DEX effect on phosphatidylinositol. In contrast to the effect on phosphatidylinositol synthesis, DEX did not alter incorporation of [³H]choline into HEPM cell lipids at any time investigated.

In order to determine whether DEX stimulated degradation of phosphatidylinositol, HEPM cells treated with DEX were incubated with [³H]inositol. After 16 hours the labeled medium was removed and replaced with unlabeled conditioned medium from parallel cultures for various times. When compared to 0 hour values, the decrease in radiolabeled phosphatidylinositol remaining in DEX-treated cells was much greater than the decrease in the untreated cells (Grove et al., 1983). Taken together with the incorporation data, these results demonstrate that DEX stimulates an increase in the rate of phosphatidylinositol degradation and synthesis in HEPM cells.

If DEX induces a decrease in cell proliferation by first altering phosphatidylinositol turnover, the dose–response curves for the two effects should be similar. Both the phosphatidylinositol effect and growth inhibition are nearly maximal at 10^{-8} M, while significant increases in both effects were induced by 10^{-10} M DEX. A good correlation also exists between the time courses for the two effects, with nearly maximal stimulation of phosphatidylinositol synthesis occurring by 30 hours (Grove et al., 1983) and nearly maximal inhibition of proliferation occurring by 24 hours. An investigation of the ability of EGF to prevent the effect of DEX on PI turnover revealed that this growth factor totally inhibited DEX-induced stimulation of PI synthesis (Grove et al., 1983). The PI data suggest that the mechanism by which DEX inhibits HEPM cell proliferation and induces cleft palate includes alterations in phosphatidylinositol turnover.

Recently, it has been postulated that glucocorticoids induce cleft palate in embryonic mice by inhibiting the release of arachidonic acid in palatal tissue (Tzortzatou et al., 1981; Goldman et al., 1981; see

Goldman, this volume). We therefore investigated the ability of DEX to inhibit serum-stimulated release of labeled arachidonic acid into the medium of cultures of CD-1 mouse palatal mesenchyme cells (R. Grove, W. Willis, and R. Pratt, unpublished). Although DEX does inhibit the release of arachidonic acid (maximally by 5 hours), this effect apparently is not involved in the mechanism of DEX-induced inhibition of mesenchyme cell proliferation. This conclusion comes from the results of experiments in which daily addition of exogenous arachidonic acid or one group of its metabolites, the prostaglandins (PGE_2, 6-keto $PGF_{1\alpha}$, $PGF_{2\alpha}$, and PGD_2 at concentrations up to 3.5 mM), were unable to prevent the effect of DEX on the proliferation of cultured palatal mesenchyme cells. That DEX-treated mesenchyme cells could synthesize prostaglandins from exogenous arachidonic acid was demonstrated by subjecting medium from cells incubated with labeled arachidonic acid to thin-layer chromatography designed to resolve authentic prostaglandins. In addition, when injected daily at 200 mg/kg, arachidonic acid was unable to prevent the induction of cleft palate in CD-1 mice treated with either triamcinolone hexacetonide or hydrocortisone. A similar lack of effect was obtained from experiments performed on the sensitive A/J strain of mice (E. F. Zimmerman, personal communication). These results are in direct conflict to results obtained by Piddington *et al.* (1983), who reported that arachidonic acid partially prevented glucocorticoid-induced cleft palate in CD-1 and A/J mice. Finally, in light of the very rapid time course for DEX-induced inhibition of arachidonic acid release (maximal by 5 hours) and the relatively long time courses for both glucocorticoid-induced inhibition of cell proliferation and cleft palate formation (3 days), it is unlikely that DEX-induced inhibition of arachidonic acid release is directly related to inhibition of palatal mesenchyme cell proliferation and glucocorticoid-induced cleft palate.

III. Epidermal Growth Factor

A. EGF INFLUENCE IN DEVELOPMENTAL SYSTEMS

While work was in progress to purify nerve growth factor (NGF) from male mouse submaxillary glands (Cohen, 1965), it was observed that certain partially purified extracts of the glands produced biological effects distinct from those attributed to NGF. When injected into newborn mice, purified extract produced biological effects quite distinct from NGF, e.g., precocious opening of the neonatal eyelids and premature eruption of the incisors, and was thus called epidermal growth factor (EGF). Following the discovery of these *in vivo* effects,

EGF was shown to be a potent mitogen (MW 6045) for a variety of cultured cells of ectodermal and mesodermal origin (Carpenter and Cohen, 1979), including ectodermal keratinocytes derived from skin, conjunctival, and pharyngeal tissue, and mesodermal granulosa and corneal endothelial cells, vascular smooth muscle, chondrocytes, and fibroblasts (Gospodarowicz et al., 1978).

The ability of EGF to trigger cell proliferation in neonatal and adult animals raised the possibility that EGF could be an embryonic/fetal growth hormone responsible for specific epithelial territories in the embryo (Gospodarowicz, 1981). This possibility has been tested in different organs such as the lung and palate. Sundell et al. (1975) showed that constant infusion of EGF into fetal lambs for 3–5 days stimulated epithelial growth in many sites, including upper and lower airways. In addition EGF appeared to afford protection against the development of hyaline membrane disease when given in utero at 123–130 days of gestation. This suggests that cell differentiation is stimulated in addition to cell growth. Injection of EGF into 24-day-old rabbit fetuses also induced accelerated maturation of the lung (Catterton et al., 1979). It therefore seems that EGF is capable of promoting not only epithelial cell growth in the fetal rabbit lung, but cell differentiation as well. It may therefore be an important hormone in the maturation of the lung and be capable of protecting the prematurely delivered fetus against the development of hyaline membrane disease.

The results of several studies demonstrate that the palate is dependent on EGF for many aspects of its growth and differentiation. In the mouse the secondary palate first becomes morphologically distinct on day 11 of gestation, at which time it exists as two bilateral processes extending from the paired maxillary processes. Between days 13 and 14 the palatal processes become reoriented from a vertical position alongside the tongue to one above it and fuse with each other along their medial surfaces. This fusion brings about the separation of the oral and nasal cavities. The medial epithelial lamina formed between the apposing palatal processes is disrupted during palatal fusion, and the mesenchymal tissues of the two processes become confluent. By day 17 of gestation the dorsal epithelium of the palate, which constitutes the floor of the nasal cavity, has differentiated into a pseudostratified ciliated columnar epithelium, and the ventral epithelium, which constitutes the roof of the oral cavity, has differentiated into a stratified squamous epithelium.

Both in vivo and in vitro studies have suggested that tissue interactions are important in the differentiation of the secondary palate. The occurrence of cell death within the medial epithelial lamina between the fusing palatal processes has been well documented (Greene and Pratt, 1976; Pratt, 1983). Cell death as a mechanism of morphogenesis has been shown to be one way of eliminating various tissues and organs during development. In the case of the palate, it appears that programmed cell death assists in the removal of the medial palatal epithelium. Organ culture studies have demonstrated that cell death within the medial palatal epithelium does not depend upon the presence of the palatal mesenchyme, at least not during the 3 days that precede the fusion events (Tyler and Koch, 1977). Cell death occurs within the medial region of cultured palatal epithelium that has been isolated from its mesenchyme and occurs in accordance with the *in vivo* schedule. EGF can inhibit the degeneration of the medial palatal epithelium and promote hypertrophy and keratinization of its cells (Hassell, 1975). The effect of EGF can therefore occur directly on the medial epithelial cells to prevent, through the keratinization process, the adhesion of the apposing palatal shelves. It has also been shown that cessation of DNA synthesis and cell death in the medial palatal epithelium can be inhibited in organ culture by addition of EGF (Pratt *et al.*, 1980d). If EGF is administered after cells have lost their ability to make DNA, although it no longer stimulates cells to divide, it can nevertheless act as a survival agent and prevent cell death in this region. In contrast, if present in the culture medium before cells have lost their ability to make DNA, EGF will both induce hyperplasia and prevent cell death in the medial epithelium. If EGF is added to isolated palatal epithelia in their final stage of differentiation (day 13 or 14 of gestation in mice), it can still affect the morphology of the isolated epithelium, but it will not stimulate DNA synthesis or prevent cell death (Tyler and Pratt, 1980). Therefore, depending on the temporal sequence of epithelial cell differentiation in the palate, some aspects of palatal shelf growth and differentiation may depend on EGF. Further evidence was provided by demonstrations that palatal shelves can be successfully cultured in serum-free medium containing EGF as well as other growth factors and hormones (Pratt *et al.*, 1980d). Removal of EGF from the medium resulted in a drastically reduced overall growth and in death of the palatal medial epithelial cells; therefore, EGF may be important for the growth and differentiation of epithelial cells of the palate.

B. EGF EFFECTS ON CULTURED PALATAL EPITHELIAL CELLS

The epithelia covering the developing palatal shelves play a key role in normal palatogenesis. Prior to palatal shelf fusion, three distinct cell regions are evident in the epithelium which covers the shelf.

These include the dorsal nasal, the ventral oral, and the medial epithelial cells. After contact, the medial cells undergo programmed cell death, and the nasal cells develop functional cilia and secrete mucus, while the oral cells become squamous and keratinize (Greene and Pratt, 1976; Meller, 1980). In addition, alterations in the growth and differentiation of the palatal epithelium have been reported to be involved in abnormal palatogenesis induced by certain teratogens (Greene and Pratt, 1977; Pratt et al., 1980a; Pratt, 1983). To facilitate a clearer understanding of epithelial development in both normal and abnormal palatogenesis, we have developed conditions which allow for growth and differentiation of palatal epithelial cells *in vitro* in the absence of the palatal mesenchyme (Grove and Pratt, 1982, 1983). It is clear that differentiation occurs *in vitro* since cilia appear on nasal cells and oral cells flattened into a squamous phenotype after 3–4 days in culture.

Palatal epithelial cell culture represents an important advance in the study of palatal epithelial development. Previous methods for studying the epithelium *in vitro* include whole shelf organ culture (Pourtois, 1972) and culture of the separated epithelium and mesenchyme grown in transfilter recombination (Tyler and Koch, 1977). Using the transfilter culture technique, EGF had been shown to stimulate DNA synthesis in the dissociated palatal epithelium (Tyler and Pratt, 1980). Recent results demonstrate that day 13 palatal epithelial cells synthesize DNA and proliferate optimally in the absence of the palatal mesenchyme when cultured on an endothelial cell-derived extracellular matrix (ECM) in DME/F-12 supplemented with fetal bovine serum and EGF (Grove and Pratt, 1982, 1983). Furthermore, epithelial cells cultured in this medium maintain their differentiation into cells characteristic of both nasal epithelium (ciliated) and oral epithelium (squamous) of the complete (fused) secondary palate. Receptors for EGF as well as an EGF-like growth factor have been found in various embryonic mouse tissues (Adamson et al., 1981) and in particular the epithelium of the day 13 mouse palatal shelf (Nexo et al., 1980). Pratt and co-workers have postulated that EGF plays a major role in regulating the growth and differentiation of the mammalian secondary palate. We have demonstrated that growth and differentiation of palatal epithelial cells cultured both on plastic and on an endothelial cell extracellular matrix (ECM) are highly dependent on the presence of EGF (Grove and Pratt, 1983). Thus EGF or some EGF-like molecule along with hormones such as the glucocorticoids (Pratt and Salomon, 1981) may regulate proliferation and differentiation of palatal epithelial cells *in vivo* as well as *in vitro*.

The culture of mouse palatal epithelial cells should provide a system in which the effect of various hormones and growth factors as well as teratogens can be investigated. Using this system, one can obtain a better understanding of the role that hormones and growth factors play in palatal epithelial development. Furthermore, for those teratogens which act on the palate epithelium, the mechanism of teratogenicity can be investigated more easily with a culture system which allows palatal epithelial cell proliferation and differentiation in the absence of its mesenchyme.

C. Cyclic AMP Levels Influence EGF Effects on the Palate

Since the initial isolation of adenosine 3',5'-monophosphate by Sutherland and Rall (1958), it has become clear that cyclic AMP plays an important role in a variety of cellular activities including growth and differentiation Pastan and Willingham (1981). Pratt and Martin (1975) demonstrated an increase in cyclic AMP in the rat secondary palate during the time of elevation and fusion, and they proposed that the programmed cell death of the medial palatal epithelium was mediated in part through this increased cyclic AMP. Hassell and Pratt (1977) demonstrated that inhibition of palatal medial epithelial death by EGF in organ culture was partially prevented by addition of cyclic AMP, suggesting that some of the EGF effects may be mediated through lowered levels of cyclic AMP. Greene and Pratt (1979) and Greene et al. (1980), using immunohistochemical localization techniques, demonstrated that the increase in palatal cyclic AMP was transient, was correlated with increased adenylate cyclase activity in medial epithelial cells, and occurred predominantly in these epithelial cells.

The transient change in level of cyclic AMP (but not cyclic GMP) observed in the palate is presumably under hormonal control. Waterman et al. (1976, 1977) examined hamster palates in vivo and in vitro to define the hormonal basis for these changes in cyclic AMP. Norepinephrine and epinephrine were the catecholamines most capable of inducing increased activation of adenylate cyclase at most periods of palatal growth. Increased enzyme activity in the presence of norepinephrine was more susceptible to antagonism by the β-adrenergic agent propranolol than to the α-adrenergic agent phentolamine. The remaining catecholamines, isoproterenol and dopamine, displayed a lesser ability to activate adenyl cyclase. Other hormones, histamine, serotonin, thyrotropin, growth hormone, thyroxine, and glucagon, were not stimulatory. Using tissue homogenates, Palmer et al. (1980) found that the most potent agents capable of activating adenylate cyclase were parathyroid hormone and calcitonin; this activity is most likely in the preosteoblastic region, which is found in the mesenchyme beneath the nasal epithelium. Palmer *et al.* (1980) also observed that prostaglandins (PG) E_1, E_2, and $F_{2\alpha}$ stimulated adenylate cyclase activity in the intact hamster palate. Chepenik and Greene (1981) reported the presence of prostaglandin-like compounds in primary cultures of mouse palatal mesenchyme.

D. EGF RECEPTOR INVOLVEMENT IN PALATAL DEVELOPMENT

Yoneda and Pratt (1981b) showed that human embryonic palatal mesenchymal cells contain a high level of EGF receptors and are quite responsive to the growth-promoting properties of EGF. This raises the distinct possibility that human palatal development is also dependent on EGF. As mentioned earlier, mouse palatal mesenchymal cells respond to EGF, and it was recently found that EGF enhances the synthesis of type V collagen when tested in organ culture (Silver *et al.*, 1984).

EGF receptor binding sites can be detected in mouse embryos as early as day 11–12 of gestation (Nexo *et al.*, 1980). Autoradiographic studies have demonstrated their presence in the palatal shelves by day 13 of gestation. Adamson *et al.* (1981) and Adamson and Warshaw (1982) found that a variety of other embryonic mouse tissues contained EGF receptors and displayed downregulation (decrease) of these receptors when EGF was injected into the amniotic sac. The appearance of an EGF-like substance as a function of the age of the embryo was analyzed by radioimmunoassay and radioreceptor assay (Nexo *et al.*, 1980); although little or no EGF was found prior to day 11, a dramatic increase occurred on day 12 and levels continued to rise through day 14. No corresponding increase occurred in the maternal serum during this time, although levels were considerably higher than those found in nonpregnant serum. This increase in an EGF-like substance closely paralleled the increase in specific binding of labeled EGF to membranes of crude embryonic homogenates, which increased 10-fold from days 12 to 14. The source and composition of the EGF present in the embryo are uncertain. The maternal level of EGF could not contribute to the fetal level since transplacental transport does not occur. The embryonic form does not cross-react to the same extent as maternal EGF with anti-EGF antibodies, although both can cross-react to the same extent with the EGF receptor. This suggests that the embryonic EGF is distinct from adult EGF immunologically. Instead, the embryonic EGF may be similar to the recently discovered transforming growth factors (Twardzik *et al.*, 1982; Proper *et al.*, 1982).

IV. Summary

The purpose of this chapter has been to discuss glucocorticoid and EGF involvement in normal and abnormal palatal development. It is to be hoped that we have made clear the important point that these hormone/growth factors and their receptors are present during normal embryonic palatal development to provide for regulation of growth and cellular differentiation. When these hormone/growth factors are administered in pharmacological or large doses that result in teratogenesis, these potent chemicals and their receptors then become inducers of cleft palate. The primary reason for this is that the hormone/growth factor receptors have unique and special areas of localizations in target (embryonic and fetal) tissues, e.g., glucocorticoids in the palate. Therefore, large amounts of these chemicals are specifically bound to receptors in these target tissues and these high levels of hormone/growth factor–receptor complexes result in aberrant development, e.g., glucocorticoids cause inhibition of palatal mesenchymal cell growth.

These effects are distinct from the interactions of physiological levels of these hormone/growth factors with their receptors in these target tissues during development, e.g., glucocorticoids cause induction of key enzymes and modulation of EGF receptor levels. The exact molecular mechanism(s) by which high levels of hormone/growth factors–receptor complexes exert harmful effects on embryos or fetuses is (are) unknown and remain(s) a challenge for the future.

Interaction of hormone/growth factors and their receptors certainly cannot provide an explanation for the mechanism of all types of craniofacial teratogenesis, but this concept certainly appears capable of providing important information relating to the mechanisms of many animal and human teratogens. The fact that these chemicals and their receptors are involved in normal development makes them all the more important since subtle alterations in their levels or activities could result in teratogenesis without an exposure to pharmacological levels of these hormone/growth factors.

It seems that progress in this area will develop quickly since the techniques of recombinant DNA research are available in conjunction with responsive *in vitro* cell systems such as the established line of human embryonic palatal mesenchymal cells. Clearly, the future looks very exciting for understanding the role that these hormone/growth factors and their receptors play in normal and abnormal palate development.

REFERENCES

Adamson, E. D., and Warshaw, J. B. (1982). *Dev. Biol.* **90**, 430–434.
Adamson, E. D., Delber, M. J., and Warshaw, J. (1981). *Nature (London)* **291**, 656–659.

Ballard, P. L., Baxter, J. D., Higgins, S. J., Rousseau, G. G., and Tomkins, G. M. (1974). *Endocrinology* **94**, 998–1015.

Baxter, J. D., and Forsham, P. H. (1972). *Am. J. Med.* **53**, 573–581.

Biddle, F. G., and Fraser, F. C. (1976). *Genetics* **84**, 743–754.

Biddle, F. G., and Fraser, F. C. (1977). *Genetics* **85**, 289–302.

Bonner, J. J., and Slavkin, H. C. (1975). *Immunogenetics* **2**, 213–218.

Butley, M. S., Erickson, R. P., and Pratt, W. B. (1978). *Nature (London)* **275**, 236–238.

Cake, M. J., and Litwack, G. (1975). *In* "Biochemical Actions of Hormones" (G. Litwack, ed.), Vol. 3, pp. 317–390. Academic Press, New York.

Carpenter, G., and Cohen, S. (1979). *Annu. Rev. Biochem.* **48**, 193–216.

Catterton, W. Z., Escobeds, M. B., Sexson, W. R., Gray, M. E., Sundell, H. W., and Stahlman, M. T. (1979). *Pediatr. Res.* **13**, 104–108.

Chepenik, K. P., and Greene, R. M. (1981). *Biochem. Biophys. Res. Commun.* **100**, 951–958.

Cohen, S. (1965). *Dev. Biol.* **12**, 394–407.

Demant, P. (1973). *Transplant. Rev.* **15**, 162–185.

Dietrich, C. P., and Armelin, H. A. (1978). *Biochem. Biophys. Res. Commun.* **84**, 794–801.

Diewert, V. M., and Pratt, R. M. (1981). *Teratology* **24**, 149–162.

DiSorbo, D. M., and Litwack, G. (1978). *In* "Endocrine Control in Neoplasma" (R. K. Sharm and W. E. Criss, eds.), pp. 249–262. Raven, New York.

Erickson, R. P., Butley, M. S., and Sing, C. F. (1979). *J. Immunogenet.* **6**, 253–262.

Farrell, P. M. (1977). *J. Steroid Biochem.* **8**, 463–470.

Francke, U., and Gehring, V. (1980). *Cell* **22**, 657–664.

Fraser, F. C., and Fainstat, T. (1951). *Pediatrics* **8**, 527.

Goldman, A. S., Katsumata, M., Yaffe, S. J., and Gasser, D. L. (1977). *Nature (London)* **265**, 643–644.

Goldman, A. S., Herold, R., and Piddington, R. (1981). *Proc. Soc. Exp. Biol. Med.* **166**, 418–421.

Gospodarowicz, D. (1981). *Annu. Rev. Physiol.* **43**, 251–263.

Gospodarowicz, D., Delgado, D., and Vlodavsky, I. (1980). *Proc. Natl. Acad. Sci. U.S.A.* **77**, 4094–4098.

Gospodarowicz, D., Greenburg, G., Bialecki, H., and Zetter, B. R. (1978). *In Vitro* **14**, 85–118.

Greene, R. M., and Kochhar, D. M. (1973). *Teratology* **8**, 153–126.

Greene, R. M., and Kochhar, D. M (1975). *Teratology* **11**, 47–55.

Greene, R. M., and Pratt, R. M. (1976). *J. Embryol. Exp. Morphol.* **36**, 225–245.

Greene, R. M., and Pratt, R. M. (1977). *Exp. Cell Res.* **105**, 27–37.

Greene, R. M., and Pratt, R. M. (1979). *J. Histochem. Cytochem.* **27**, 924–931.

Greene, R. M., Shanfeld, J. L., Davidovitch, Z., and Pratt, R. M. (1980). *J. Embryol. Exp. Morphol.* **60**, 271–281.

Greene, R. M., Goldman, A. S., Lloyd, M., Baker, M., Brown, K. S., Shanfeld, J. L., and Davidovitch, Z. (1981). *J. Craniofac. Genet. Dev. Biol.* **1**, 31–44.

Greengard, O. (1969). *Science* **163**, 891–895.

Grove, R. I., and Pratt, R. M. (1982). *J. Cell Biol.* **95**, 40.

Grove, R. I., and Pratt, R. M. (1983). *Exp. Cell Res.* **148**, 195–205.

Grove, R. I., and Schimmel, S. D. (1982). *Biochim. Biophys. Acta* **711**, 272–280.

Grove, R. I., Willis, W. D., and Pratt, R. M. (1983). *Biochem. Biophys. Res. Commun.* **110**, 200–207.

Habenicht, J. R., Glomset, J. A., King, W. C., Nist, C., Mitchell, C. D., and Ross, R. (1981). *J. Biol. Chem.* **256**, 12329–12335.

Hackney, J. F. (1980). *Teratology* **21**, 39–51.

Haswgawa-Sasaki, H., and Sasaki, T. (1981). *Biochim. Biophys. Acta* **666**, 252–258.
Hassell, J. R. (1975). *Dev. Biol.* **45**, 90–103.
Hassell, J. R., and Pratt, R. M. (1977). *Exp. Cell Res.* **106**, 55–62.
Herold, R. C., and Futran, N. (1980). *Arch. Oral Biol.* **25**, 423–429.
Hill, J. D. (1981). *J. Endocrinol.* **88**, 425–435.
Hollenberg, M. D. (1979). *Vit Horm.* **37**, 69–110.
Hollenberg, M. D. (1981). *Trends Pharm. Sci.* **2**, 320–322.
Kalter, H. (1954). *Genetics* **39**, 185–196.
Kalter, H. (1965). *In* "Teratology Principles and Techniques" (J. G. Wilson and J. Warkany, eds.), pp. 57–64. Univ. of Chicago Press, Chicago, Illinois.
Kalter, H. (1981). *Teratology* **24**, 79–86.
Katsumata, M., Baker, M. K., and Goldman, A. J. (1981). *Biochim. Biophys. Acta* **676**, 245–256.
Kim, C. S., and Pratt, R. M. (1983). *Teratology* **27**, 57A.
Kurisu, K., Shimuzu, K., and Wada, K. (1977). *Jpn. J. Oral Biol.* **19**, 288–299.
Kurisu, K. S., Sasaki, K., Shimazaki, Y., and Wada, R. (1981). *J. Craniofac. Genet. Dev. Biol.* **1**, 273–284.
Lahti, A., and Saxén, (1967). *Nature (London)* **216**, 1217–1218.
Lahti, A., Antila, E., and Saxén, L. (1972). *Teratology* **6**, 37–42.
Lapetina, E. G. (1982). *Trends Pharm. Sci.* **3**, 115–118.
Leach, K. L., Erickson, R. P., and Pratt, W. B. (1982). *J. Steroid Biochem.* **17**, 121–123.
Lieberman, M. A., Ruben, D., and Glaser, L. (1981). *Exp. Cell Res.* **133**, 413–419.
Meller, S. M. (1980). *In* "Current Research Trends in Prenatal Craniofacial Development" (R. M. Pratt and R. L. Christiansen, eds.), pp. 221–235. Elsevier, Amsterdam.
Meruelo, D., and Edidin, M. (1975). *Proc. Natl. Acad. Sci. U.S.A.* **72**, 2644–2648.
Moscona, A. A. (1975). *J. Steroid Biochem.* **6**, 633–641.
Nanda, W. J., Vander Linden, F. P. G. M., and Jansen, H. W. B. (1970). *Experientia* **26**, 1111–1115.
Nexo, E., Hollenberg, M. D., Figueroa, A., and Pratt, R. M. (1980). *Proc. Natl. Acad. Sci. U.S.A.* **77**, 2782–2785.
Nordeen, S. K., Lan, N. C., Showers, M. O., and Baxter, J. D. (1981). *J. Biol. Chem.* **256**, 10503–10508.
Nortraj, C. V., and Datta, P. (1978). *Proc. Natl. Acad. Sci. U.S.A.* **75**, 6115–6119.
Palmer, G. C., Palmer, S. J., Waterman, R. E., and Palmer, S. M. (1980). *Pediatr. Pharm.* **1**, 45–54.
Pastan, I. H., and Willingham, M. C. (1981). *Science* **214**, 504–509.
Piddington, R., Herold, R., and Goldman, A. F. (1983). *Proc. Soc. Exp. Biol. Med.* **174**, 336–342.
Pinsky, L., and DiGeorge, A. M. (1965). *Science* **147**, 402–405.
Pourtois, M. (1972). *In* "Developmental Aspects of Oral Biology" (H. C. Slavkin and L. A. Bavetta, eds.), pp. 81–108. Academic Press, New York.
Pratt, R. M. (1980). *In* "Development of Mammals" (M. H. Johnson, ed.), Vol. 4, pp. 203–231. Elsevier, Amsterdam.
Pratt, R. M. (1983). *Trends Pharm. Sci.* **4**, 160–162.
Pratt, R. M., and Hassell, J. R. (1975). *Dev. Biol.* **45**, 192–198.
Pratt, R. M., and Martin, G. R. (1975). *Proc. Natl. Acad. Sci. U.S.A.* **72**, 874.
Pratt, R. M., and Salomon, D. S. (1981). *In* "Biochemical Basis of Chemical Teratogenesis" (M. R. Juchau, ed.), pp. 179–193. Elsevier/North Holland, Amsterdam.
Pratt, R. M., Goggins, J. R., Wilk, A. L., and King, C. T. G. (1973). *Dev. Biol.* **32**, 230–237.

Pratt, R. M., Dencker, L., Yoneda, T., and Diewert, V. M. (1980a). *Teratology* **21**, 62a.
Pratt, R. M., Salomon, D. S., Diewert, V. M., Erickson, R. R., Burns, R., and Brown, K. S. (1980b). *Teratogen. Carcinogen. Mutagen.* **1**, 15–24.
Pratt, R. M., Wilk, A. L., Horigan, E. H., Greenberg, J. H., and Martin, G. R. (1980c). *In* "Etiology of Cleft Lip and Cleft Palate" (M. Melnick, D. Bixler, and E. Shields, eds.), pp. 169–172. Liss, New York.
Pratt, R. M., and Salomon, D. S. (1981). *In* "Biochemical Basis of Chemical Teratogenesis" (M. R. Juchau, ed.), pp. 179–193. Elsevier/North Holland, Amsterdam.
Pratt, R. M., Yoneda, T., Silver, M. H., and Salomon, D. S. (1980d). *In* "Research Trends in Prenatal Craniofacial Development" (R. M. Pratt and R. L. Christiansen, eds.), pp. 235–252. Elsevier, Amsterdam.
Proper. J. A., Bjornson, C. L., and Moses, H. L. (1982). *J. Cell. Physiol.* **110**, 169–174.
Roth, J., and Taylor, S. I. (1982). *Annu. Rev. Physiol.* **44**, 639–651.
Salomon, D. W., and Pratt, R. M. (1976). *Nature (London)* **264**, 174–177.
Salomon, D. S., and Pratt, R. M. (1978). *J. Cell. Physiol.* **97**, 315–328.
Salomon, D. S., and Pratt, R. M. (1979). *Differentiation* **13**, 141–154.
Salomon, D. S., and Pratt, R. M. (1980). *In* "Current Research Trends in Prenatal Craniofacial Development" (R. M. Pratt and R. L. Christiansen, eds.), pp. 367–386. Elsevier, Amsterdam.
Salomon, D. S., Yubairi, Y., and Thompson, E. G. (1978). *J. Steroid Biochem.* **9**, 95–115.
Salomon, D. S., Gift, V. D., and Pratt, R. M. (1979). *Endocrinology* **104**, 154.
Saxén, I. (1973). *Arch. Oral Biol.* **18**, 1469–1480.
Schmidt, T. J., and Litwack, G. (1982). *Physiol. Rev.* **62**, 1132–1191.
Shah, R. M., and Travill, A. A. (1976). *J. Embryol. Exp. Morphol.* **35**, 213–224.
Silver, M. H., Murray, C., and Pratt, R. M. (1984). *Differentiation* (in press).
Sugimoto, M., Kojima, A., and Endo, H. (1976). *Dev. Growth Differ.* **18**, 319–339.
Sundell, H., Serenius, F. G., Barthe, P., Friedman, Z., Kanarek, K. S., Esobedo, M. B., Orth, D. N., and Stahlman, M. T. (1975). *Pediatr. Res.* **9**, 371–376.
Sutherland, E. W., and Rall, T. W. (1958). *J. Biol. Chem.* **232**, 1077–1086.
Tyler, M. S., and Koch, W. E. (1977). *J. Embryol. Exp. Morphol.* **38**, 19–34.
Tyler, M. S., and Pratt, R. M. (1980). *J. Embryol. Exp. Morphol.* **58**, 93–106.
Twardzik, D. R., Ranchalis, J. E., and Todaro, G. J. (1982). *Cancer Res.* **42**, 590–593.
Tzortzaton, G. G., Goldman, A. S., and Boutwell, W. C. (1981). *Proc. Soc. Exp. Biol. Med.* **166**, 321–324.
Vekemans, M., Taylor, B. A., and Fraser, F. C. (1981). *Genet. Res.* **38**, 327–331.
Walker, B. E. (1967). *Proc. Soc. Exp. Biol. Med.* **125**, 12–20.
Walker, B. E., and Fraser, F. C. (1957). *J. Embryol. Exp. Morphol.* **5**, 201–210.
Waterman, R. E., Palmer, G. C., Palmer, S. J., and Palmer, S. M. (1976). *Anat. Rec.* **185**, 125–138.
Waterman, R. E., Palmer, G. C., Palmer, S. J., and Palmer, S. M. (1977). *Anat. Rec.* **188**, 431–444.
Yoneda, T., and Pratt, R. M. (1981a). *J. Cran. Genet. Dev. Biol.* **1**, 229–234.
Yoneda, T., and Pratt, R. M. (1981b). *Science* **213**, 563–565.
Yoneda, T., and Pratt, R. M. (1981c). *Differentiation* **19**, 194–198.
Yoneda, T., and Pratt, R. M. (1982). *Teratology* **26**, 255–258.
Yoneda, T., Goldman, A. S., Van Dyke, D. C., Wilson, L. S., and Pratt, R. M. (1981). *J. Cran. Genet. Dev. Biol.* **1**, 229–234.
Zimmerman, E. F., and Bowen, D. (1972). *Teratology* **5**, 335–347.

CHAPTER 6

MORPHOLOGICAL, CELLULAR, AND BIOCHEMICAL ASPECTS OF DIFFERENTIATION OF NORMAL AND TERATOGEN-TREATED PALATE IN HAMSTER AND CHICK EMBRYOS

Ravindra M. Shah

DEPARTMENT OF ORAL BIOLOGY
FACULTY OF DENTISTRY
THE UNIVERSITY OF BRITISH COLUMBIA
VANCOUVER, BRITISH COLUMBIA, CANADA

I. Introduction

This chapter was prepared with the concept that knowledge of development at all levels of biology, i.e., molecular, cellular, and tissue (or organ), is essential for understanding the nature of the issues involved in embryogenesis of the palate, and the pathogenesis of cleft palate. Questions such as what the genes are for palate development, where they are located, and how they make a palate are as crucial as how the epithelial and mesenchymal cells "behave" during reorienta-

CURRENT TOPICS IN DEVELOPMENTAL BIOLOGY, VOL. 19

ISBN 0-12-153119-8

tion, what regulates the programmed death of cells in medial edge epithelium (MEE), and what role the matrix plays in palate morphogenesis. Some of these questions have been extensively debated (see reviews by Greene and Pratt, 1976; Shah, 1979b; Zimmerman, 1979; Pratt, 1980; Zimmerman et al., 1980), while others remain unexplored.

Very little information is available on the evolution of vertebrate palate (Gregory, 1929; Parrington and Westoll, 1940). Recently, some indirect experimental approaches have been initiated to explore the link between evolution and development, with the hope that a better understanding of the regulatory mechanisms involved in normal and cleft palate development would accrue (see work on chick by Shah and Crawford, 1980; Koch and Smiley, 1981; Greene et al., 1983; Shah et al., 1984a,b; and on alligator by Ferguson, 1981). Questions such as why, and how, the mammalian palate develops on the side of the tongue when its ultimate position is over the tongue (Shah, 1977b; Ferguson, 1981) and how programmed death in mammalian MEE is regulated have received little attention. These questions are significant in light of recent observations that there are important differences (discussed below in Sections II and III) in palatogenesis between mammals and birds from morphological, cellular, and biochemical aspects.

During the past four decades numerous teratogens which induce cleft palate in a variety of animals have been recognized (Kalter and Warkany, 1959; Cohen, 1964; Dagg, 1966; Warkany, 1971; Shah, 1979c). During this period, however, most studies on the pathogenesis of drug-induced cleft palate dealt with either morphological or biochemical aspects of differentiation (Walker and Fraser, 1957; Larsson, 1962; Jacobs, 1964; Dostal and Jelinek, 1974; Shah and Travill, 1976b; Shah, 1979d; Diewert, 1979; Diewert and Pratt, 1981; Greene et al., 1981; Greene and Salomon, 1981; Goldman and Katsumata, 1980; Katsumata et al., 1981; Sonawane and Goldman, 1981; Yoneda et al., 1981; Yoneda and Pratt, 1981a,b; Brinkley and Vickerman, 1982; Shah and Burton, 1984). Surprisingly, only a few studies have approached the problem from the standpoint of cytodifferentiation (Mato and Uchiyama, 1972; Mato et al., 1975; Hassell, 1975; Shah and Travill, 1976c; Morgan, 1976; Morgan and Pratt, 1976; Hassell and Pratt, 1977; Shah, 1980; Kurisu et al., 1981; Montenegro and Paz de la Vega, 1982). In this context, it is important to recognize that an understanding of the cytodifferentiation of cleft palate is essential for at least two reasons: (1) In order to understand the nature of the problem, the cellular aspects of cleft palate development should be understood prior to the molecular aspects, because until the cellular behavior (response) is correctly understood, appropriate molecular issues are difficult to raise, let alone discuss (Wolpert, 1971). (2) Since in the biological hierarchy cells occupy a position between the level of organ (or tissue) and molecule, knowledge of cytodifferentiation is crucial in relating the morphological and molecular aspects (Jacob and Monod, 1963).

The following chapter is concerned with some of the issues related to normal palate embryogenesis and drug-induced cleft palate pathogenesis in mammals and birds. Since this approach is significant from an evolutionary viewpoint, it may allow the correlation of evolutionary, embryological, and pathological aspects of palate development.

The discussion focuses on normal and abnormal morphogenesis and differentiation at cellular, subcellular, and biochemical levels. Earlier work from my laboratory has been already reviewed elsewhere (Shah, 1979b) and this chapter describes recent work. Finally, an effort is made to unify findings and interpretations within a framework of a working hypothesis, so that appropriate questions can be raised, answered, and evaluated.

II. An Evolutionary Overview of Palate Morphogenesis in Hamster and Chick

A. MORPHOGENESIS

Palatal morphogenesis is similar in hamsters and other mammals. The secondary palate originates as two vertical projections (shelves) on each side of the midline from the roof of the oronasal cavity (Fig. 1). The tongue arises from the floor of the oronasal cavity and eventually occupies a position between the two developing shelves (Fig. 2). Later, the shelves change the direction of their development and approach one another horizontally over the dorsal surface of the tongue (Fig. 3). Ultimately, the two horizontally developing shelves come in contact and unite to form a continuous structure separating the oronasal cavity into an upper nasal and a lower oral space (Fig. 4).

Chronologically, the events of hamster palatal morphogenesis occur between days 10 and 13 of gestation. The development of two vertical projections begins on early day 10 and continues until day 12 of gestation. During the next 6 hours (12 days and 6 hours), the shelves become horizontal. By the middle of day 12, they fuse in the middle third of the palate. Subsequently, the posterior and then the anterior thirds of the secondary palate close by day 13 of gestation.

We have correlated morphological events of palatogenesis with other developmental parameters such as crown–rump length, embry-

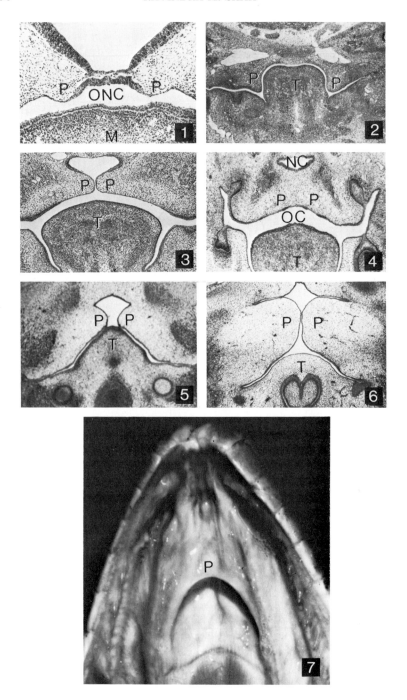

onic weight, and a numerical rating system, and the reliability of these data has been confirmed (Shah and Chaudhry, 1974a; Shah and Travill, 1976a; Shah, 1979a; Shah and Wong, 1980).

In contrast to the hamster, chick palatal shelves originate as a horizontal outgrowth from the maxillary process over the dorsal surface of the tongue (Fig. 5) and continue to develop toward one another until they come into contact (Fig. 6). Unlike hamster palatal shelves, however, the shelves do not unite, and a space between the shelves persists, allowing communication between the oral and nasal cavities (Shah and Crawford,1980). Chronologically, these events occur between days 6 and 8 of incubation (Hamilton–Hamburger stages 30–35) and have been confirmed by Koch and Smiley (1981).

Thus there are important differences in palatal morphogenesis between representative mammals and birds. These differences are significant from both developmental and evolutionary standpoints, and permit the raising of basic questions. For example, why does the direction of origin of palatal shelves differ between mammals and birds? Are there different intra- and extracellular mechanism(s) which govern the direction of shelf development, or are these differences purely related to the presence of different palatal genes and their expression? Why do contacting chick palatal shelves not form a mammalian-type epithelial seam? Answers to these questions have been hitherto unavailable, and a meaningful understanding of the regulatory mechanisms that operate during normal and abnormal palatal development is needed.

FIG. 1. Frontal section of a hamster embryo on day 10 of gestation. Two palatal shelves (P) are developing vertically from the roof of the oronasal cavity (ONC). Tongue development has not yet started from the floor of the mouth (M). ×88.

FIG. 2. Frontal section of a hamster embryo on day 10½ of gestation. The tongue (T) has developed between two vertically developing palatal shelves (P). ×87.

FIG. 3. Frontal section of a hamster embryo at 12 days and 4 hours of gestation. The palatal shelves (P) are horizontal over the tongue (T). ×87.

FIG. 4. Frontal section of a hamster embryo at 12 days and 20 hours of gestation. A mesenchymal union has occurred following fusion between two palatal shelves (P), and thus the oral (OC) and nasal cavities (NC) are separated. ×112.

FIG. 5. Frontal section of a chick embryo at 6 days and 12 hours of incubation. The palatal shelves (P) have begun to develop in a horizontal direction above the tongue (T). ×37.

FIG. 6. Frontal section of a chick embryo on day 8 of incubation. The palatal shelves (P) are meeting over the tongue (T). ×40.

FIG. 7. An intraoral view of the snake palate. The palate (P) is developed in the anterior half but not in the posterior half of the mouth. ×3.

B. Evolution of the Palate

Although the literature on the subject is meager, it is certain that the development of the secondary palate has undergone evolutionary changes (Gregory, 1929; Parrington and Westoll, 1940). Fish and amphibians lack a secondary palate. We have examined the palate from some species of reptiles. Lizards show some evidence of secondary palate development in the form of a horizontal ridge. Palatal shelves, however, never come into contact, and a large space persists between them during ontogeny. Snakes, on the other hand, have a closed palate in the anterior half of the oral cavity, but in the posterior half there is no evidence of palate development (Fig. 7). Recently, Ferguson (1981) has indicated that an ancient reptile, the American *Alligator mississippiensis*, has a mammal-like closed palate (see the chapter by Ferguson and Honig, this volume). In birds (i.e., chick), as already noted, the secondary palatal shelves are well developed, but they do not fuse. Like those of the chick, the alligator's palatal shelves grow horizontally from the beginning (Ferguson, 1981), but their subsequent morphogenesis is different. In the ontogeny of the palate in mammals, there are at least three unique additional observable developmental events, absent in other vertebrates. First, initial mammalian secondary palate development is in a vertical direction, which subsequently becomes horizontal. There is no precedent phylogenetically for vertical development and subsequent reorientation of the palatal shelf. Thus arises the question of why mammalian palatal shelves initially develop vertically when their ultimate orientation is horizontal (Shah, 1977b; Ferguson, 1981). Second, the mammalian tongue originates after the appearance of the secondary palatal shelves. And third, there is an epithelial fusion of the two palatal shelves followed by programmed death of cells in the seam, macrophage activity, and mesenchymal continuity. Ferguson (1981) reports that in the alligator epithelial contact followed by mesenchymal continuity between palatal shelves occurs, but programmed death of epithelial cells and macrophage activity are lacking. The alligator palate seems to unite by the process of "mergence." These differences between mammalian and lower vertebrate palatogenesis deserve further investigation.

C. Why Does the Mammalian Palate Develop Vertically?

From a morphological standpoint, it may be possible to obtain some insight into the vertical development of mammalian shelves. Hayward and Avery (1957) assumed that prior to palatal development, the tongue occupied the oronasal cavity. Lack of space over the tongue would force the palatal shelves to grow vertically along the sides of the tongue. This assumption, however, was made after examining frontal sections of developing heads in which the tongue was already occupying a position between the vertical shelves. Similar views had also been expressed in early textbooks of embryology. It would seem that these were post hoc observations. Recent unpublished studies from my laboratory indicate that in the hamster, when palatal primordia develop from the roof of the oronasal cavity, tongue development has not yet started (Fig. 1). Two lingual swellings, the precursors of the tongue, begin their development subsequent to the start of palatal development. By the time the tongue precursors unite and start to occupy a large proportion of the space in the oronasal cavity, the vertical palatal shelves are already well developed (Fig. 2). Thus Hayward and Avery's (1957) assumption that lack of space due to the tongue's position in the oronasal cavity forces the palatal shelves to grow vertically must be erroneous. In the hamster, the palatal shelves appear before the tongue. This observation also implies that genes coding for the origin of hamster palatal primordia are active in the epithelial and/or mesenchymal tissues of the roof of the oronasal cavity. But the mechanism of modulation of gene expression that triggers the development of palatal primordia is unknown. It is, however, reasonable to suggest that the tongue has no role in controlling vertical hamster palatal growth. Indeed, an earlier analysis of human cases of aglossia, microglossia, and cleft palate also indicate that the tongue may not be involved in early palate morphogenesis (Shah, 1977b).

Recent observations on lower vertebrates also minimize the role of the tongue in governing initial development of the palatal primordia in a vertical and not a horizontal direction. In the chick and alligator, a large tongue is already present prior to the appearance of the horizontal palatal shelves (Shah and Crawford, 1980; Koch and Smiley, 1981; Ferguson, 1981). This observation provides evidence against Hayward and Avery's (1957) postulate.

Thus from both developmental and evolutionary viewpoints, these observations (see Shah 1977b; Ferguson, 1981) suggest that initiation of mammalian palatal development in the vertical direction is determined genetically and is not dependent on simple extrinsic forces.

III. Cellular and Biochemical Aspects of Palate Embryogenesis in Hamster and Chick

A. MEDIAL EDGE EPITHELIAL DIFFERENTIATION

The medial edge epithelium (MEE) of hamster secondary palate constitutes a highly specialized and easily identifiable group of cells whose developmental fate is fairly well understood. The bilaminar MEE can be easily distinguished from the nasal epithelial cells, which are columnar. Differentiating MEE, in contrast to the oral epithelium, (1) does not show further stratification with advancing development, (2) contains less glycogen, (3) has no hemidesmosomes, (4) forms lysosomes with progressive differentiation, (5) does not incorporate [^{3}H]thymidine and thus has stopped proliferating earlier in development, (6) shows Ruthenium red-bound complex carbohydrates on the cell surface which later disappear just prior to palatal closure, (7) shows an increased activity of cAMP with advancing palatogenesis, and (8) fuses with its counterpart and is ultimately eliminated (Chaudhry and Shah, 1973, 1979; Shah and Chaudhry 1974a,b; Shah, 1979a,e; Shah et al., 1984a). Similar observations have been made in other mammalian species (for review see Greene and Pratt, 1976; Shah, 1979b).

On the other hand, chick MEE is not very specialized (Shah and Crawford, 1980; Koch and Smiley, 1981; Greene et al., 1983; Shah et al., 1984a). Differentiating chick MEE, unlike hamster (mammalian) MEE, (1) shows gradual stratification, becoming four to six layers of cells during development, (2) contains little or no glycogen, (3) develops hemidesmosomes during development, (4) never shows lysosomes, i.e., programmed cell death does not occur, (5) continues to proliferate throughout palatogenesis, as evidenced by [^{3}H]thymidine incorporations, (6) shows the presence of Ruthenium red-bound complex carbohydrates on the cell surface which do not disappear, (7) shows no alteration in cAMP activity during palatogenesis, and (8) does not fuse with its counterpart and is not normally eliminated during development.

It is obvious that a complex series of events is taking place on the cell surface and in the plasma membrane during contact of opposing MEE in mammals, the functions of which are still unclear. Complex glycoconjugates may have a role in initial adherence between two shelves (Shah, 1979e; Shah and Crawford, 1980; Greene et al., 1983; Pratt, 1983), but they are not responsible for the formation of an epithelial seam. The seam is formed via desmosomal development (Shah, 1979e). Recent observations, however, suggest that the process of seam formation is more complex. In a series of experiments we observed that the in vitro behavior of homotypic chick and hamster palatal tissues resembles that in vivo (Shah et al., 1984a). Homotypic hamster palatal shelves, when placed in contact in vitro, established mesenchymal continuity, whereas those from chick did not. However, when MEE of hamster and chick were placed in contact in vitro, an epithelial seam

was formed, and mesenchymal continuity was subsequently established between the two palatal shelves. Thus, it seems that changes
which allow the formation of a seam can be induced in chick MEE by
the presence of mammalian palatal tissues. Whether molecules such as
calcium ions are involved in the development of an epithelial seam, or
if there are any specific electrophysiological properties of epithelial
cells which may determine when and where the desmosomes develop,
is not yet known. The heterotypic *in vitro* model, however, could be
very useful in understanding developmental and evolutionary aspects
of palatogenesis.

B. MESENCHYMAL DIFFERENTIATION

During the past few years, we have begun an analysis of the mesenchymal component of the hamster palate and have found that both
cellular and matrix components of the mesenchyme differentiate with
advancing palatogenesis. The main subcellular alterations in mesenchymal cells were observed during the remodeling of palatal shelves
from a vertical to a horizontal direction (Shah, 1979a). The stellate
mesenchymal cells elongate and form junctions with one another. In
the subplasma membrane area bundles of fine filaments, which are
oriented along the long axis of the elongated cell, appear. While intracellular differentiation is progressing, the extracellular matrix also
shows important alterations (Jacobson and Shah, 1981; Jacobson,
1982). There is a significant increase in the synthesis of glycosaminoglycans (mainly hyaluronic acid) during palate reorientation and a
subsequent decrease as the shelves became horizontal. Mesenchymal
cells assume a stellate morphology again. These cellular and biochemical changes were interpreted as facilitating the reorientation of
the palate (Shah, 1979a; Jacobson, 1982). In addition, the mesenchymal cells continue to proliferate at a low but constant rate during
palatogenesis, as evidenced by [³H]thymidine incorporation. Such cellular proliferation may serve to maintain palatal growth in harmony
with the orofacial and general physical growth of the hamster embryo.
These cellular and biochemical features of hamster mesenchymal differentiation, with the exception of continued cell proliferation, are absent during chick palatogenesis (R. Shah, unpublished observations).

C. EVIDENCE FOR AN EPITHELIAL–MESENCHYMAL INTERACTION

It is obvious from this analysis that there is a well-defined developmental history for both palatal MEE and mesenchymal cell populations from different phylogenetic classes. Moreover, both MEE and
mesenchyme have undergone significant alterations in their biological

behavior during vertebrate evolution. Further analysis of these cell populations, therefore, may be useful in answering several important questions. For example, since mammalian palatal MEE is different from oral and nasal epithelia, and since MEE is programmed to die in mammals but not in lower vertebrates, one may ask (1) how developmental restrictions (or promotions) are established within MEE cells to make them different from other epithelial cells of the secondary palate, (2) how programmed cell death is regulated at the cellular and molecular levels, and (3) how developmental restrictions (or promotions) are established in mammalian MEE which makes it differ in behavior from lower vertebrate MEE.

We recently undertook a series of experiments concerning transfilter epithelial–mesenchymal interactions during palate development in chick and hamster. Since one of the main differences between hamster and chick MEE differentiation is the development of lysosomes, we used the appearance of lysosomes as a marker of phenotypic expression in order to see how the process of differentiation was being regulated. The results are described elsewhere (Shah *et al.*, 1984b) but may be summarized as follows:

1. In homochronic recombinations of hamster palatal epithelial and mesenchymal tissues from day 11 (when palatal shelves are still developing vertically), lysosomes did not form in MEE, but in similar recombinations from day $11\frac{1}{2}$ and 12 (immediately prior to shelf reorientation) they did, suggesting that there had been an epithelial–mesenchymal interaction.

2. In heterochronic recombinations of hamster palatal tissues, i.e., day 11 epithelium with day $11\frac{1}{2}$ mesenchyme and vice versa MEE showed lysosomes in the presence of the older mesenchyme only, indicating that temporal restrictions were involved in the developmental regulation.

3. In homochronic and heterochronic recombinations of chick palatal tissues from days 6–9, lysosomes never formed in MEE, which corresponds to their *in vivo* behavior, i.e., a lack of programmed cell death. This result suggests that there is also an epithelial–mesenchymal interaction in chick palatal tissues which restricts mammalian-type MEE differentiation.

4. When isolated hamster or chick MEE cells of different ages were grown alone on Millipore filters, epithelial cells developed lysosomes, albeit at different times. At zero hour there were no lysosomes in any epithelia. Thus we felt that an inherent propensity

for programmed cell death is present in MEE cells of both chick and hamster.

5.   When hamster and chick palatal tissues were reciprocally recombined, it became obvious that MEE behavior depended on the age and source of mesenchyme (Table I). Hamster mesenchyme from day $11\frac{1}{2}$ and 12 allowed lysosome formation in day 7 and 8 chick MEE but not in day 6 and 9 chick MEE. Chick mesenchyme, on the other hand, never allowed lysosome formation in hamster MEE.

Similar examples of epithelial reaction to foreign mesenchyme (and vice versa) have also been documented in other chimeric recombination studies (Coulombre and Coulombre, 1971; Dhouailly, 1973, 1975; Sengel, 1976; Hata and Slavkin, 1978; Kollar and Fisher, 1980). These observations indicate that in spite of genetic diversity among different classes of animals inductive signals produced by tissues of one species can be interpreted by target tissues of a very different species.

It may be useful to discuss the results of these experiments in relation to the morphological, cellular, and biochemical aspects analyzed earlier in this chapter. The observations summarized in items 1–3 suggest that perhaps there may be either a message in day $11\frac{1}{2}$ and 12 hamster mesenchyme which would *promote* lysosomal formation in MEE or one in chick mesenchyme and in day 11 and younger hamster mesenchyme which would *prevent* lysosomal formation. If the message promotes cell death, then one may ask why chick mesenchyme and day 11 hamster mesenchyme did not do so. It could be argued that perhaps there are significant class differences such that the molecular messages promoting cell death are not available in chick; day 11 hamster mesenchyme may be premature and hence would lack these factors. In an earlier study, however, when two day 11 hamster palatal shelves, or a chick and a day 11 hamster shelf, were placed in contact, their MEE

TABLE I

BEHAVIOR OF MEDIAL EDGE EPITHELIUM FOLLOWING RECIPROCAL RECOMBINATION
OF CHICK AND HAMSTER PALATAL TISSUES

Source and age of mesenchyme	Source and age of epithelium	Lysosomes
Hamster, day 11	Chick, days 6–9	Absent
Hamster, day 11½ and 12	Chick, days 6 and 9	Absent
Hamster, day 11½ and 12	Chick, days 7 and 8	Present
Chick, days 6–9	Hamster, days 11, 11½, and 12	Absent

formed a seam which was subsequently eliminated (Shah *et al.*, 1984a). This would happen only if day 11 mesenchyme were capable of further *in vitro* differentiation. Yet it does not allow lysosomal formation in MEE following transfilter recombination!

On this basis, one may suggest that day 11 mesenchyme may contain inhibitors of lysosomal formation. Spemann (1924) suggested that a mesenchymal factor may promote or maintain epithelial differentiation, but not suppress it. Indeed, there does not appear to be any example in the literature in which the mesenchyme of any tissue has been shown to promote cell death in the epithelium. However, there are numerous reports reviewed elsewhere (Grobstein, 1967; Deucher, 1975; Wessells, 1977; Saxén *et al.*, 1976; Saxén, 1977; Sawyer and Fallon, 1983) which support Spemann's suggestion. Thus, one may propose that a mesenchymal factor which "maintains" and "protects" MEE is continuously available in chick but only until day 11 in hamster palate. Subsequently, however, in day 11½ and older hamster palate, due to changes taking place just prior to reorientation (i.e., increased glycosaminoglycan synthesis, cell movement, etc.), the regulatory effect of the mesenchyme factor may be either minimized or lost, and consequently, MEE cells gradually differentiate toward programmed cell death. This hypothesis would be consistent with observations noted in items 4 and 5.

This hypothesis also allows interpretation of palatal tissue interactions from the standpoint of adaptation during evolution. Mederson (1975, 1983), Ho and Saunders (1979), Alberch *et al.* (1979), and Hall (1983) have expressed a view that, during evolution, morphological alterations are based on tissue interactions. These alterations may be modulated in such a way that the functional adaptation of the organism may be improved. Such modulation may produce forms which are potentially important to an organism's survival in a changed environment (Mederson, 1983). Within this context, it is suggested that the loss of an inductive message or loss of a regulatory effect by an inductive message at a specific stage of mammalian palatogenesis would be desirable since it would allow programmed cell death in MEE. This leads to an enhancement of the biological function of palate in mammals. The adaptive significance of such an evolutionary change in palatogenesis from birds to mammals is the separation of the oral and nasal cavities in mammals, which permits chewing, swallowing, and breathing to be performed concurrently as required.

In summary, one may suggest that during mammalian and avian palatal development (1) a mesenchymal message may play a crucial role in MEE differentiation by maintaining epithelial integrity; (2)

there appear to be temporal, environmental, and evolutionary restrictions on the effectiveness of the mesenchymal factor on MEE; and (3) the MEE seems to have an inherent capacity to undergo cell death. The capacity is completely restricted by mesenchyme in birds, but only restricted during early mammalian palatogenesis (see the discussion by Ferguson and Honig, this volume).

IV. Morphogenesis of Cleft Palate in Hamster

It may be useful to recall four crucial morphological events of normal secondary palate development in hamster: (1) initiation of palatal primordia and development of the vertical shelves, (2) reorientation of shelves, (3) approximation and fusion of MEE of the opposing shelves to form a seam, and (4) removal of the seam and establishment of mesenchymal continuity. Theoretically, a cleft palate could develop by affecting any one of these events. My colleagues and I have attempted to induce cleft palate by independently affecting some of these morphological processes.

We have so far analyzed the effect of six drugs on hamster palate development (Table II). These drugs induced cleft palate in 100% of the hamster fetuses without a significantly high incidence of resorption (Shah and Chaudry, 1973; Shah and Travill, 1976a; Shah and Kilistoff, 1976; Shah, 1977a; Shah and MacKay, 1978; Shah and Burdatt, 1979). The treatment schedule, dose, and mode of drug administration are outlined in Table II. The developmental parameters (age, weight, crown–rump length, and numerical rating) which were used for studying normal palate morphogenesis were utilized to analyze drug-induced cleft palate development. The details of the morphological analysis are presented elsewhere (Shah and Travill, 1976b; Shah, 1979d; Shah and Wong, 1980; Burdett and Shah, 1980, 1983; King and Shah,

TABLE II

Experimental Schedule for Cleft Palate Induction in Hamster

Drug	Dose	Gestational day of treatment	Mode of administration
Hydrocortisone	40 mg	11	Intramuscular
Triamcinolone	4 mg	11	Intramuscular
5-Fluorouracil	81 mg/kg	11	Intramuscular
5-Bromo-2-deoxyuridine	900 mg/kg	9	Intraperitoneal
6-Mercaptopurine	70 mg/kg	9	Intraperitoneal
Hadacidin	250 mg	9	Intraperitoneal

1981; Shah and Burdett, 1983), but a summary is presented in Table III. Of the six drugs that were analyzed, hadacidin and 6-mercaptopurine affected initiation and subsequently delayed vertical development of the shelves. At term, i.e., on day 15 of gestation, the palatal shelves remained vertically oriented. Following bromodeoxyuridine treatment, shelves developed vertically until day 12, as did shelves in the controls, but the reorientation was "prevented" by the drug. Consequently, like shelves in animals given hadacidin and 6-mercaptopurine, the shelves remained vertical at term, albeit through a different morphological pathway. Triamcinolone and 5-fluorouracil "delayed" reorientation of the shelves by several hours but did not prevent it. When the shelves became horizontal, a large gap persisted between them, and shelves never made contact until term. Hydrocortisone was the only agent tested which allowed approximation of palatal shelves in most instances, but it prevented the fusion of the opposing MEE.

V. Cellular Aspects of the Pathogenesis of Teratogen-Induced Cleft Palate in Hamster

Even though several teratogens which induce cleft palate in animals have been recognized during the past four decades, surprisingly few studies describe pathogenesis of cleft palate at the ultrastructural level (Mato and Uchiyama, 1972; Mato et al., 1975; Hassell, 1975; Shah and Travill, 1976c; Morgan, 1976; Morgan and Pratt, 1977; Hassell and Pratt, 1977; Shah, 1980; Kurisu et al., 1981; Montenegro and Paz de la Vega, 1982). The studies show two major deficiencies: (1) In most of them, palatal tissues were examined at 24-hour intervals after drug exposure. Such an interval probably would not allow recognition of the

TABLE III

EFFECT OF VARIOUS DRUGS ON MORPHOGENESIS
OF PALATE IN HAMSTER

Drug	Morphological effect
Hadacidin	Interferes with initial vertical shelf development
6-Mercaptopurine	Interferes with initial vertical shelf development
5-Bromo-2-deoxyuridine	Prevents reorientation
5-Fluorouracil	Delays reorientation
Triamcinolone	Delays reorientation
Hydrocortisone	Prevents fusion

initial cytoplasmic and/or nuclear alterations at the subcellular level, which may occur within a few hours of injection. Hence the sequence of changes leading to ultimate cellular injury cannot be reconstructed. (2) Also in most studies, the subcellular alterations, if any, were examined only in MEE and not in mesenchyme. Indeed, these studies have concentrated only on the issue of alteration of programmed cell death after teratogenic assault. No doubt the issue is important, but even during normal development, programmed cell death is only a terminal event in the differentiation of MEE. It is preceded by many alterations in epithelial and mesenchymal cells and in the extracellular matrix, as indicated in Section III of this chapter. If mechanisms are to be identified at the subcellular level, then it is essential that initial ultrastructural changes, followed by sequential alterations in the cytodifferentiation of the affected cells, should be analyzed. Also, alterations in the other areas of the palate should be considered in a sequential manner in order to ultimately describe the overall pathogenesis of the defect at the subcellular level.

A. Cleft Palate Due to Interference in the Initial Vertical Shelf Development

Although a theoretical possibility always existed that a cleft palate could develop from an assault on initial shelf development, there are no studies in the literature which describes cleft palate development by this mechanism. Recently, we have recognized that hadacidin and 6-mercaptopurine interfere with initial development of vertical palatal shelves.

Hadacidin (N-formyl-N-hydroxyglycine) was synthesized by Kaczka et al. (1962) from a broth culture of Penicillium frequentans. Shigura and Gordon (1962a,b) suggested that the drug specifically inhibits an enzyme, adenylosuccinate synthetase, and consequently blocks purine synthesis de novo. 6-Mercaptopurine was synthesized by Ellion et al. (1952), who later (1967) suggested that the drug may act as a purine antagonist, inhibiting the incorporation of adenine and hypoxanthine into nucleic acids during their synthesis.

For comparison, ultrastructural observations of the initial development of vertical palatal shelves in the normal hamster are described. On day 9 of gestation, the oronasal cavity is lined with a simple epithelium in which cells are roughly cuboidal (Fig. 8) and contain a large nucleus, numerous polyribosomes, a few cisternae of rough endoplasmic reticulum, a few mitochondria, and a small Golgi complex. Although many large spaces intervene between the epithelial cells, their continuity is maintained by desmosomes. The epithelial–mesen-

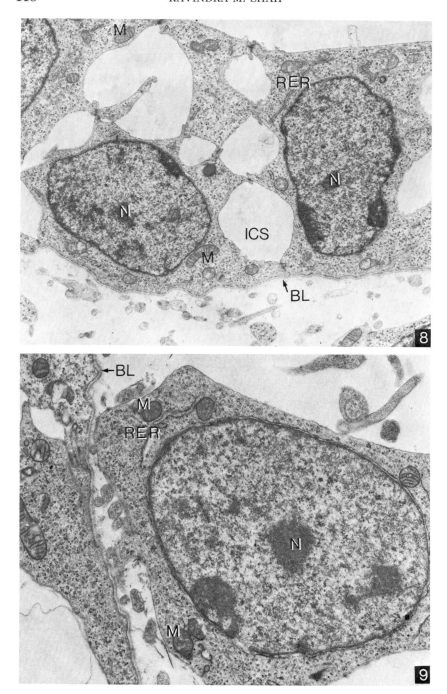

chymal interface is smooth, and the basal lamina is continuous. The mesenchymal cells are stellate and contain organelles similar to those in the epithelial cells (Fig. 9).

When the initial palatal primordia appear on the tenth day of gestation, the precursor MEE is bilaminar. The outer cells are flat, and deeper cells are irregular. The cellular content in both epithelium and mesenchyme, however, is unchanged. Subsequently, the same cellular morphology persists until day 12 in the vertically developing shelves. The shelves then undergo reorientation and fusion. The epithelial and mesenchymal changes during these stages have been described previously (Chaudhry and Shah, 1973, 1979; Shah and Caudhry, 1974a,b; Shah, 1979a,b) and in Section III.

1. Hadacidin Treatment

Twelve hours after hadacidin treatment (Table I), the first changes were seen in the mesenchymal cells. In some mesenchymal cells, the nuclear membrane was swollen, and clumps of chromatin material were dispersed throughout the nucleoplasm (Fig. 10). Other mesenchymal cells were normal in appearance. Eighteen hours after the treatment, one could recognize the aggregation of electron-dense material in the cytoplasm of the affected mesenchymal cells (Fig. 11). Following localization of the enzyme acid phosphatase, these aggregations were identified as lysosomes.

As time after treatment increased, more palatal mesenchymal cells showed nuclear changes followed by cytoplasmic lysosomal alterations. Twenty-four hours after treatment, a similar sequence of changes was seen in the precursor MEE cells (Fig. 12). Later, alterations were also seen in the basal lamina. In some areas between MEE and mesenchyme, the basal lamina separated from the epithelium (Fig. 13). The lamina densa, however, was always continuous. In other areas between MEE and mesenchyme, the basal lamina appeared to be multiplying (Fig. 14). Subsequently, the lysosomal activity became reduced in the epithelium but persisted in the mesenchyme.

The epithelial, mesenchymal, and basal laminar alterations in the hadacidin-treated developing palate gradually disappeared, and on

---

Fig. 8. Electron micrograph of simple epithelium on the roof of the oronasal cavity at day 9 of gestation in hamster showing undifferentiated cells. N, Nucleus; M, mitochondria; RER, rough endoplasmic reticulum; ICS, intercellular space; BL, basal lamina. ×8120.

Fig. 9. Electron micrograph of a mesenchymal cell subjacent to the epithelium on the roof of the oronasal cavity at day 9 of gestation in hamster. N, Nucleus; M, mitochondria; RER, rough endoplasmic reticulum; BL, basal lamina, ×12,600.

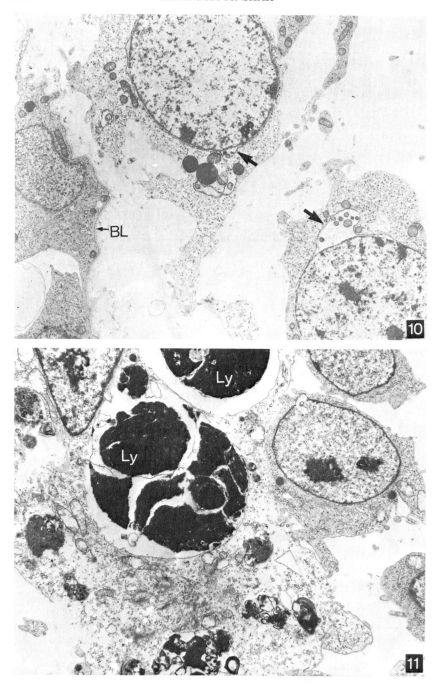

day 12 the palatal shelves, like those of controls, were vertical. Reorientation of the two shelves never occurred. The treated shelves thus remained vertical until term, and a cleft persisted.

2. 6-Mercaptopurine Treatment

Eighteen hours after 6-mercaptopurine (6-MP) injection, the initial changes were seen in the mesenchymal cells and resembled those described following hadacidin treatment, i.e., swollen nuclear membrane, chromatin clumping, and lysosomal formation in cytoplasm. Subsequently, similar changes appeared in the precursor MEE. Both the mesenchymal and epithelial intracellular changes were, however, more extensive, more severe, and longer lasting than after hadacidin treatment. Also, the mesenchymal cells were rounded after 6-mercaptopurine treatment. The basal laminar alterations seen after hadacidin treatment were absent.

These observations indicate that the initial assault at the tissue and cellular level following hadacidin and 6-mercaptopurine treatment is similar. In both instances, it appears that in comparison to controls, the direction of mesenchymal and then epithelial cellular differentiation is altered *de novo* in treated animals. Mesenchymal nuclear alterations may, perhaps, set in motion the teratological actions. The cytoplasmic lysosomal changes are terminal effects. The epithelial alterations (and the basal laminar changes after hadacidin treatment) follow mesenchymal changes in a similar manner. These observations also suggest that there are epithelial–mesenchymal interactions during which these tissues may exert regulatory effects on one another. Also, changes in mesenchymal cytodifferentiation may affect subsequent extracellular matrix synthesis and thus subsequent palatal development. These issues need to be investigated further.

B. CLEFT PALATE DUE TO INTERFERENCE IN PALATAL SHELF REORIENTATION

Since Walker and Fraser (1957) indicated that cortisone treatment of pregnant mice delayed palatal shelf reorientation in the fetuses,

---

FIG. 10. Electron micrograph of a hadacidin-treated mesenchymal cell on the roof of the oronasal cavity at 9 days and 12 hours of gestation in hamster showing peripheral clumping of nuclear chromatin material, swollen nuclear membrane (arrows) (cf. Fig. 9). BL, Basal lamina. ×6525.

FIG. 11. Electron micrograph of a hadacidin-treated mesenchymal cell on the roof of the oronasal cavity at 9 days and 18 hours of gestation in hamster showing development of lysosomes (Ly). ×5655.

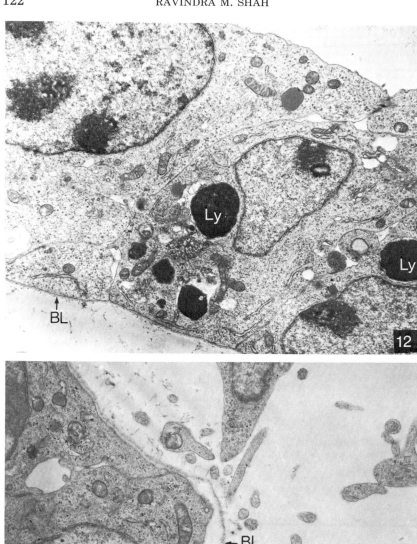

several other agents have been recognized which may also induce cleft palate by this morphological mechanism (Walker and Crain, 1960; Callas and Walker, 1963; Kochhar and Johnson, 1965; Nanda, 1970, 1971; Diewert, 1979, 1981; Diewert and Pratt, 1979).

During the past few years, we have recognized that bromodeoxyuridine (BrdU) induces cleft palate in hamster by "preventing," and triamcinolone and 5-fluorouracil (5-FU) by "delaying," shelf reorientation (Shah, 1979d; Shah and Wong, 1980; King and Shah, 1981). Both BrdU and 5-FU are growth inhibitors. Ellison (1961) suggested that 5-FU may interfere with DNA synthesis by preventing the methylation reaction mediated by thymidylate synthetase, which converts deoxyuridylic acid to thymidylic acid. Another reported action of 5-FU is indirect inhibition of RNA (Bosch *et al.*, 1958). The mechanism of BrdU action is unclear, although it is suggested that incorporation of BrdU into DNA probably leads to defective cytodifferentiation (Tencer and Brachet, 1973; Lee *et al.*, 1974). The effects of triamcinolone, like those of other glucocorticoid hormones, vary among tissues and are not clearly understood. The possibilities are discussed by Shah (1980).

1. Bromodeoxyuridine Treatment

Eighteen hours after treatment (Table II), swollen nuclear membranes in some of the mesenchymal cells were the first ultrastructural alterations to be observed. This was followed by the appearance of lysosomes in some mesenchymal cells. Other mesenchymal cells resembled their control counterparts. Subsequently, lysosomes appeared in the precursor MEE and continued to increase until day $10\frac{1}{2}$ of gestation in both epithelial and mesenchymal cells. In the affected cells, other organelles did not show any ultrastructural damage. The lysosomal activity was then progressively reduced, and between days 11 and 15 of gestation, it was absent in both the epithelial and mesenchymal cells of the vertical palate. During this period, the basal lamina remained continuous.

2. 5-Fluorouracil Treatment

Six hours after treatment (Table II), lysosomes first appeared in some of the precursor MEE (Fig. 15) and then in mesenchymal cells of

FIG. 12. Electron micrograph of hadacidin-treated precursor MEE of palate at 10 days of gestation in hamster showing development of hysosomes (Ly). BL, Basal lamina. ×8120.

FIG. 13. Electron micrograph of hadacidin-treated palatal epithelium at 10 days and 6 hours of gestation in hamster showing separation of the basal lamina (BL) from epithelium. ×14,000.

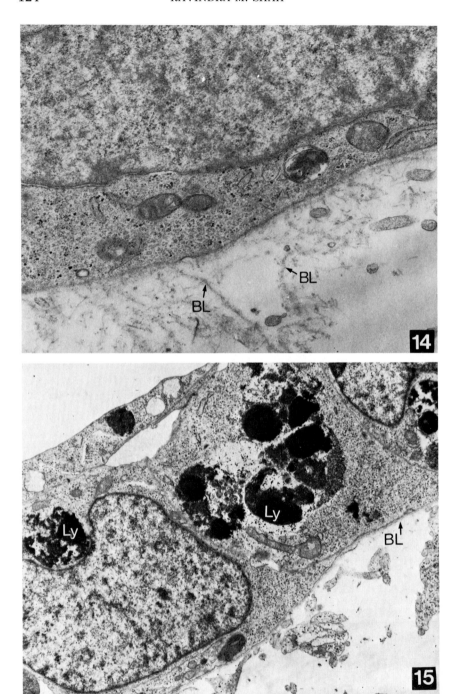

the vertical palatal shelf (Shah *et al.*, 1984c). As time progressed, all prospective MEE cells showed lysosomes, but the predominant activity was in the mesenchyme. Eighteen hours after treatment, lysosomal activity gradually began to subside, first in mesenchymal cells and then in epithelial cells. At this time, however, the basal lamina was missing below the precursor MEE (Fig. 16). Subsequently, 30 hours after treatment, lysosomal activity had disappeared, and the basal lamina had begun to reappear. Thereafter, the palatal shelves became horizontal, but they never fused and a cleft persisted.

3. Triamcinolone Treatment

Unlike the aforementioned drugs, the initial effect of triamcinolone was seen at the epithelial–mesenchymal interface (Shah, 1980). Twenty hours after the treatment, the basal lamina was disrupted in the precursor MEE area of the vertical shelf (Fig. 17). Epithelial and mesenchymal cells, however, were normal in appearance. Thirty-two hours after the treatment, some of the basal cells showed reduced polyribosomes (Fig. 18) in cytoplasm and peripheral condensation of the chromatin material in the nucleus. The rough endoplasmic reticular cisternae and mitochondria were swollen. Later, as the shelves underwent a delayed reorientation, i.e., 36–40 hours after the treatment (Shah, 1979d), more basal cells of MEE showed nuclear and cytoplasmic alterations. The basal lamina adjacent to all such cells was missing. The adjacent mesenchymal cells were still normal looking. The basal cells disintegrated with time. Subsequently, the MEE regenerated on the horizontal shelves, but the shelves did not contact their counterparts, and a cleft persisted. It should be noted that following triamcinolone treatment differentiation of mesenchymal cells was delayed temporally in comparison to controls. Unlike BrdU and 5-FU, however, which also affected shelf reorientation, triamcinolone induced neither premature lysosomal formation nor ultrastructural signs of injury in the mesenchymal cells. Indeed, the observable effects following tramcinolone treatment were limited to the epithelium and basal lamina.

In summary, although the initial lesions at the tissue and cellular levels following treatment with growth inhibitors BrdU and 5-FU are

FIG. 14. Electron micrograph of hadacidin-treated palatal epithelium at 10 days and 6 hours of gestation in hamster showing duplication of the basal lamina (BL). ×20,000.

FIG. 15. Electron micrograph of 5-fluorouracil-treated precursor MEE of palate at 11 days and 6 hours of gestation in hamster showing lysosome (Ly) in the cells. Basal lamina (BL) is intact. ×8120.

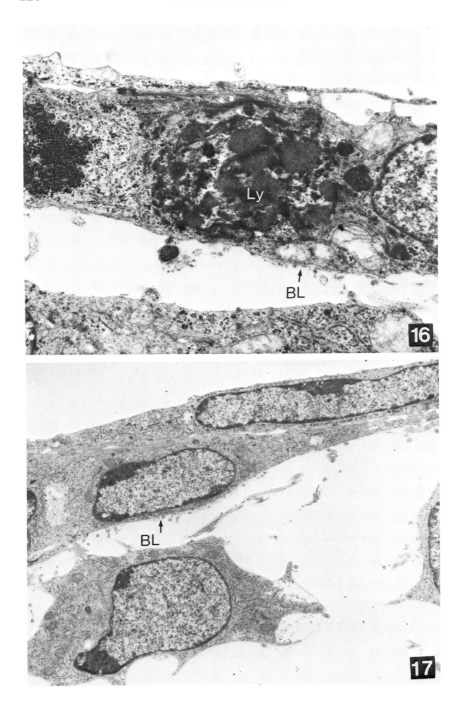

different, eventually both epithelium and mesenchyme are affected. These observations are consistent with those seen following 6-MP and hadacidin treatment. The effect of triamcinolone seems to be limited to the epithelial cells. In all instances, however, both the timing and nature of programmed cell death in MEE are affected, which perhaps reflects misregulation of the epithelial–mesenchymal interaction.

C. CLEFT PALATE DUE TO INTERFERENCE WITH THE FUSION PROCESS

Hydrocortisone Treatment

Hydrocortisone is the only agent that we have identified which induces cleft palate in hamster by affecting the fusion of opposing shelves (Shah and Travill, 1976a). The initial effect of hydrocortisone was on the basal cells of precursor MEE (Fig. 19). Initial changes in nuclei consisted of peripheral condensation of the chromatin material and reduced electron density of nucleoplasm. Subsequently, the cytoplasm showed reduced polyribosomes and swelling of mitochondria and rough endoplasmic reticulum cisternae. These alterations were interpreted as irreversible degenerative changes (Kerr, 1971; Trump et al., 1974). The epithelial changes were followed by loss of the subjacent basal lamina of the vertical shelves. As the shelves became horizontal and approached one another, increasing numbers of basal cells showed degeneration in MEE. Later, the basal cells disintegrated. Ultimately, however, the MEE regenerated and became stratified. The mesenchymal differentiation does not seem to have been affected, at least at the ultrastructural level, by hydrocortisone treatment.

D. UNIFICATION

Observations on the pathogenesis of cleft palate at a cellular level are summarized in Table IV. Several generalizations may be made. (1) Depending on the nature of teratogenic agent, either epithelium or both epithelium and mesenchyme may be affected. (2) Growth inhibitors induce cellular injury to both epithelium and mesenchyme,

---

FIG. 16. Electron micrograph of 5-fluorouracil-treated precursor MEE of palate at 11 days and 18 hours of gestation in hamster showing lysosome (Ll) and disintegrating basal lamina (BL). ×8910.

FIG. 17. Electron micrograph of triamcinolone-treated palatal epithelium and mesenchyme at 11 days and 20 hours of gestation in hamster. The precursor MEE and mesenchymal cells are unaltered but the basal lamina (BL) is discontinuous. ×6525.

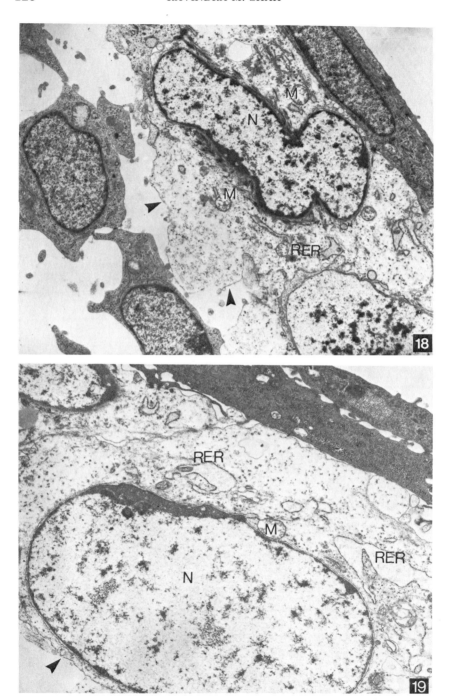

whereas steroid-induced injury is limited to the epithelium. (3) Ultimate cellular alterations are irreversible and differ with different agents—steroids affect polyribosomes and thus may depress protein synthesis, whereas growth inhibitors induce precocious lysosomal activities and thus may alter intracellular homeostasis. (4) Treatment with steroids leads to elimination of cells, whereas following treatment with growth inhibitors the response varies; hadacidin and BrdU appear to have a mild effect on a few cells, while 5-FU and 6-MP seem to have severe effects on most cells. In the latter instances, however, cells do not appear to be eliminated.

From the standpoint of cytodifferentiation, lysosomal development in both epithelial and mesenchymal cells of the palate following teratogen treatment is precocious and is absent at a comparable time during normal development (except at the time of epithelial seam fragmentation). A question, therefore, arises: Following BrdU and hadacidin treatment, why are some palatal cells affected and others not? Two possibilities may be considered. First, the difference may be related to varying sensitivities of cells from different germ layers. Since palatal epithelial and mesenchymal cells are derived from different germ layers, they may react differently to a teratogenic agent. The observation that hadacidin and BrdU affect some mesenchymal cells, but not all, suggests that perhaps the palatal mesenchyme contains two distinct cell populations which were derived from the neural crest and the primary mesoderm (LeLievre, 1978; Been and Lieuw Kie Song, 1978; Noden, 1980). Second, it is also possible that the affected mesenchymal cells were differentiated to a greater or lesser degree than unaffected ones, and this may be related to variation in their nutritional status (Harley, 1978) or proliferative state. Scott (1977) has indicated that cytotoxic response due to growth inhibitors is usually preceded by reduced DNA synthesis.

The foregoing analysis of abnormal morphogenesis (Section IV) and alterations at the tissue and cellular levels also raises three interesting questions of a general nature in regard to drug-induced cleft palate

---

FIG. 18. Electron micrograph of triamcinolone-treated palatal epithelium at 12 days and 8 hours of gestation in hamster. The basal epithelial cells show reduced polyribosomes, swollen mitochondria (M) and rough endoplasmic reticulum cisternae (RER), and peripheral clumping of the chromatin material in nucleus (N). The basal lamina is missing (arrowheads). Mesenchymal cells appear unaltered. ×6525.

FIG. 19. Electron micrograph of hydrocortisone-treated palatal epithelium at 12 days of gestation in hamster. The basal cells show peripheral clumping of chromatin in nucleus (N), reduced polyribosomes, and swollen mitochondria (M) and cisternae of rough endoplasmic reticula (RER). The basal lamina is missing (arrowheads). ×10,230.

TABLE IV

SUMMARY OF DRUG-INDUCED CLEFT PALATE PATHOGENESIS IN HAMSTER

Agent	First tissue affected	Initial cellular alteration	Other evidence of cell injury	Alterations in the other tissue	Effect on basal lamina
Hadacidin	Mesenchyme	Swollen nuclear membrane	Lysosomes	Lysosomes in epithelium	Folding and duplication
6-Mercaptopurine	Mesenchyme	Swollen nuclear membrane	Lysosomes	Lysosomes in epithelium	—
Bromodeoxyuridine	Mesenchyme	Swollen nuclear membrane	Lysosomes	Lysosomes in epithelium	—
5-Fluorouracil	Epithelium	Lysosomes	—	Lysosomes in mesenchyme	Missing
Triamcinolone	Epithelium	Reduced polyribosomes	Swollen RER and mitochondria	—	Missing
Hydrocortisone	Epithelium	Nuclear chromatin condensation	Reduced polyribosomes and swollen RER and mitochondria	—	Missing

pathogenesis: (1) Could more than one pathologic cellular alteration lead to an identical morphological mechanism? (2) Could identical pathologic cellular alterations lead to different morphological mechanisms? (3) Could different pathologic cellular alterations lead to different morphological mechanisms? Examination of Tables III and IV indicates that the answer to all these questions is obviously yes. For example, the morphological mechanism by which 5-FU and triamcinolone induce cleft palate is the same, i.e., delayed reorientation, but the cellular alterations are different. The morphological mechanisms by which hadacidin and BrdU induce cleft palate are different, but the cellular alterations are similar. Hydrocortisone and 6-mercaptopurine induce cleft palate by different morphological mechanisms, and the underlying cellular alterations are also different. Indeed, there may be other cellular changes associated with the initiation and subsequent differentiation of the cleft palate defect. The significance of cellular alterations, however, remains unclear. For example, clumping of chromatin material may or may not be associated with swelling of the nuclear membrane, as was seen after treatment with growth inhibitors and glucocorticoids, respectively. Obviously, in both instances nuclear–cytoplasmic interactions, which govern cytodifferentiation, must have been affected. Also, some cytoplasmic alterations are suggestive of altered differentiation, whereas others seem to reflect cell death.

Cell death is important in the normal pathogenesis of many tissues and organs (Glucksmann, 1951; Saunders, 1966; Forsberg and Kallen, 1968; Webster and Goss, 1970; Schweichel and Merker, 1973; Lockshin and Beaulaton, 1974; Pexieder, 1975). The mechanisms regulating physiological cell death are, however, not yet clear. During palate development, cell death is useful in the removal of epithelium which intervenes between two opposing shelves so that mesenchymal continuity may be established. Palatal mesenchymal cells, on the other hand, are not programmed to die at any time during normal development. In Section III,C, evidence was discussed regarding involvement of the mesenchyme in the regulation of programmed cell death in palatal MEE.

Also, cell death during teratogenesis is not uncommon (Grunewald, 1958; Menkes et al., 1970; Scott, 1977). However, knowledge concerning how cell death leads to malformation is incomplete. Wilson (1977), Saxen (1977), Scott (1977), and others have suggested that during abnormal morphogenesis excessive or insufficient cell death can lead to malformations. Our results with drug-induced cleft palate development suggest that cell death can also be abnormal in location and precocious, and may be mediated via either lysosomal or nonlysosomal pathways.

Undoubtedly, in addition to cytodifferentiation and cell death, various other aspects of cell and tissue behavior, e.g., cell multiplication, cell movement, cell–cell and cell–matrix interactions, and matrix synthesis, should also be studied after teratogenic assault in order to arrive at an understanding of the cellular basis of cleft palate development. As in other developing systems, some of this behavior may be preprogrammed in precursor cells, while other behaviors may develop in response to external signals provided by the microenvironment (Toole, 1982; Jacobson, 1982), including positional information (Wolpert, 1971) and contact relationships of the cells. Final understanding of cleft palate pathogenesis awaits evaluation of these factors.

In conclusion, two major points emerge from experimental studies on two different classes of animals. First, normal palate development results from a preprogrammed series of events in cell populations of diverse embryological origin, a series which involves proliferation, interaction, differentiation, movement, and matrix synthesis. Second, normal palate development can be manipulated by affecting any of the preprogrammed series of events. Because of differences in their biological behavior, comparative studies of palatogenesis in the hamster (a placental animal) and chick (a nonplacental animal) offer a unique opportunity to explore and manipulate these preprogrammed events.

ACKNOWLEDGMENTS

The work reported in this chapter was supported by research grants from the Medical Research Council of Canada and British Columbia Health Sciences Research Foundation. I am indebted to Roger Suen, Linda Skibo, and David Burdett for their patience, generosity, and excellent assistance during the preparation of this chapter.

REFERENCES

Alberch, P., Gould, S. J., Oster, G. F., and Wake, D. B. (1979). *Paleobiology* **5**, 296–317.
Been, W., and Lieuw Kie Song, S.H. (1978). *Acta Morphol. Neerl. Scand.* **16**, 145–255.
Bosch, L., Herbers, E., and Heidelberger, C. (1958). *Cancer Res.* **18**, 334–343.
Brinkley, L., and Vickerman, M. M. (1982). *J. Embryol. Exp. Morphol.* **69**, 193–213.
Burdett, D. N., and Shah, R. M. (1980). *J. Dent. Res.* **59**, 302.
Burdett, D. N., and Shah, R. M. (1983). *J. Dent. Res.* **62**, 237.
Callas, G., and Walker, B. E. (1963). *Anat. Rec.* **145**, 61–70.
Chaudhry, A. P., and Shah, R. M. (1973). *J. Morphol.* **139**, 329–350.
Chaudhry, A. P., and Shah, R. M. (1979). *Acta Anat.* **103**, 384–394.
Cohen, R. L. (1964). *Clin. Pharmacol. Ther.* **5**, 480–496.
Coulombre, J. L., and Coulombre, A. J. (1971). *Dev. Biol.* **25**, 464–478.
Dagg, C. P. (1966). *In* "Biology of the Laboratory Mouse" (E. L. Green, ed.), pp. 309–328. McGraw-Hill, New York.

Deucher, E. (1975). "Cellular Interactions in Animal Development." Chapman & Hall, London.

Dhouailly, D. (1973). *J. Embryol. Exp. Morphol.* **30**, 587–603.

Dhouailly, D. (1975). *Roux's Arch. Dev. Biol.* **177**, 323–340.

Diewert, V. (1979). *Teratology* **19**, 213–228.

Diewert, V. (1981). *Teratology* **24**, 43–52.

Diewert, V., and Pratt, R. M. (1979). *Teratology* **20**, 37–52.

Diewert, V., and Pratt, R. M. (1981). *Teratology* **24**, 149–162.

Dostal, M., and Jelinek (1974). *Folia Morphol.* **20**, 362–374.

Ellion, G. B. (1967). *Fed. Proc. Fed. Am. Soc. Exp. Biol.* **26**, 898–903.

Ellion, G. B., Burgi, E., and Hitchings, G. H. (1952). *J. Am. Chem. Soc.* **74**, 411–414.

Ellison, R. R. (1961). *Med. Clin. N. Am.* **45**, 677–688.

Ferguson, M. J. (1979). *Med. Hypotheses* **5**, 1079–1090.

Ferguson, M. J. (1981). *J. Craniofac. Genet. Dev. Biol.* **1**, 123–144.

Forsberg, J. G., and Kallen, B. (1968). *Rev. Roum. Embryol. Cytol-Ser. Embryol.* **5**, 91–111.

Glucksmann, A. (1951). *Biol. Rev.* **26**, 59–103.

Goldman, A., and Katsumata, M. (1980). *In* "Etiology of Cleft Lip and Cleft Palate" (M. Melnick, D. Bixler, and E. Shield, eds.), pp. 91–120. Liss, New York.

Greene, R. M., and Pratt, R. M. (1976). *J. Embryol. Exp. Morphol.* **36**, 225–240.

Greene, R. M., and Salomon, D. S. (1981). *Cell Differ.* **10**, 193–199.

Greene, R. M., Goldman, A. S., Lloyd, M., Baker, M., Brown, K. S., Shanfeld, J. L., and Davidovitch, Z. (1981). *J. Craniofac. Genet. Dev. Biol.* **1**, 31–44.

Greene, R. M., Shah, R. M., Lloyd, M. R., Crawford, B. J., Suen, R., Shanfeld, J. L., and Davidovitch, Z. (1983). *J. Exp. Zool.* **225**, 43–52.

Gregory, W. (1929). "Our Faces from Fish to Man." Putnam, New York.

Grobstein, C. (1967). *Natl. Cancer Inst. Monogr.* **26**, 279–299.

Grunewald, P. (1958). *Am. J. Pathol.* **34**, 77–95.

Hall, B. K. (1983). *J. Craniofac. Genet. Dev. Biol.* **3**, 75–82.

Hamburger, V., and Hamilton, H. L. (1951). *J. Morphol.* **88**, 49–92.

Harley, L. (1978). *In* "Molecular Basis of Biological Degradative Processes" (R. Berlin, H. Herrmann, I. Lepow, and J. Tanzer, eds.), pp. 1–24. Academic Press, New York.

Hassell, J. R. (1975). *Dev. Biol.* **45**, 90–102.

Hassell, J., and Pratt, R. M. (1977). *Exp. Cell Res.* **106**, 55–62.

Hata, R. I., and Slavkin, H. (1978). *Proc. Natl. Acad. Sci. U.S.A.* **75**, 2790–2793.

Hayward, J., and Avery, J. (1957). *J. Oral Surg.* **15**, 320–326.

Ho, M. W., and Saunders, P. T. (1979). *J. Theor. Biol.* **78**, 573–592.

Jacob, F., and Monod, J. (1963). *In* "Cytodifferentiation and Macromulecular Synthesis" (M. Locke ed.), pp. 30–64. Academic Press, New York.

Jacobs, R. M. (1964). *Anat. Rec.* **150**, 271–278.

Jacobson, B. (1982). *Mol. Aspects Med.* **5**, 401–459.

Jacobson, B., and Shah, R. M. (1981). *Teratology* **23**, 42A–43A.

Kaczka, E. A., Gitterman, C. O., Dulaney, E. L., and Folkers, K. (1962). *Biochemistry* **1**, 340–343.

Kalter, H., and Warkany, J. (1959). *Physiol. Rev.* **39**, 69–115.

Katsumata, M., Baker, M. K., Goldman, A. S., and Gasser, D. L. (1981). *Immunogenetics* **13**, 319–325.

Kerr, J. F. R. (1971). *J. Pathol.* **105**, 13–20.

King, K., and Shah, R. M. (1981). *Teratology,* **23**, 47A.

Koch, W., and Smiley, G. R. (1981). *Arch. Oral Biol.* **26**, 181–189.

Kochhar, D. M., and Johnson, E. M. (1965). *J. Embryol. Exp. Morphol.* **14**, 223–238.

Kollar, E. J., and Fisher, C. (1980). *Science* **207**, 993–995.

Kurisu, K., Sasaki, S., Shimazaki, K., Ohsaki, Y., and Wada, K. (1981). *J. Craniofac. Genet. Dev. Biol.* **1**, 273–284.

Larsson, K. S. (1962). *Acta Morphol. Neerl. Scand.* **4**, 349–367.

Lee, H., Deshpande, A., and Kalmus, G. (1974). *J. Embryol. Exp. Morphol.* **32**, 835–848.

LeLievre, C. S. (1978). *J. Embryol. Exp. Morphol.* **47**, 17–37.

Lockshin, R. A., and Beaulaton, J. (1974). *Life Sci.* **15**, 1549–1566.

Mato, M., and Uchiyama, Y. (1972). *Gunma Rep. Med. Sci.* **3**, 377–380.

Mato, M., Uchiyama, Y., Aikawa, E., and Smiley, G. R. (1975). *Teratology* **11**, 153–168.

Mederson, P. F. A. (1975). *Am. Zool.* **15**, 315–328.

Mederson, P. F. A. (1983). *In* "Epithelial–Mesenchymal Interactions in Development" (R. H. Sawyer and J. F. Fallon, eds.), pp. 215–240. Praeger, New York.

Menkes, B., Sandor, S., and Ilies, A. (1970). *In* "Advances in Teratology" (D. H. M. Woollam, ed.), pp. 165–215. Logos Press, London.

Montenegro, M. A., and Paz De La Vega, Y. (1982). *Arch. Oral Biol.* **27**, 771–775.

Morgan, P. (1976). *Dev. Biol.* **51**, 225–240.

Morgan, P., and Pratt, R. M. (1977). *Teratology* **15**, 281–290.

Nanda, R. (1970). *Teratology* **3**, 237–244.

Nanda, R. (1971). *Arch. Oral Biol.* **16**, 435–444.

Noden, D. M. (1980). *In* "Current Research Trends in Prenatal Craniofacial Development" (R. M. Pratt and R. L. Christiansen, eds.), pp. 3–26. Elsevier, Amsterdam.

Parrington, F. R., and Westoll, T. S. (1940). *Philos. Trans. R. Soc. London Ser. B* **230**, 305–355.

Pexieder, T. (1975). *Adv. Anat. Embryol. Cell Biol.* **51**, 1–100.

Pratt, R. M. (1980). *In* "Development in Mammals" (M. H. Johnson, ed.), Vol. 4, 203–232. Elsevier, Amsterdam.

Pratt, R. M. (1983). *Trends Pharm. Sci.*, 160–162.

Saunders, J. W. (1966). *Science* **154**, 604–612.

Sawyer, R. H., and Fallon, J. F. (1983). "Epithelial–Mesenchymal Interactions in Development." Praeger, New York.

Saxen, L. (1977). *In* "Cell and Tissue Interactions" (J. W. Lash and M. M. Berger, eds.), pp. 1–9. Raven, New York.

Saxen, L., Karkinen-Jaaskelainen, M., Lehtonen, E., Nordling, S., and Wartiovaara, J. (1976). *In* "The Cell Surface in Animal Embryogenesis and Development" (G. Poste and G. L. Nicolson, eds.), pp. 331–407. North-Holland Publ., Amsterdam.

Schweichel, J. M., and Merker, H. J. (1973). *Tertology* **7**, 253–266.

Scott, W. J. (1977). *Handb. Teratol.* **2**, 81–98.

Sengel, P. (1976). "Morphogenesis of Skin." Cambridge Univ. Press, London and New York.

Shah, R. M. (1977a). *J. Embryol. Exp. Morphol.* **39**, 203–220.

Shah, R. M. (1977b). *Teratology* **15**, 261–272.

Shah, R. M. (1979a). *J. Embryol. Exp. Morphol.* **53**, 1–13.

Shah, R. M. (1979b). *In* "Advances in the Study of Birth Defects" (T. V. N. Persaud, ed.), Vol. 1, pp. 69–84. MTP Press, Lancaster.

Shah, R. M. (1979c). *In* "Advances in the Study of Birth Defects" (T. V. N. Persaud, ed.), Vol. 2, pp. 25–39. MTP Press, Lancaster.

Shah, R. M. (1979d). *J. Anat.* **129**, 531–539.

Shah, R. M. (1979e). *Invest. Cell Pathol.* **2**, 319–331.

Shah, R. M. (1980). *Invest. Cell Pathol.* **3**, 281–294.

Shah, R. M., and Burdett, D. N. (1979). *Can. J. Physiol. Pharmacol.* **57**, 53–58.

Shah, R. M., and Burton, A. (1984). Submitted.
Shah, R. M., and Chaudhry, A. P. (1973). *Teratology* **7**, 191–194.
Shah, R. M., and Chaudhry, A. P. (1974a). *J. Anat.* **117**, 1–15.
Shah, R. M., and Chaudhry, A. P. (1974b). *Teratology* **10**, 17–30.
Shah, R. M., and Crawford, B. J. (1980). *Invest. Cell Pathol.* **3**, 319–328.
Shah, R. M., and Killistoff, A. J. (1976). *J. Embryol. exp. Morphol.* **36**, 101–108.
Shah, R. M., and MacKay, R. A. (1978). *J. Embryol. Exp. Morphol.* **43**, 47–54.
Shah, R. M., and Travill, A. A. (1976a). *J. Embryol. Exp. Morphol.* **35**, 213–224.
Shah, R. M., and Travill, A. A. (1976b). *Teratology* **13**, 71–84.
Shah, R. M., and Travill, A. A. (1976c). *Am. J. Anat.* **145**, 149–166.
Shah, R. M., and Wong, D. T. W. (1980). *J. Embryol. Exp. Morphol.* **57**, 119–128.
Shah, R. M., Crawford, B. J., Greene, R. M., Suen, R., Burdett, D. N., King, K. O., and Wong, D. T. W. (1984a). Submitted.
Shah, R. M., Crawford, B. J., Suen, R., and Wong, A. (1984b). Submitted.
Shah, R. M., Wong, D. T. W., and Suen, R. (1984c). *Am. J. Anat.* (in press).
Shigura, H. T., and Gordon, C. N. (1962a). *J. Biol. Chem.* **237**, 1932–1936.
Shigura, H. T., and Gordon, C. N. (1962b). *J. Biol. Chem.* **237**, 1937–1940.
Sonawane, B. R., and Goldman, A. (1981). *Proc. Soc. Exp. Biol. Med.* **168**, 175–179.
Spemann, H. (1924). "Embryonic Development and Induction." Yale Univ. Press, New Haven, Connecticut.
Tencer, R., and Brachet, J. (1973). *Differentiation* **1**, 51–64.
Toole, B. P. (1982). *Connect. Tissue Res.* **10**, 93–100.
Trump, B., Laiho, K., Mergner, W., and Arstila, A. (1974). *Beitr. Pathol.* **152**, 243–271.
Walker, B. E., and Crain, B. (1960). *Am. J. Anat.* **107**, 49–58.
Walker, B. E., and Fraser, F. C. (1957). *J. Embryol. Exp. Morphol.* **5**, 201–209.
Warkany, J. (1971). "Congenital Malformations. Notes and Comments." Yearbook Publ., Chicago, Illinois.
Webster, D. A., and Goss, A. (1970). *Dev. Biol.* **22**, 154–184.
Wessells, N. K. (1977). "Tissue Interactions and Development." Benjamin/Cummings, Menlo Park, California.
Wilson, J. G. (1977). *Handb. Teratol.* **1**, 47–73.
Yoneda, T., and Pratt, R. M. (1981a). *J. Craniofac. Genet. Dev. Biol.* **1**, 411–423.
Yoneda, T., and Pratt, R. M. (1981b). *Differentiation* **19**, 194–198.
Yoneda, T., Goldman, A., Van Dyke, D. C., Wilson, L. S., and Pratt, R. M. (1981). *J. Craniofac. Genet. Dev. Biol.* **1**, 229–234.
Zimmerman, E. F. (1979). *In* "Advances in the Study of Birth Defects" (T. V. N. Persaud, ed.), Vol. 3, pp. 143–160. M. T. P. Press, Lancaster.
Zimmerman, E. F., Wee, E. L., Clark, R. L., and Verkatasubramanian, K. (1980). *In* "Current Research Trends in Prenatal Craniofacial Development" (R. M. Pratt and R. L. Christiansen, eds.), pp. 187–202. Elsevier, Amsterdam.

CHAPTER 7

EPITHELIAL–MESENCHYMAL INTERACTIONS DURING VERTEBRATE PALATOGENESIS

*Mark W. J. Ferguson**

DEPARTMENT OF ANATOMY
MEDICAL BIOLOGY CENTRE
THE QUEEN'S UNIVERSITY OF BELFAST
BELFAST, NORTHERN IRELAND

and

Lawrence S. Honig†

LABORATORY FOR DEVELOPMENTAL BIOLOGY
ANDRUS GERONTOLOGY CENTER
UNIVERSITY OF SOUTHERN CALIFORNIA
LOS ANGELES, CALIFORNIA

* Present address: Department of Basic Dental Science, University of Manchester, Dental School, Manchester, England.
† Present address: Department of Anatomy and Cell Biology, University of Miami School of Medicine, Miami, Florida.

CURRENT TOPICS IN
DEVELOPMENTAL BIOLOGY, VOL. 19

I. Introduction and Review

During normal development, the palatal epithelium of any vertebrate consists of three distinct regions: nasal, medial, and oral, each with different developmental fates. In most, if not all, vertebrates the nasal epithelia differentiates into pseudostratified ciliated columnar cells and the oral epithelia into keratinized stratified squamous cells. However, the fate of the medial edge epithelial cells (MEE) of embryonic palatal shelves varies among different vertebrate species (see Ferguson et al., 1984, for review). In mammals (e.g., mice, rats, rabbits, and man) the MEE die, in alligators they migrate, and in chicks the MEE keratinize. In each case the MEE express different and clearly distinguishable phenotypes.

Thus, terminally differentiating mammalian MEE exhibit a number of characteristic changes including the appearance of a carbohydrate-rich glycoprotein surface coat, cessation of DNA synthesis, transient increases in the levels of cAMP, accumulation of intracellular lysosomes, loss of distinct cell boundaries, and flattening and necrosis of the MEE (see chapters by Greene and Garbarino, and Pratt et al., this volume). Clearly, MEE differentiation in mammals is characterized by preparatory changes for and actual physiological cell death. Such phenomena result in fusion of paired palatal shelves, formation and disruption of an epithelial seam, and mesenchymal continuity across the palate.

However, while cell death is characteristic of terminal MEE differentiation in mammals, this is not the case in all vertebrates. Thus, in alligator embryos the MEE do not show extensive cell death; rather, they contact each other and progressively migrate out of the closure zone in a posteronasal direction (Ferguson, 1981a,b, 1984a,b; Ferguson et al., 1984). Precontact alligator MEE develop a characteristic cobblestoned appearance, with distinct cell boundaries, numerous microvilli on the cell surface and at the cell boundaries, and very little cell necrosis (Ferguson, 1981a,b, 1984a,b; Ferguson et al., 1984). Contrariwise, in chicken embryos, the MEE of each palatal shelf contact each other but neither adhere, fuse, migrate, nor die but rather keratinize, so that chickens have a natural cleft palate with a midline choana joining the oral and nasal cavities (Shah and Crawford, 1980; Koch and Smiley, 1981; Greene et al., 1983).

It is widely recognized that the epithelia of most, if not all, tissues and organs are dependent upon tissue interactions with the adjacent mesenchyme for their differentiation and morphogenesis (Wessells, 1977). An enormous literature concerning such interactions has evolved and in general mesenchyme may be classified as instructive, i.e., instructing an epithelium to express a program of development different from its normal fate, or permissive, i.e., providing conditions which permit the expression of previously determined developmental programming.

The differentiation of palatal epithelium could involve epithelial–mesenchymal interactions. The nature of such interactions has been investigated by Tyler and Koch (1977a,b), but both of their studies were limited to mice. Thus, Tyler and Koch (1977a) reported that day 12 embryonic mouse palatal epithelium separated from its mesenchyme and cultured in isolation still underwent limited differentiation into nasal, medial, and oral types. They also found that palatal epithelium cultured transfilter to the oral surface of palatal mesenchyme differentiated in a pattern identical to that of palatal epithelium cultured transfilter to the nasal surface of palatal mesenchyme. Moreover, in heterochronic recombinations of epithelium and mesenchyme from day 12, 13, and 14 mouse embryos, the epithelium differentiated according to a schedule appropriate for the age of the epithelium rather than for the age of the mesenchyme (Tyler and Koch, 1977a), thus suggesting that palatal epithelium is determined as early as 12 days of mouse gestation. In a subsequent experiment Tyler and Koch (1977b) showed that in heterotypic recombinations between palatal epithelium and either tongue, incisor, or salivary gland mesenchyme, the histodifferentiation of the epithelium was palatal in character, whereas the morphogenesis was characteristic of the mesenchyme. This was certainly true of the nasal and oral epithelium but little mention was made of medial edge epithelial cell death (Tyler and Koch, 1977b). Tyler and Koch (1977a,b) concluded that mouse palatal epithelial differentiation was independent of mesenchymal influences by 12 days of gestation, could be supported by various types of mesenchyme, and was an example of a permissive epithelial–mesenchymal interaction. This interpretation has led many to consider that palatal MEE differentiation is a fairly autonomous event, and the term "programmed cell death" is widespread in the recent palatal MEE literature (Hudson and Shapiro, 1973; Pratt and Martin, 1975; Tyler and Koch, 1977a,b; Tyler and Pratt, 1980).

However, recent studies have shown that epidermal growth factor influences mouse palatal MEE differentiation via an action on the underlying mesenchyme (Tyler and Pratt, 1980; Yoneda and Pratt, 1981), so that the role of the mesenchyme in normal MEE differentiation requires reexamination. The emphasis of Tyler and Koch's (1977a,b) studies was on total palatal epithelial differentiation, principally oral and nasal, with only limited observations on MEE differ-entiation. Moreover, Tyler and Koch (1977a,b) did not study the effects of recombining a heterotypic epithelium with palatal shelf mesenchyme.

No one has addressed the evolutionary issues of palatal MEE differ-entiation in different vertebrate species, e.g., will the mesenchyme of a mouse palatal shelf instruct the MEE of a chick palatal epithelium (which normally keratinizes) to undergo cell death? Such issues are of considerable interest, for it has been shown that embryonic rabbit mammary gland mesenchyme instructs embryonic chick flank epi-thelium to differentiate into a mammary gland-like structure (Prop-per, 1969; Propper and Gomet, 1973) and that embryonic mouse molar dental papilla mesenchyme instructs embryonic chick pharyngeal epi-thelium to differentiate into ameloblast-like cells (Kollar and Fischer, 1980; Kollar, 1982). Normally, Aves express neither mammary glands nor teeth, and controversy (Cummings et al., 1981) surrounds the con-clusion that avian oral epithelium has retained the genes for enamel protein synthesis (Kollar and Fischer, 1980; Kollar, 1982). The system of mammalian hair/reptilian scale/avian feather has been used with great effect in investigations of epithelial–mesenchymal interactions during amniote skin morphogenesis (Sengel, 1975, 1976; Sengel and Dhouailly, 1977; Dhouailly, 1975, 1977; Dhouailly et al., 1978). Clear-ly, the differing phenotypes expressed by MEE in mouse (cell death), alligator (cobblestoned morphology, distinct cell boundaries, numerous microvilli, little cell death), and chicken (keratinization, no cell death, no cobblestoning) embryos provide an excellent experimental system for the analysis of putative palatal epithelial–mesenchymal interac-tions.

II. Experimental Strategy

We have previously shown that alligator, chicken, and mouse em-bryonic palatal shelves will differentiate normally under identical, chemically defined culture conditions (Ferguson et al., 1984). We have now analyzed putative epithelial–mesenchymal interactions during vertebrate palatogenesis by performing heterotypic, heterochronic, ho-motypic, and isochronic recombinations of palatal epithelium and mes-enchyme, followed by culture of the recombinants under conditions described by Ferguson et al. (1982, 1983, 1984). This review summa-rizes a number of results described elsewhere (Ferguson and Honig, 1984); further information and details of technique can be found there.

In different experiments, palatal shelves and lower jaws were dis-sected under sterile conditions from Hamburger and Hamilton (1951) stage 31 (day 7) and 34 (day 8) chicken embryos, Ferguson (1984a) stage 17 (day 22), 18 (days 24–26) and 19 (day 27) alligator embryos, and Theiler (1972) stage 20 (day 12) 21 (day 13), and 22 (day 14) mouse embryos. Epithelia and mesenchymes were cleanly separated with fine tungsten needles following incubation of the tissue in 1% trypsin at 4°C for 75 minutes. Care was taken to preserve the shape of the palatal shelf mesenchyme and to note the position of the medial edges of both the separated epithelium and mesenchyme. Large numbers of experimental recombinations of epithelia and mesenchymes were performed as described in Sections III–VI. In each experimental set (e.g., mouse mandibular epithelium and mouse palatal mesenchyme) at least 20 recombinations were performed and frequently as many as 50. The location and direction of the original medial edge of either the epithelium or the mesenchyme or both were marked by punching fine holes (with tungsten needles) in the filter adjacent to the tissue. Recombinants were organ cultured on Millipore filters using the method previously described for palatal shelves (Ferguson et al., 1984). They were removed from culture after either 1, 2, 3, 4, 5, or 6 days and assayed for MEE differentiation by vital staining with neutral red (for cell death) followed by either histological or SEM analysis (Ferguson et al., 1984). In each set approximately 80% of recombinations were successful and the results homogeneous. Unsuccessful recombinants included those in which the epithelial sheet had either slipped off or curled up on the mesenchyme. Most difficulty was experienced in interspecies recombinations involving mouse palatal shelves, owing to the size disparity between these and either chick or alligator shelves. Contaminant epithelia or mesenchymes due to unclean separations were not a problem, and in heterotypic recombinations between alligator, chick, and mouse tissues an internal check for contamination exists, as there is a considerable disparity in epithelial cell size between the three vertebrates.

III. Palate Epithelium and Mesenchyme Cultured in Isolation

Examination of the separated epithelial and mesenchymal surfaces both immediately after separation and following organ culture for 2–3 days consistently revealed no evidence of contamination due to unclean separations (Figs. 1 and 2). Palatal epithelium from all three species performed poorly when organ cultured in isolation (either in chemically defined or serum-supplemented media) (Ferguson et al., 1984). The epithelial sheets underwent progressive degeneration and were usually completely necrotic and disrupted by 3 days in culture.

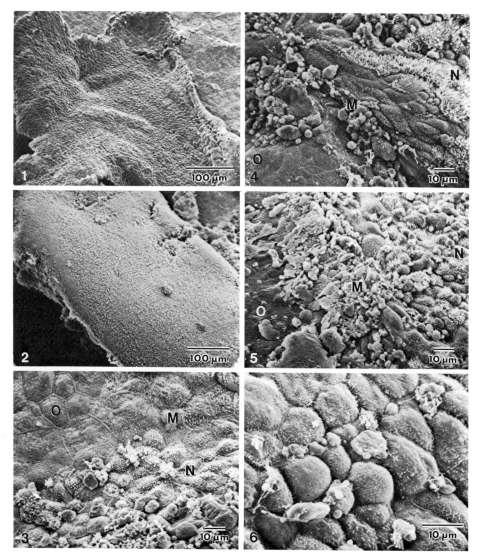

FIG. 1. SEM of the undersurface of a freshly separated mouse palatal epithelium. Note the lack of mesenchymal contamination.

FIG. 2. SEM of an alligator palatal shelf mesenchyme cultured (without epithelium) for 2 days. Note the lack of epithelial cell contamination.

FIG. 3. SEM of a recombination between stage 18 (day 24) alligator mandibular epithelium and stage 18 alligator palatal mesenchyme after 3.5 days culture. Note the differentiation of the mandibular epithelium (which normally keratinizes) into oral stratified squamous (O), medial cobblestoned, villous (M), and nasal pseudostratified ciliated columnar epithelium (N). Differentiation is thus similar to that of the normal alligator palate.

During this period little normal palatal epithelial differentiation could be detected. Of course, the mouse MEE cells died, but then so did the rest of the epithelial sheets, so little significance can be attached to this observation.

By contrast, the separated palatal mesenchymes remained healthy when cultured in isolation. In all three species the mesenchyme differentiated into bone, cartilage, and muscle in a fashion comparable to that described for cultured intact palatal shelves (Ferguson *et al.*, 1984).

IV. Intraspecies Palate/Mandible Recombinations

A. ALLIGATOR

Epithelial—mesenchymal recombinations were performed between the palatal shelves and mandibles (external, posterior—lateral margins) of stage 18 (day 24) alligator embryos. When mandibular epithelium was placed over palatal mesenchyme it subsequently differentiated into oral stratified squamous keratinizing cells, medial cobblestoned, villous, migrating cells, and nasal pseudostratified ciliated columnar cells (Fig. 3). This pattern is typical of normal alligator palatal differentiation (i.e., of the mesenchyme) but atypical of normal mandibular differentiation, in which the epithelium normally develops into heavily keratinized stratified squamous cells. In the reverse recombination, in which palatal epithelium was placed over mandibular mesenchyme, the former differentiated entirely into heavily keratinized stratified squamous cells, i.e., in a pattern typical of the mandible but not of the palate. Alligator mesenchyme appears to be directing epithelial differentiation.

FIG. 4. SEM of a recombination between stage 17 (day 9) mouse mandibular epithelium and stage 20 (day 12) mouse palatal mesenchyme after 3.5 days culture. Note the differentiation of the mandibular epithelium (which normally keratinizes) into oral stratified squamous epithelium (O), medial cell death (M), and nasal pseudostratified ciliated colunar epithelium (N). Differentiation is similar to that of the normal mouse palate.

FIG. 5. SEM of a recombination between stage 20 (day 12) mouse palatal epithelium and stage 20 mouse mandibular mesenchyme after 3.5 days culture. Note the keratinized stratified squamous oral epithelium (O), death of the MEE (M), and the pseudostratified ciliated columnar nasal epithelium (N). Differentiation is similar to that of the normal mouse palate.

FIG. 6. SEM of the medial edge of a recombination between stage 18 (day 24) alligator palatal epithelium and stage 18 alligator palatal mesenchyme with the medial edges crossed after 3 days organ culture. Note the cobblestoned, microvillous epithelial cells and limited cell death typical of alligator MEE differentiation.

B. Chick

Epithelial–mesenchymal recombinations were performed between the palatal shelves and mandibles (external, posterior–lateral margins) of stage 31 (day 7) chicken embryos. The results were similar to those obtained from comparable alligator recombinations described above. Thus, in recombinations of mandibular epithelium and palatal mesenchyme, the epithelium differentiated into oral and medial keratinizing stratified squamous epithelium and nasal pseudostratified ciliated columnar epithelium, with a sharp junction between the two epithelial types. This is typical of normal chick palatal epithelial differentiation. As with alligator, the reverse recombination of chick palatal epithelium and mandibular mesenchyme resulted in extensively keratinized stratified squamous epithelial differentiation.

C. Mouse

Epithelial–mesenchymal recombinations were made between the palatal shelves of either stage 20 (day 12) or stage 21 (day 13) mouse embryos and the mandibles (external lateral margins) of either stage 17 (day 9) or stage 20 (day 12) mouse embryos. Keratinization of the stratified squamous mandibular epithelium is already underway at stage 20 (day 12), so that recombinations of this with palatal mesenchyme merely maintain the former pattern of differentiation. However, when stage 17 (day 9) mandibular epithelium (which is not overtly differentiated) is recombined with palatal mesenchyme from either stage 20 (day 12) or stage 21 (day 13) embryos a different result is found. In these cases epithelial differentiation is typified by oral keratinized stratified squamous epithelium, medial cell death, and nasal pseudostratified ciliated columnar epithelium (Fig. 4). Both ages of palatal mesenchyme produce this result. The differentiation pattern appears to be specified by the mesenchyme.

In the reverse recombinations of either stage 20 (day 12) or stage 21 (day 13) palatal epithelium on either stage 17 (day 9) or stage 20 (day 12) mandibular mesenchymes, a result different from the pattern observed in alligator and chick is found. In these recombinations, the mouse palatal epithelium differentiates into oral stratified squamous keratinizing cells, medial cell death, and nasal pseudostratified ciliated columnar cells (Fig. 5) i.e., in a pattern characteristic of the epithelium and not of the mandibular mesenchyme. It appears that mouse palatal epithelium is already determined by stage 20 (day 12) and that this program cannot be altered by the mandibular mesenchyme. However, the mouse palatal mesenchyme is still capable of signaling normal palatal epithelial differentiation to a heterotypic mandibular epithelium, even as late as stage 21 (day 13).

V. Intraspecies Palate/Palate Recombinations

A. MEDIAL EDGES COINCIDENT, MEDIAL EDGES CROSSED, AND UPSIDE-DOWN EPITHELIA

1. General

Homotypic, isochronic recombinations [e.g., stage 21 (day 13) mouse palatal mesenchyme with stage 21 mouse palatal epithelium] with the medial edges of the epithelium and mesenchyme placed coincident were performed as controls in each species in order to determine whether or not the experimental procedures of separation, etc., had any effect on normal palatal differentiation, particularly on MEE differentiation. Similar recombinations were performed with the medial edge of the epithelium placed at right angles to the medial edge of the mesenchyme (hereafter called medial edges crossed). The objective of this experiment was to observe if the epithelium became reprogrammed by the mesenchyme to form "new" oral, nasal, and medial surfaces or if the epithelium expressed any differentiation characteristic of its "old" position. This was a particularly critical experiment in the case of the mouse, as the palate/mandible recombinations had shown a palatal mesenchyme capable of signaling but a palatal epithelium which was determined early—would we therefore observe two medial edges (i.e., an old and a new one) in these crossed palatal recombinations? Finally, recombinations were performed in each species with the sheet of epithelium placed upside down on the mesenchyme, i.e., with the separated basement membrane surface uppermost (the medial edges were coincident in some cases and crossed in others). The objective here was to determine if the palatal epithelium could change its polarity and express normal differentiation.

2. Alligator

Recombinations were performed between the palatal epithelia and mesenchymes of either stage 17 (day 22–23) or stage 18 (days 24–25) alligator embryos. Regardless of the type of recombination (i.e., medial edges coincident, crossed, or upside-down epithelia), the epithelium differentiated in a normal palatal fashion of oral keratinized stratified squamous epithelium; medial cobblestoned, villous, migrating epithelium; and nasal pseudostratified ciliated columnar epithelium (Fig. 6). The pattern of differentiation corresponded to the orientation of the

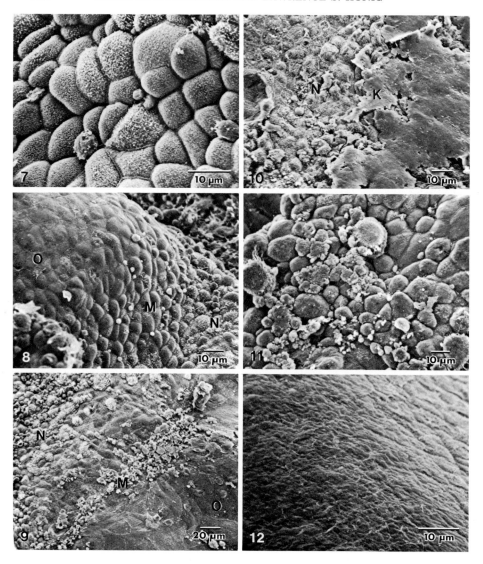

FIG. 7. SEM of the medial edge of a recombination between stage 18 (day 25) posterior (unclosed) alligator palatal epithelium and stage 18 anterior (closed) alligator palatal mesenchyme after 3 days organ culture. Note the cobblestoned, microvillous epithelial cells typical of alligator MEE differentiation (compare with Fig. 6).

FIG. 8. SEM of a recombination between stage 18 (day 25) alligator anterior (closed) palatal oral epithelium and stage 18 alligator posterior (unclosed) palatal mesenchyme after 3.5 days organ culture. Note the epithelial differentiation into oral stratified squamous (O), medial cobblestoned, microvillous (M), and nasal pseudostratified ciliated columnar cells (N).

mesenchyme. The original orientation of the palatal epithelium before separation and recombination had no obvious effects. Clearly, the experimental manipulations had little effect on alligator MEE differentiation, the palatal mesenchyme appeared to be directing epithelial differentiation, and the palatal epithelium could change its polarity.

3. Chick

Recombinations were made between the palatal epithelium and mesenchymes of either stage 31 (day 7) or stage 34 (day 8) chick embryos. Results similar to those described above for alligator were obtained, i.e., regardless of the type of recombination the epithelium differentiated in a normal palatal pattern (which corresponded to the orientation of the mesenchyme) of oral and medial keratinized stratified squamous cells and nasal pseudostratified ciliated columnar cells with a sharp junction between the two (Fig. 10). The same general conclusions apply to chick as to alligator.

4. Mouse

Recombinations were made between the palatal epithelia and mesenchymes of either stage 20 (day 12) or stage 21 (day 13) mouse embryos. Results similar in principle to those observed in alligator and chick were obtained. Thus, regardless of the type of recombination the epithelium differentiated in a normal palatal fashion of oral ker-

---

FIG. 9. SEM of a recombination between stage 21 (day 13) mouse palatal epithelium and stage 21 mouse lateral palatal mesenchyme after 3.5 days organ culture. The medial edge of the epithelial sheet was not apposed to the border of the lateral mesenchyme but rather crossed it at 90°. Note differentiation of the epithelium into oral stratified squamous cells (O), medial cell death (M), and nasal pseudostratified ciliated columnar cells (N), typical of normal mouse palatal development.

FIG. 10. SEM of a recombination between stage 31 (day 7) chick palatal epithelium and stage 31 chick palatal mesenchyme after 4.5 days organ culture. Note the sharp transition between the keratinizing stratified squamous oral and medial edge epithelium (K) and the pseudostratified ciliated columnar nasal epithelium (N). This pattern is typical of chick palatal development.

FIG. 11. SEM of the medial edge of a recombination between stage 18 (day 24) alligator palatal epithelium and stage 21 (day 13) mouse palatal mesenchyme after 3 days organ culture. The medial edges of the epithelia and mesenchyme were apposed. Note that cell death, typical of the mouse, is far more abundant than during normal alligator medial edge differentiation. Compare with Figs. 5, 6, and 7.

FIG. 12. SEM of the medial edge of a recombination between stage 18 (day 24) alligator palatal epithelium and stage 31 (day 7) chick palatal mesenchyme after 5 days organ culture. The medial edges of the epithelium and mesenchyme were apposed. Note the extensive keratinization typical of chick MEE differentiation but not of alligator. Compare with Figs. 6, 7, and 10.

atinized stratified squamous epithelium, medial cell death, and nasal pseudostratified ciliated columnar epithelium (similar to Fig. 9). The pattern of differentiation corresponded to the orientation of the mesenchyme, the original epithelial orientation appeared to have no effect, and two medial edges at right angles to each other were never observed in the crossed recombinations. Clearly, if mouse palatal epithelium is determined at stages 20 and 21 (as suggested by the palate/mandible recombinations), then this program can be altered by a mouse palatal mesenchyme. These recombinations also confirm the notion that the mouse palatal mesenchyme can specify epithelial differentiation at both stages 20 (day 12) and 21 (day 13).

B. MEDIAL AND LATERAL MESENCHYMES

The foregoing experiments suggested that palatal medial edge mesenchymal cells specified MEE differentiation in all three species. We were interested to learn if this was a special property of the palatal medial edge mesenchymal cells or if other palatal mesenchymal cells possessed this ability but only those on the medial edge expressed it, perhaps as a result of their position in relation to, and interaction with, other cells. We therefore devised the following experiment.

Palatal shelves were excised and the epithelia separated as described earlier. The palatal shelf mesenchyme was then cut longitudinally (i.e., from anterior to posterior with respect to the head) into two segments: a medial segment which had one edge which was the original palatal medial edge and the other the cut edge; and a lateral segment which had one edge which was the bisected palatal surface ("new" medial edge) and the other the edge where it had been cut from the lateral mass of the maxillary process. The separated epithelium was then recombined with either the original medial edge of the medial segment or the "new" medial edge of the lateral segment. Epithelia were recombined with their medial edges either coincident or crossed with respect to the mesenchymal edges. Clearly, this experiment utilizes twice the number of epithelia to mesenchymes. Recombinations were made between the same stages of alligator, chick, and mouse embryos as described in Section V,A. In every case palatal epithelial differentiation proceeded normally, i.e., into keratinized stratified squamous oral epithelia, pseudostratified ciliated columnar nasal epithelia, and the appropriate vertebrate medial edge phenotype, i.e., cobblestoned, villous, migrating epithelia in the alligator, keratinized stratified squamous epithelia in the chick, and cell death in the mouse (Fig. 9). MEE differentiation proceeded normally when placed on either the original medial edge of the medial segment or on the "new" medial edge of the lateral segment in all three species (Fig. 9). The crossed recombinations did not produce two medial edges, but rather one medial edge which corresponded to the orientation of the mesenchyme. It is remarkable that the "new" medial edge of the lateral mouse mesenchyme could alter the differentiation of the supposedly determined mouse palatal epithelium in crossed recombinations.

Clearly, the ability to signal MEE differentiation is not restricted to a special subpopulation of palatal mesenchymal cells beneath the medial edge. Rather, it appears to be a general property of palatal mesenchymal cells and only those on an edge express it, perhaps as a result of their position or of their interactions with surrounding cells and the overlying reconstituted basement membrane. The hypothesis that there is a gradient of some "morphogen" with a high point either medially or laterally cannot be excluded by these experiments. Removal of the mesenchymal medial edge might result in a reformed gradient (e.g., Meinhardt, 1982). Another possibility is that it is the contact between presumptive oral and nasal mesenchymal cells that generates an effective new medial edge. The role of the reformed basement membrane is also unknown in these experiments. However, the composition of the palatal basement membrane in all three species and alterations in the former with developmental time are currently under investigation *in vivo, in vitro,* and in recombinations.

C. Fused Palatal Epithelium and Mesenchyme

1. Alligator

In order to understand further the nature of interactions between palatal mesenchyme and epithelium with regard to MEE differentiation, we decided to exploit the fact that the alligator palate closes in a progressive antero–posterior sequence over several days (Ferguson, 1981a,b, 1982, 1984a,b). At stage 18 (day 24) the anterior half of the palate is closed, while posteriorly the shelves are still widely separated (and do not close fully until day 28). We therefore excised the palates from stage 18 (day 24) alligator embryos and cut them transversely into closed and unclosed segments. The oral and nasal epithelia were separated from the closed segments and the latter discarded (since it separates off into small sheets owing to the presence of the nasal septum and nasopharyngeal ducts on the nasal surface of the palate). The closed mesenchyme was then bisected longitudinally along the line where palatal closure had taken place to give two shelves of "fused mesenchyme." The posterior unclosed shelves were separated into epithelia and mesenchymes. The unclosed posterior palatal epithelia were recombined with the anterior fused palatal mesenchymes and the anterior oral epithelial sheets recombined with the posterior palatal shelf mesenchymes. In both cases palatal epithelial differentiation proceeded normally, i.e., into keratinized stratified squamous oral epithelia; cobblestoned, villous, migrating medial epithelia; and pseudostratified ciliated columnar nasal epithelia (Figs. 7 and 8). This means that recently closed palatal mesenchyme, which has already specified medial edge, oral, and nasal differentiation, still retains the capacity to specify such differentiation again (Fig. 7). At what stage the mesenchyme loses this ability is unknown, but it is clearly after overt palatal closure. Equally, the oral palatal epithelium from a recently closed palate can be induced to differentiate into nasal, medial, and oral types by a suitable palatal mesenchyme (Fig. 8).

2. Mouse

A comparable experiment to the above was performed by separating the recently fused palates of stage 22 (day 14) mouse embryos into oral epithelia and longitudinally bisected fused palatal mesenchymes, followed by recombination of these with the separated palatal mesenchymes and epithelia of stage 21 (day 13) mouse embryos. A result similar in principle to that observed with alligators was obtained, i.e., in both cases the epithelia differentiated into oral keratinized stratified squamous cells, medial cell death, and nasal pseudostratified ciliated columnar cells. The orientation of the mesenchyme specified the pattern of differentiation. Once again, recently fused palatal mesenchyme can specify MEE (and nasal and oral) differentiation, while recently fused oral palatal epithelium can be made to differentiate into nasal, medial, and oral types by a suitable palatal mesenchyme. These results are in accord with the suggestions made in Section V,B concerning the way in which palatal mesenchyme could specify palatal epithelial differentiation.

VI. Interspecies Palate/Palate Recombinations

A. MEDIAL EDGES COINCIDENT

In all interspecies recombinations, oral and nasal epithelial differentiation were always normal, i.e., keratinized stratified squamous cells and pseudostratified ciliated columnar cells, respectively. For brevity only MEE differentiation will be described in the following sections. The difference in size between alligator, chick, and mouse cells enabled one to keep an internal check for contamination (due to unclean separations) in these interspecies recombinations (none was found).

All recombinations of stage 18 alligator epithelium and either stage 20 or stage 21 mouse mesenchyme exhibited MEE differentiation which was more characteristic of the mouse, i.e., more extensive cell death than the alligator (Fig. 11). MEE differentiation appeared to be specified by the mesenchyme, which is the general principle that applies to all recombinations in this section.

For recombinations of stage 18 alligator epithelium and stage 31 chick mesenchyme, MEE differentiation was characteristic of the chick, i.e., extensive keratinization, rather than of the alligator (Fig. 12).

In all recombinations of either stage 20 or stage 21 mouse epithelium and stage 18 alligator mesenchyme, MEE differentiation was characteristic of the alligator, i.e., cobblestoned, villous, migrating cells with very limited cell death, and not of the mouse (extensive cell death) (Fig. 13).

In recombinations of either stage 20 or stage 21 mouse epithelium and stage 31 chick mesenchyme, there was a sharp transition between the keratinized stratified squamous epithelium and the pseudostratified ciliated columnar epithelium, with no signs of cobblestoning or cell death (Figs. 15 and 17). This pattern is characteristic of the chick, in which the MEE become keratinized stratified squamous cells, but not of the mouse, in which the MEE die.

In recombinations of stage 31 chick epithelium and stage 18 alligator mesenchyme, MEE differentiation was characteristic of the alligator, i.e., the chick epithelial cells became cobblestoned and villous, and showed signs of migration with limited cell death (Fig. 16). This is in contrast to the normal pattern of chick MEE differentiation, which produces keratinized stratified squamous cells.

In all recombinations of stage 31 chick epithelium and either stage 20 or stage 21 mouse mesenchyme, MEE differentiation was characteristic of the mouse, i.e., cell death, rather than of the chick (Fig. 18).

It is evident that when the palatal epithelia and mesenchymes of alligator, chick, and mouse embryos are recombined with their medial edges coincident, the MEE differentiates in a pattern characteristic of the vertebrate from which the mesenchyme originated. Thus, palatal mesenchyme appears to be instructing MEE differentiation and such instructions go across selected species of the vertebrate classes: Reptilia, Aves, and Mammalia. If the fate of mouse palatal epithelium is specified by stage 20, as suggested by the palate/mandible recombination experiments, then the program may be altered if the epithelium is recombined with its medial edge coincident with the medial edge of

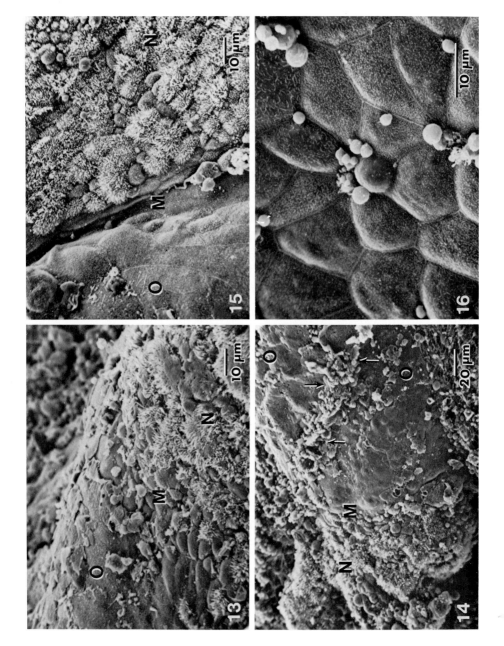

either an alligator or a chick palatal mesenchyme. Moreover, the program of mouse palatal epithelial differentiation may also be altered if it is recombined with its medial edge crossed over that of a mouse palatal mesenchyme (see Section V,A,4). This raises the possibility that there is a "hierarchy" of mesenchymes, some of which can alter the program of mouse MEE differentiation and others of which cannot. As this may give an insight into the possible mechanisms whereby the mesenchyme influences epithelial differentiation, we decided to assay the "strengths" of alligator, chick, and mouse palatal mesenchymal "signaling" by performing interspecies recombinations with the medial edges of the epithelia and mesenchymes crossed.

B. MEDIAL EDGES CROSSED

Recombinations were performed as specified in Section VI,A except that the medial edges were crossed. All recombinations, except those involving mouse palatal epithelia, gave the same result regardless of whether the medial edges were coincident or crossed. Thus, the palatal mesenchyme accurately specified nasal, oral, and medial edge epithelial differentiation.

The exceptions were recombinations involving mouse palatal epi-

---

FIG. 13. SEM of a recombination between stage 20 (day 12) mouse palatal epithelium and stage 18 (day 24) alligator palatal mesenchyme after 3.5 days organ culture. The medial edges of the epithelia and mesenchyme were apposed. Note the oral keratinized stratified squamous epithelia (O), nasal pseudostratified ciliated columnar epithelia (N), and the cobblestoned medial edge epithelia (M) exhibiting little cell death. This pattern is similar to the alligator (e.g., Fig. 6) but different from the massive cell death usually seen in the mouse (e.g., Figs. 5 and 9).

FIG. 14. SEM of a recombination between stage 21 (day 13) mouse palatal epithelium and stage 18 (day 24) alligator palatal mesenchyme after 3.5 days organ culture. The medial edges of the epithelia and mesenchymes were not apposed but rather crossed at right angles. Note the oral stratified squamous (O) and nasal pseudostratified ciliated columnar (N) epithelia. The "new" medial edge of the shelf (M) has cobblestoned, villous cells typical of alligator MEE differentiation. However, the "old" medial edge of the mouse epithelium (arrowed) has undergone cell death. Compare with Fig. 13, in which the medial edges were apposed.

FIG. 15. SEM of a recombination between stage 21 (day 13) mouse palatal epithelium and stage 31 (day 7) chick palatal mesenchyme (with the medial edges of both apposed) after 3.5 days organ culture. Note the sharp transition between the keratinized stratified squamous epithelium of the oral (O) and medial (M) edges and the pseudostratified ciliated columnar nasal epithelium (N). There is a lack of MEE cell death, which is typical of the chick (e.g., Fig. 10) but not of the mouse (e.g., Figs. 5 and 9).

FIG. 16. SEM of the medial edge of a recombination between stage 31 (day 7) chick palatal epithelium and stage 18 (day 24) alligator palatal mesenchyme (with the medial edges of both apposed) after 3 days organ culture. Note the cobblestoned, villous epithelial cells and the limited cell death characteristic of alligator MEE differentiation.

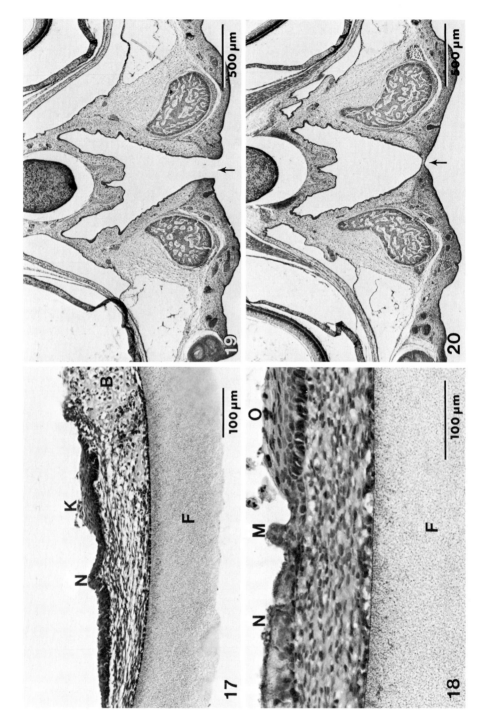

thelium and either alligator or chick palatal mesenchyme. In these cases two medial edges were observed (Fig. 14). The mesenchyme specified a "new" medial edge, the epithelial cells of which had a phenotype typical of the vertebrate from which the mesenchyme was derived, i.e., cobblestoned, villous, migrating cells in the case of alligator and keratinized stratified squamous cells in the case of the chick (Fig. 14). The mesenchyme also specified nasal and oral epithelial differentiation into pseudostratified ciliated columnar epithelium and keratinized stratified squamous epithelium, respectively (Fig. 14). However, it did not reprogram the original mouse MEE, and so a line of cell death ("old" medial edge) was observed at right angles to the "new" medial edge (Fig. 14). The "old" medial edge did not separate nasal and oral epithelial phenotypes; rather, these corresponded to the orientation of the "new" mesenchyme and were separated by the "new" medial edge.

Clearly, alligator and chick palatal mesenchyme can (1) specify the type of MEE differentiation in a mouse palatal epithelia, (2) alter the determined mouse MEE phenotype if the medial edges are placed coincident, (3) produce a new medial edge, oral, and nasal surfaces if the epithelia and mesenchymes are crossed, but (4) cannot alter the determined mouse MEE phenotype in a crossed recombination. However, a mouse palatal mesenchyme can alter the determined mouse MEE phenotype in a crossed recombination (see Section V,A,4). These results suggest that the "signaling capability" of mouse oral and nasal mesenchyme is such that it can redetermine mouse MEE differentiation, whereas that of alligator and chick oral and nasal mesenchyme is

---

Fig. 17. Histological section of a recombination between stage 21 (day 13) mouse palatal epithelium and stage 31 (day 7) chick palatal mesenchyme (with the medial edges of both apposed) after 3 days organ culture. Note the sharp transition from the keratinized stratified squamous epithelia of the oral and medial edges (K) to the pseudostratified ciliated columnar nasal epithelia (N). Cell death and areas of denuded mesenchyme (see Ferguson *et al.,* 1984) are absent. The pattern is typical of chick and not of mouse. B, Bone; F, filter.

Fig. 18. Histological section of a recombination between stage 31 (day 7) chick palatal epithelia and stage 21 (day 13) mouse palatal mesenchyme (with the medial edges of both apposed) after 3 days organ culture. Note the oral stratified squamous epithelia (O), nasal pseudostratified ciliated columnar epithelia (N), and medial edge epithelial cell death (M). This pattern is typical of mouse, not chick. F, Filter.

Fig. 19. Histological section through the anterior half of a day 13 embryonic chick palate. Note the natural cleft (arrowed).

Fig. 20. Histological section through a similar region to that illustrated in Fig. 19 of a day 13 embryonic chick whose palatal medial edge epithelium had been surgically lacerated at day 9. Note the fusion of the palatal shelves (arrowed) to produce an abnormal intact chicken palate.

insufficient. The signaling capability of any vertebrate palatal mesenchyme is such that it can redetermine mouse MEE differentiation if
it is recombined with its medial edge coincident with that of the mouse
palatal epithelium. These results suggest that the pattern of MEE
differentiation may be related in some way to the reconstitution and
altering composition of the palatal basement membrane. Certainly,
whatever the mechanism, palatal mesenchymal specificity extends
across vertebrate species with a remarkable degree of accuracy for
both epithelial cytodifferentiation and the patterning of the latter.

VII. Experimental Production of Noncleft Palates in Chicken Embryos

The normal chick MEE phenotype is that of keratinized stratified
squamous cells. However, chick MEE is capable of undergoing either
cell death or cell migration if it receives the appropriate instructions
from an underlying mesenchyme. We therefore postulated that the
natural condition of cleft palate in the chick (Fig. 19) may result from
an absence of such instructions as opposed to other reasons, e.g.,
failure of quiescent shelf contact for closure. To test this hypothesis we
operated on the palatal shelves of stage 35 (day 9) chick embryos both
in ovo and *in vitro* (Ferguson and Honig, 1984). The operation consisted
of a surgical laceration of the MEE with tungsten needles so as to
produce epithelial cell death and exposed mesenchymal surfaces. Embryos were killed 4 days after operation and their palates examined
(Figs. 19 and 20). The experimental embryos showed palatal closure in
the region of operation (Fig. 20). Thus the "abnormal" condition of an
intact (noncleft) chick palate was produced (Figs. 19 and 20). This
experiment demonstrates that conditions such as shelf contact and
growth in head width are favorable for chick palatal closure but that
the latter does not occur because the MEE are not directed to die or
migrate by the chick palatal mesenchyme. Thus, certain cell–cell interactions result in an intact palate in mammals and alligators whereas others result in cleft palate in birds. If one views MEE keratinization, as seen in chicks, as a "default state" due to a failure of the
epithelium to receive instructions to die or migrate, then a loss (or
change) in one "set" of mesenchymal–epithelial interactions results in
cleft palate with all its attendant physiological, anatomical, behav-
ioral, and ecological ramifications. Such a "default" may arise because
of an alteration in the timing, migration, and interactions which the
palatal mesenchymal cells undergo during their migration from the

mesencephalic neural crest to the palate. This hypothesis is currently being tested in experimental embryonic chimeras.

VIII. Discussion

Space does not permit a discussion of the full ramifications of these experiments, which will appear in the definitive report of this work (Ferguson and Honig, 1984). (See also the experiments described by Shah on hamster and chick interactions, this volume.) Summarized, the events in *alligator* and *chick* palatal epithelial differentiation appear straightforward. The epithelium plays a passive role and responds to an underlying mesenchyme by differentiating into the phenotypes appropriate for that mesenchyme. The mesenchyme can induce appropriate oral, nasal, and medial phenotypes in a heterotypic epithelium. Mesenchyme from both early and late (even postclosure) stages of palatogenesis is capable of signaling normal palatal epithelial differentiation. Mesenchymal specificity extends not only across species but also across vertebrate classes. At neither early nor late stages of palatogenesis does alligator or chick epithelium appear "determined" or "biased," but rather it seems to be dependent on the continuing presence of the appropriate palatal mesenchyme for its continuing differentiation. The ability to signal palatal medial edge epithelial differentiation does not appear to be restricted to a subpopulation of palatal mesenchymal cells and is present even in recently fused palatal mesenchymes.

Mouse palatal epithelial differentiation is more complex. Similar generalizations to the above apply except that mouse palatal epithelium appears to be "determined" or biased from the earliest stages of overt palatogenesis. This determination can be completely altered by the influence of some mesenchymes (e.g., mouse palatal in a crossed recombination or chick and alligator palatal in coincident recombinations), partly altered by the influence of other mesenchymes (e.g., chick and alligator palatal in crossed recombinations), and completely unaffected by yet other (neutral) mesenchymes (e.g., mouse mandibular). Throughout the period of mouse palatogenesis the palatal mesenchyme can still induce appropriate palatal differentiation in a heterotypic epithelium, despite the fact that the mouse palatal epithelium already appears to be determined at these stages. In this regard, the events in mouse palatal epithelial differentiation may be likened to those in lens induction (reviewed by Kratochwil, 1983), wherein the head ectoderm becomes progressively biased toward lens differentiation by the synergistic action of at least three tissues: foregut endoderm, heart mesoderm, and the optic vesicle. We suggest that early mouse palatal epithelium is not determined but rather biased toward a particular pattern of epithelial differentiation, for this bias can be altered by an appropriate heterotypic mesenchyme. Presumably, during normal palatogenesis, mouse epithelium becomes progressively more biased under the continuing influences of the mouse mesenchyme. Interestingly, Hudson and Shapiro (1973) and Pratt and Martin (1975) have shown that mouse palatal MEE cease DNA synthesis 24 hours prior to fusion. It would be productive to investigate whether recombination of mouse palatal epithelium with chick mesenchyme prevents and/or reverses such a phenomenon.

Our conclusions are somewhat different from those reached by Tyler and Koch (1977a,b), who ascribed a permissive role to palatal mesenchyme and suggested that the epithelium was determined for a particular developmental fate from the onset of palatogenesis. However, it must be realized that our experimental results complement rather than contradict those of Tyler and Koch (1977a,b) since we report here the effects of (1) recombining heterotypic epithelium with palatal mesenchyme, (2) interspecies palate/palate recombinations, and (3) crossed, fused, medial, and lateral recombinations. Credence to the idea that palatal mesenchyme induces epithelial differentiation is also given by Pourtois (1972), who reported that epithelial disruption occurred in heterochronic recombinations of mouse palatal shelves only if the mesenchyme was excised at the time of *in vivo* palatal fusion; palatal epithelia recombined with young mesenchymes apparently remained intact. Although his conclusions on the inductive role of palatal mesenchyme are in accord with ours, his experimental results are not (nor are they in accord with Tyler and Koch, 1977a,b). Unfortunately Pourtois (1972) never reported any details of his experimental method, the numbers of recombinants studied, or the precise culture conditions, so that further comment and comparisons are impossible. Nevertheless, it is known that epidermal growth factor stimulates mouse MEE DNA synthesis and prevents cell death via an action on the mesenchyme (Tyler and Pratt, 1980; Yoneda and Pratt, 1981). Such studies support the idea that palatal mesenchyme plays more of an instructive than a permissive role in palatal MEE differentiation. Certainly, the epithelium enjoys considerably less autonomy than is currently implied in the phrase "programmed cell death" (Hudson and Shapiro, 1973; Pratt and Martin, 1975; Tyler and Koch, 1977a,b).

Such discussions raise the broader question of instructive (or directive) and permissive epithelial–mesenchymal interactions. At the level of phenomenology observed in histological preparations such a dichotomy appears clear; thus, the ability of heterotypic mesenchymes to support pancreatic morphogenesis is an example of a permissive interaction (Golosow and Grobstein, 1962), whereas development of a uterine-like columnar epithelium and associated glands from vaginal epithelium recombined with uterine mesenchyme is an example of an instructive interaction (Cunha and Lung, 1978, 1979, 1980). However, when critically assessed it remains unclear whether either of these reactions are inductive in the molecular definition of derepression of unique structural gene products, and the terms instructive, directive, and permissive are perhaps premature and unhelpful (Kratochwil, 1983). The heart of the problem resides in whether (1) cells contain and store intrinsic information which is expressed in a favorable environment or (2) developmental information is produced *de novo* and expressed following intercellular communication.

Our results argue against the extreme permissive, minimalistic view of induction suggested by Kratochwil (1983). Palatal medial edge epithelial cells (and indeed mandibular epithelia) appear to have at least three developmental options (keratinized stratified squamous cells; cobblestoned, villous, migrating cells; or cell death) which are expressed under the influence of different tissues. Under these circumstances it is difficult to escape the conclusion that the mesenchyme specifies a specific epithelial differentiation rather than affecting a simple yes–no decision for a preexisting developmental program. Nevertheless, it is unknown from our experiments whether an individual medial edge epithelial cell has more than one developmental option or whether the different phenotypes of MEE differentiation are achieved by a series of binary cell decisions, with intervening cell division. Such possibilities will be investigated in future experiments. An instructive role for the palatal mesenchyme would also be expected on theoretical grounds, for it has to affect a high degree of architectural coordination within a very small area, i.e., nasal epithelium must become pseudostratified ciliated columnar epithelium; oral, stratified squamous epithelium; and medial, the appropriate vertebrate phenotype. Moreover, MEE differentiation must be accurately specified on the medial edge of the shelf; otherwise palatal closure cannot take place in alligator and mouse embryos.

An interesting paradigm for the present study is the development of vertebrate skin *in vivo* and *in vitro* (Sengel, 1975, 1976; Dhouailly, 1975, 1977a,b; Dhouailly *et al.*, 1978; Sengel and Dhouailly, 1977). These experiments involved heterotypic recombinations between the epithelia and mesenchymes of avian, reptilian, and mammalian embryos, utilizing the general assay of mammalian hair, reptilian scale, and avian feather. In general, the conclusion from these experiments, and from others involving scaleless mutants (McAleese and Sawyer, 1981) and the mammary gland (Sakakura et al., 1976), is that morphogenetic form is regulated by the mesenchyme, whereas cytodifferentiation of the epithelium and its biosynthetic functions are specific to the organ from which it originated. Sakakura et al. (1976) suggested that there was little evidence that epithelium could be induced by heterotypic mesenchyme to synthesize, in quantity, any product "strange" to the organ from which the epithelial anlage was taken.

The present results on MEE differentiation reveal that both morphogenetic form *and* epithelial cytodifferentiation are regulated by the underlying mesenchyme. Thus, MEE differentiation appears to be an exception to previous generalizations. However, the cytodifferentiation expressed by MEE is not highly specialized and is well within the repertoire of that possessed by most epithelial cells. Herein may lie the answer. Thus, general features of epithelial cytodifferentiation, e.g., cell death, microvilli, cell swelling, may be regulated almost exclusively by the mesenchyme, whereas more specialized functions such as casein or enamel protein secretion may depend more heavily upon the nature and previous developmental history of the epithelium.

The mechanisms by which embryonic mesenchyme "instructs" adjacent epithelia are unknown for any developmental system. Current ideas include diffusible morphogenetic substances, cell surface-associated matrix material, direct cell–cell contacts and communication, changing composition of the extracellular matrix, e.g., the basal lamina, alterations in the cell membrane, and changes in cell shape and the intracellular cytoskeleton (for further information see reviews by Hay, 1977; Wessells, 1977; Bernfield and Banerjee, 1978; Saxen et al., 1980; Slavkin, 1979, 1982; Kratochwil, 1983). Not surprisingly, our data do not reveal the molecular mechanism for palatal tissue interactions. However, they do suggest that future investigations should include a thorough analysis of the structure and developmental alterations of the basement membrane during palatogenesis in all three species. In other organ systems, alterations in basement membrane composition (such as changes in the type of collagen, distribution of fibronectin, proteoglycans, and laminin) generally precede and many indeed signal epithelial differentiation (Bernfield and Banerjee, 1978; Thesleff, 1979; Thesleff and Hurmerinta, 1981; Thesleff et al., 1979, 1981; Brownell and Slavkin, 1980; Gordon and Bernfield, 1980; Ekblom et al., 1981; Lesot et al., 1981). Furthermore, degradation of the basement membrane, followed by direct mesenchymal–epithelial cell contact, may precede and signal epithelial differentiation (Mathan et al., 1972;

Cutler and Chaudhry, 1973; Slavkin and Bringas, 1976; Slavkin *et al.*, 1977; Slavkin, 1979). The point is interesting because palatal shelf mesenchyme swells considerably (due to hydration of extracellular glycosaminoglycans; Ferguson, 1977, 1978a,b; Brinkley, 1980; Diewert, 1980) during the period of palatogenesis and MEE differentiation. Such swelling may assist, or be causally related to, disruption of the basal lamina beneath the MEE. There is controversy as to the status of the basal lamina during murine MEE differentiation, De Angelis and Nallandian (1968), Shapiro and Sweeney (1969), and Smiley and Koch (1971, 1972) stating that it is complete, while Farbman (1968, 1969), Smiley and Dixon (1968), and Chippendale and Johnson (1979) state that it becomes discontinuous and that direct epithelial–mesenchymal cell contacts occur through the discontinuities. Certainly, the basal lamina must disappear at some point during normal palatal closure in mouse and alligator but not in chick, in which the palatal shelves do not close. It would be of interest to compare and contrast the composition and sequential changes in the basal lamina beneath the MEE of mouse, alligator, and chicken embryonic palatal shelves (and in heterotypic recombinations of the latter), each of which exhibits a different pattern of MEE differentiation and a different developmental fate.

It is possible that the signaling of medial edge epithelial differentiation is a "passive" rather than an active event. Medial edge epithelial differentiation may result where the mesenchymal influences which specify nasal and oral phenotypes come together. This could explain many of our experimental findings, particularly those involving medial, lateral, or fused palatal mesenchymes. Also, although nasal and oral epithelial differentiation has been collectively described as producing pseudostratified ciliated columnar epithelia and keratinized stratified squamous epithelia throughout this chapter, there are species-specific differences, particularly in nasal phenotypes. Thus, mouse nasal cells have long cilia which are very abundant, alligator cells have much smaller cilia which are less numerous, and chick nasal cells have few cilia but many long microvilli. Moreover, the timing of terminal nasal epithelial differentiation with regard to MEE differentiation varies among the three species. It is therefore possible that the various MEE phenotypes observed in the three species result from differences in the specification of the oral and nasal surfaces, whose fields of influence interact at the medial edge of the mesenchyme. Such a hypothesis can be tested experimentally in recombinations in which the separated palatal mesenchyme is split horizontally into nasal and oral segments. Epithelial–epithelial interactions of the determined nasal and oral surfaces may also play some role in the specification of palatal MEE differentiation. Moreover, the changes in mesenchymal cell shape and intracellular cytoskeletal architecture which occur at the medial edge of a shelf may enable these mesenchymal cells to influence epithelial differentiation in a manner different from those adjacent to the flat oral and nasal surfaces. Future attention should be paid to the differing shapes and cytoskeletal architecture of mesenchymal cells beneath the oral, nasal, and medial edges, for the notion that these parameters can influence a cell's differentiative state is relatively new.

Finally, our experiments reveal that cleft palate in the chick may result from altered (? failed) cell–cell interactions, whereby the MEE is not induced to die or migrate. A similar upset in the nature and timing of developmental interactions has been postulated to account for the toothless condition of modern birds (Kollar and Fischer, 1980; Kollar, 1982). The cleft avian palate is yet another example of how a small alteration in a subtle developmental process can have a profound effect on the structure, physiology, and evolution of any animal (Gould, 1983). In many senses cleft palate may be as much an atavism as a developmental malformation.

ACKNOWLEDGMENTS

These experiments were principally conducted in the Laboratory for Developmental Biology, University of Southern California, whose director, Professor H. C. Slavkin, we warmly thank for his generous hospitality, encouragement, criticism, and discussion.

We thank Mr. Ted Joanen, Mr. Larry McNease, and staff of the Rockefeller Wildlife Refuge, Louisiana, for their outstanding help in the collection and transportation of alligator eggs. Collection and specimen export were performed under United States Federal Fish and Wildlife Permit PRT2-2511 and Northern Ireland Permit B/WL2/80 issued to M.W.J.F. Mr. Pablo Bringas provided valuable technical assistance, for which we are grateful. Collaborative study was made possible by the award of a 1981 Research Travelling Scholarship from The Wellcome Trust to M.W.J.F. This work is supported by Grant 8113610CB from the Medical Research Council of Great Britain, Grant EP109.74–75 from the Northern Ireland Eastern Health and Social Services Board, and NIH Grants DE-02848 and DE-03569. Miss A. Richardson kindly typed the manuscript.

REFERENCES

Bernfield, M. R., and Banerjee, S. D. (1978). In "Biology and Chemistry of Basement Membranes" (N. A. Kefalides, ed.), pp. 137–152. Academic Press, New York.
Brinkley, L. L. (1980). In "Current Research Trends in Prenatal Craniofacial Development" (R. M. Pratt and R. L. Christiansen, eds.), pp. 203–220. Elsevier, Amsterdam.
Brownell, A. G., and Slavkin, H. C. (1980). In "Renal Physiology" (G. M. Berlyne and S. Thomas, eds.), pp. 193–204. Karger, Basel.
Chippindale, A. J., and Johnson, D. R. (1979). Experientia 35, 1101–1102.
Cummings, E. G., Bringas, P., Grodin, M. S., and Slavkin, H. C. (1981). Differentiation 20, 1–9.

Cunha, G. R., and Lung, B. (1978). *J. Exp. Zool.* **205,** 181–194.

Cunha, G. R., and Lung, B. (1979). *In Vitro* **15,** 50–71.

Cunha, G. R., and Lung, B. (1980). *In* "Male Accessory Sex Glands" (E. Spring-Mills and E. S. E. Hafez, eds.), pp. 39–59. Elsevier, Amsterdam.

Cutler, L. S., and Chaudhry, A. P. (1973). *Dev. Biol.* **33,** 229–240.

DeAngelis, V., and Nallandian, J. (1968). *Arch. Oral Biol.* **13,** 601–608.

Dhouailly, D. (1975). *Wilhelm Roux's Arch.* **177,** 323–340.

Dhouailly, D. (1977). *Front Matrix Biol.* **4,** 86–121.

Dhouailly, D., Rogers, G. E., and Sengel, P. (1978). *Dev. Biol.* **65,** 58–69.

Diewert, V. M. (1980). *In* "Current Research Trends in Prenatal Craniofacial Development" (R. M. Pratt and R. L. Christiansen, eds.), pp. 165–186. Elsevier, Amsterdam.

Ekblom, P., Thesleff, I., Miettinen, A., and Saxen, L. (1981). *Cell Differ.* **10,** 281–288.

Farbman, A. I. (1968). *Dev. Biol.* **18,** 93–116.

Farbman, A. I. (1969). *J. Dent. Res.* **48,** 617–624.

Ferguson, M. W. J. (1977). *Virchows Arch. Abt. A Pathol. Anat. Histol.* **375,** 97–113.

Ferguson, M. W. J. (1978a). *J. Anat.* **125,** 555–577.

Ferguson, M. W. J. (1978b). *J. Anat.* **126,** 37–49.

Ferguson, M. W. J. (1981a). *Arch. Oral Biol.* **26,** 427–443.

Ferguson, M. W. J. (1981b). *J. Craniofac. Genet. Dev. Biol.* **1,** 123–144.

Ferguson, M. W. J. (1982). "The Structure and Development of the Palate in *Alligator mississippiensis.*" Ph.D. thesis, The Queen's University of Belfast.

Ferguson, M. W. J. (1984a). *In* "Biology of the Reptilia" (C. Gans, F. S. Billett, and P. Maderson, eds.), Vol. 14. Wiley, New York.

Ferguson, M. W. J. (1984b). *In* "The Structure, Development and Evolution of Reptiles" (M. W. J. Ferguson, ed.), pp. 223–273. Academic Press, New York.

Ferguson, M. W. J., and Honig, L. S. (1984). In preparation.

Ferguson, M. W. J., Honig, L. S., Bringas, P., and Slavkin, H. C. (1982). *In* "Factors and Mechanisms Influencing Bone Growth" (A. D. Dixon and B. G. Sarnat, eds.), pp. 275–286. Liss, New York.

Ferguson, M. W. J., Honig, L. S., Bringas, P., and Slavkin, H. C. (1983). *In Vitro* **19,** 385–393.

Ferguson, M. W. J., Honig, L. S., and Slavkin, H. C. (1984). *Anat. Rec.* **209,** 1–19.

Golosow, N., and Grobstein, C. (1962). *Dev. Biol.* **4,** 242–255.

Gordon, J. R., and Bernfield, M. R. (1980). *Dev. Biol.* **74,** 118–135.

Gould, S. J. (1983). "Hen's Teeth and Horse's Toes," pp. 177–186. Norton, New York.

Greene, R. M., Shah, R. M., Lloyd, M. R., Crawford, B. J., Suen, R., Shanfeld, J. L., and Davidovitch, Z. (1983). *J. Exp. Zool.* **225,** 43–52.

Hamburger, V., and Hamilton, H. L. (1951). *J. Morphol.* **88,** 49–92.

Hay, E. D. (1977). *In* "International Cell Biology 1976–1977" (B. R. Brinkley and K. R. Porter, eds.), pp. 50–57. Rockefeller Univ. Press, New York.

Hudson, C. D., and Shapiro, B. L. (1973). *Arch. Oral Biol.* **18,** 77–84.

Koch, W. E., and Smiley, G. R. (1981). *Arch. Oral Biol.* **26,** 181–187.

Kollar, E. J. (1982). *In* "Teeth: Form, Function and Evolution" (B. Kurten, ed.), pp. 21–31. Columbia Univ. Press, New York.

Kollar, E. J., and Fischer, C. (1980). *Science* **207,** 993–995.

Kratochwil, K. (1983). *In* "Cell Interactions and Development" (K. M. Yamada, ed.), pp. 99–122. Wiley, New York.

Lesot, H., Osman, M., and Ruch, J. V. (1981). *Dev. Biol.* **82,** 371–381.

Mathan, M., Hermos, J. A., and Trier, J. S. (1972). *J. Cell Biol.* **52,** 577–588.

McAleese, S. R., and Sawyer, R. H. (1981). *Science* **214,** 1033–1034.

Meinhardt, M. (1982). "Models of Biological Pattern Formation." Academic Press, New York.

Pourtois, M. (1972). *In* "Developmental Aspects of Oral Biology" (H. C. Slavkin and L. A. Bavetta, eds.), pp. 81–108. Academic Press, New York.

Pratt, R. M., and Martin, G. R. (1975). *Proc. Natl. Acad. Sci. U.S.A.* **72**, 874–877.

Propper, A. (1969). *C. R. Hebd. Seances Acad. Sci. Paris Ser. D.* **268**, 1423–1426.

Propper, A., and Gomot, L. (1973). *Experientia* **29**, 1543–1544.

Sakakura, T., Nishizuka, Y., and Dawe, C. J. (1976). *Science* **194**, 1439–1441.

Saxen, L., Ekblom, P., and Thesleff, I. (1980). *In* "Development in Mammals" (M. H. Johnson, ed.), Vol. 4, pp. 161–202. Elsevier, Amsterdam.

Sengel, P. (1975). *Ciba Found. Symp.* **29**, 51–70.

Sengel, P. (1976). *In* "Organ Culture in Biomedical Research" (M. Balls and M. A. Monnickendam, eds.), pp. 111–147. Cambridge Univ. Press, London and New York.

Sengel, P., and Dhouailly, D. (1977). *In* "Cell Interactions in Differentiation" (M. Karkinen-Jääskeläinen, L. Saxen, and L. Weiss, eds.), pp. 153–169. Academic Press, New York.

Shah, R. M., and Crawford, B. J. (1980). *Invest. Cell Pathol.* **3**, 319–328.

Shapiro, B. L., and Sweeney, L. (1969). *J. Dent. Res.* **48**, 652–660.

Slavkin, H. C. (1979). *J. Biol. Buccale* **6**, 189–203.

Slavkin, H. C. (1982). *J. Craniofac. Genet. Dev. Biol.* **2**, 179–189.

Slavkin, H. C., and Bringas, P. (1976). *Dev. Biol.* **50**, 428–442.

Slavkin, H. C., Trump, G. N., Brownell, A., and Sorgente, N. (1977). *In* "Cell and Tissue Interactions" (J. W. Lash and M. M. Burger, eds.). Raven, New York.

Smiley, G. R., and Dixon, A. D. (1968). *Anat. Rec.* **161**, 293–310.

Smiley, G. R., and Koch, W. E. (1971). *J. Dent. Res.* **50**, 1671–1677.

Smiley, G. R., and Koch, W. E. (1972). *Anat. Rec.* **173**, 405–416.

Theiler, K. (1972). "The House Mouse. Development and Normal Stages from Fertilization to 4 Weeks of Age." Springer-Verlag, Berlin and New York.

Thesleff, I. (1979). *J. Biol. Buccale* **6**, 241–249.

Thesleff, I. and Hurmerinta, K. (1981). *Differentiation* **18**, 75–88.

Thesleff, I., Stenman, S., Vaheri, A., and Timpl, R. (1979). *Dev. Biol.* **70**, 116–126.

Thesleff, I., Barrach, H. J., Foidart, J. M., Vaheri, A., Pratt, R. M., and Martin, G. R. (1981). *Dev. Biol.* **81**, 182–192.

Tyler, M. S., and Koch, W. E. (1977a). *J. Embryol. Exp. Morphol.* **38**, 19–36.

Tyler, M. S., and Koch, W. E. (1977b). *J. Embryol. Exp. Morphol.* **38**, 37–48.

Tyler, M. S., and Pratt, R. M. (1980). *J. Embryol. Exp. Morphol.* **58**, 93–106.

Wessells, N. K. (1977). "Tissue Interactions and Development." Benjamin/Cummings, London.

Yoneda, T., and Pratt, R. M. (1981). *Science* **213**, 563–565.

CHAPTER 8

GENETICS OF PALATE DEVELOPMENT*

Michel J. J. Vekemans

MCGILL UNIVERSITY-MONTREAL CHILDREN'S HOSPITAL RESEARCH INSTITUTE
CENTRE FOR HUMAN GENETICS
AND DEPARTMENTS OF PATHOLOGY, PEDIATRICS, AND BIOLOGY
MCGILL UNIVERSITY
MONTREAL, QUEBEC, CANADA

and

Fred G. Biddle

DEPARTMENTS OF PEDIATRICS AND MEDICAL BIOCHEMISTRY
ALBERTA CHILDREN'S HOSPITAL RESEARCH CENTRE
UNIVERSITY OF CALGARY
CALGARY, ALBERTA, CANADA

*This chapter is dedicated with appreciation to Dr. F. Clarke Fraser.

165

I. Introduction

The prerequisite for the genetic analysis of any biological process is a heritable difference or heritable variation in the process. If palate development is a normal biological process, how can the genetic mechanisms that regulate it be identified and studied? In this chapter, a framework for the genetic study of normal palate development is discussed.

The laboratory mouse provides a mammalian system for which the embryonic pathway of palate development has been examined and a maternal–embryonic system is available to study interaction between mother and conceptus. More importantly, the mouse provides a rich and growing library of genetically defined strains and mutant stocks that continues to be characterized.

In the study of cleft palate teratogenesis, it is usual to consider the process of cleft palate induction and the mechanisms by which the teratogens act. Therefore, genetic studies of differences in response to teratogens tend to be framed in terms of the cleft palate reaction and what the teratogens do. In this chapter, we attempt to shift the emphasis to the normal process of palate development. We would like to return to the framework embodied in the concepts of *developmental homeostasis* and *canalization* (Waddington, 1942) and suggest how the apparent genetic architecture of palate development may already provide evidence for this concept. We deal only with the glucocorticoid cortisone acetate, since most of the genetic studies of the cleft palate reaction have been done with it.

In a single species and in the absence of major genes or teratogens that disrupt the normal developmental process, palate development is normal. We can envisage different control mechanisms that are specified by the genetic information in the species and that direct this process on a pathway that is normal. By starting with the normal process, we can then ask the questions: What are the genetic components of the mechanisms that maintain development within the boundaries that we call normal? What do mutations (point mutations and genomic mutations) and teratogens do to this normal development? We can interpret mutations and teratogens as probes of the normal developmental process.

This chapter will not be a review of the teratological genetics of palate development in mice. Instead, we attempt to put our studies into a genetic framework to ask whether the framework is leading to answers. Is the framework adequate, and if it is not, why not?

II. Historical Perspectives of the Mouse Model for Palate Development

A. STRAIN DIFFERENCES IN CORTISONE-INDUCED CLEFT PALATE ("SINGLE-DOSE" STUDIES)

Treatment of pregnant mice with cortisone acetate caused cleft palate in the embryos (Baxter and Fraser, 1950). When several genetically different strains were examined with the same dosage regime of cortisone, large differences in the frequency of induced cleft palate were found (Fraser and Fainstat, 1951). To the geneticist, stable differences between strains in the frequency of induced cleft palate present a model system for genetic analysis: What is the cause of the *differences* in frequency of the cleft palate response?

The first analysis of the genetic cause of the strain differences in frequency of cortisone-induced cleft palate used the A/J and C57BL/6J strain pair (Kalter, 1954). This study and several others will be summarized briefly, but first an important concept must be emphasized. When a genetic analysis is made of the difference between a strain pair in a quantitative trait, such as cortisone-induced cleft palate, any inferences about the genetic control of the trait are valid only for the specific strain pair. No extrapolation and generalization of the differences between the original two strains to other strains can be made until the appropriate crosses between them have been made.

The A/J strain is more sensitive than C57BL/6J, that is, a higher frequency of cleft palate is induced in A/J than in C57BL/6J embryos with the same treatment. Reciprocal crosses demonstrated a significant maternal effect in the strain pair; F_1 embryos in A/J mothers expressed a higher frequency of cleft palate than the F_1 embryos in C57BL/6J mothers. Further matings of reciprocal F_1 females to A/J males to recover embryonic genes for sensitivity to induced cleft palate demonstrated that cytoplasmic factors were not involved in the maternal effect trait. Subsequent studies demonstrated that X chromosome-linked factors were not responsible for the maternal effect with this strain pair (Biddle and Fraser, 1977a). Therefore, two genetic traits were identified: a *maternal effect trait* in which A/J mothers, relative to C57BL/6J mothers, caused a higher frequency of induced cleft palate in the embryos; and an *embryonic response trait* in which A/J embryos were more sensitive than C57BL/6J embryos. The concepts of maternal and cytoplasmic effect traits in teratology have been reviewed (Biddle and Fraser, 1977b) and will not be discussed here.

A mating study with the A/J and C57BL/6J strains demonstrated that the resistance of C57BL/6J embryos relative to A/J embryos was dominant. Sensitivity of A/J embryos was a recessive character and, in order to recover genes for sensitivity, backcross matings were made to the A/J strain, but there was no evidence for the segregation of a single genetic factor (Kalter, 1954). This first study may have been complicated by the fact that segregation of the cleft palate sensitivity trait was followed through females that were crossed and backcrossed to A/J males. Both the maternal effect trait and the embryonic response trait would be segregating and both traits are measured by the frequency of induced cleft palate in the fetuses.

A search was made for other strain differences in frequency of cortisone-induced cleft palate. Cortisone was administered as a milligrams per mouse dosage on days 11 through 14 of gestation. In one series at 1.25 mg/mouse/day, the following order of sensitivity was found: A/St > BALB/c > C3H (Loevy, 1963). In another series at 2.5 mg/mouse/day, the following order of sensitivity was found: A/J > DBA/1 > C3H > C57BL/6J > CBA (Kalter, 1965).

A minor controversy arose when the A strains (either A/J or A/St) were mated reciprocally with C3H and tested with cortisone (Loevy, 1963, 1968; Kalter, 1965). A maternal effect was found with the A strains and C3H, but the direction of the effect was opposite to that found with the A/J and C57BL/6J strain pair. It was assumed that the strain order of the maternal effect should follow the strain order of sensitivity to cortisone-induced cleft palate. The discrepancy could be due to X chromosome-linked factors that determine embryonic sensitivity, since they have been found with some strain pairs (Francis, 1973), or to the fact that the maternal effect trait and the embryonic response trait are genetically independent systems. This remains to be resolved. We will return to a discussion of these historical data (Section VI,A,2) because some important information appears to have been completely overlooked.

B. Strain Differences in Normal Palate Development

The ability to induce cleft palate with cortisone in all embryos of the A/J mouse provided the embryologist with the first useful model for the study of the clefting process (Walker and Fraser, 1957). The morphogenetic events of normal palate development (without teratogen) were documented first in three different strains of mice (A/J, DBA/1, and C57BL/Fr) (Walker and Fraser, 1956). A qualitative score was assigned to the stages of palate closure and litters were examined at different chronological times during closure. The matrix of numbers of embryos in the different qualitative stages against gestational age suggested that the palate closed early in C57BL, late in A/J, and at an intermediate time in DBA/1. Therefore, there are genetic differences in the normal embryology of the process. When cortisone was administered to two of the strains, A/J and C57BL, and the embryology of the palate closure was followed, there appeared to be a delay in both strains.

III. Palate Development: A Homeostatic Process

A. A MODEL OF PALATE DEVELOPMENT

In the mouse, the secondary palate appears initially as two antero-posterior ridges of tissue on the medial surface of the maxillary process, forming the shelves that first grow vertically, passing downward and lateral to the tongue. During closure, the shelves reorient themselves to a horizontal plane above the dorsum of the tongue to fuse with each other and with the nasal septum, forming a single continuous structure, the secondary palate (see reviews by Burdi *et al.,* 1972; Greene and Pratt, 1976; Trasler and Fraser, 1977).

Single major genes have been very informative in identifying the basic processes involved in the formation of the secondary palate. For example, it is clear that the reorientation of the shelves involves a force intrinsic to the shelves since in the phocomelic mouse mutant (*pc*) the shelves are unable to move in time because of reduced shelf force, and a cleft palate results (Fitch, 1957). Opposing this shelf force is the growing tongue, which impedes the movement of the shelves to the horizontal. Thus, in the chondrodysplastic mouse mutant (*cho*), shelf movement is delayed and morphological observations at the time of palate closure suggest that the delay is caused by increased tongue resistance, which is due to reduced growth of Meckel's cartilage and of forward movement of the lower jaw (Seegmiller and Fraser, 1977). The probability of an embryo having cleft palate also depends on shelf width and head width. For example, in the urogenital mouse mutant (*ur*), the shelves reach the horizontal normally, but a cleft palate occurs because the shelves are too narrow to reach each other (Fitch, 1957). Similarly, a large head width, as found in the patch mouse mutant (*Ph*), requires the shelves to become horizontal relatively early in order to close successfully (Gruneberg and Truslove, 1960).

A simplistic representation of these ontogenetic events is illustrated in Fig. 1. The frequency distribution on the left represents the stage at which the shelves achieve the horizontal. This occurs relatively early in some embryos and late in others. The frequency distribution on the right represents the threshold. It is the last stage at

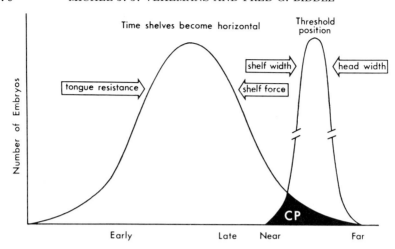

FIG. 1. A representation of part of the homeostatic or multifactorial model for palate development. (Modified from Fraser, 1976; see text for details.)

which the shelves can reach the horizontal and still fuse. Reorientation of the shelves later than this results in cleft palate. The diagram illustrates the position of the distribution (relative to the threshold) as being determined primarily by the interaction of the shelf force and the resistance of the tongue. The stronger the shelf force, the earlier the shelves will move. The stronger the resistance of the tongue, the later the shelves will move. The position of the threshold is determined by the interaction of shelf width and head width; in some embryos the threshold is reached early and in some others relatively later. All vectors (shelf force, tongue resistance, shelf and head width) of the model are presumably influenced by several genetic and environmental factors. Thus, there are several mechanisms involved in palate closure and only a discrete proportion of them will eventually lead to cleft palate. This is an example of a multifactorial threshold model in which at least one component of liability to cleft palate (stage of palate closure) can be measured and the nature of the developmental threshold is clearly defined (Fraser, 1976).

B. Quantitation of Palate Development

The model can be analyzed quantitatively and compared between different genotypes. If embryos are examined in litters that are collected at different times during palate closure, the embryos can be assigned to one or another of the different stages (Walker and Fraser, 1956). The cumulative frequencies of embryos at different stages at each time can be fitted to a normal distribution so that closure can be defined in terms of the rate of closure and the median time for closure. Differences between strains and embryos have been found so far only in the time at which palate closure occurs (Vekemans and Fraser, 1979; Biddle, 1980). In addition, cortisone treatment appears to cause a delay in the time of the closure process (Vekemans and Fraser, 1979). These results were predicted by the threshold model (Fraser, 1977). A question that remains is whether the genetic differences in the cleft palate reaction to cortisone simply reflect the genetic differences in the underlying homeostatic model for palate development.

C. Quantitation of the Cleft Palate Norm of Reaction

If there are genetic differences in the cleft palate reaction of the mouse to cortisone, we need to consider the concept of the *norm of reaction* and *dose–effect models*. The norm of reaction is an underlying principle in teratology and teratological genetics (Biddle, 1979, 1981). It is the standard mode of reaction to treatment that an individual inherits. In genetics, it is the correspondence or relationship between phenotype and different genotype–environment combinations.

The importance of the norm of reaction in teratology is illustrated in Fig. 2 by comparing two sets of hypothetical dose–effect curves for

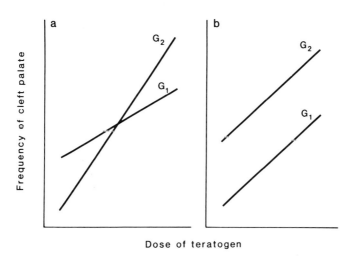

Fig. 2. Two sets of hypothetical dose–effect curves for cortisone-induced cleft palate for two different strains or genotypes (G_1 and G_2). (a) The dose–effect lines intersect and demonstrate interaction between genotype and teratogen. (b) The dose–effect lines are parallel and demonstrate an additive relationship between genotype and teratogen. (From Biddle, 1979.)

cleft palate induced by a teratogen in two different strains or genotypes, G_1 and G_2. For the cleft palate reaction, the phenotype is not
the fact that an individual has expressed cleft palate in response to the
teratogen, rather it is the frequency of cleft palate at a specific dose.
(The dose–effect relationships in Fig. 2 are drawn linearly for the
purpose of discussion.) In Fig. 2a, the dose–effect lines for the two
genotypes are different and in this illustration they intersect. Therefore, depending on dosage, the two strains could express the same or
very different frequencies of cleft palate. In addition, the ranked order
of cleft palate sensitivity of the two strains would change with dosage.
In a genetical sense there is *interaction* between genotype and dosage
of teratogen in the expression of cleft palate. In Fig. 2b, the dose–effect
lines are parallel. The difference between the two strains, measured by
the cleft palate response, is the same for all dosages and the difference
between dosages is the same for all frequencies of cleft palate. In this
case an *additive* relationship is found between genotype and dosage of
teratogen.

In both hypothetical examples (Fig. 2a and b), the cause of the
difference in the cleft palate response between the two genotypes is the
subject for genetic study. Is the difference between genotypes in their
norms of reaction due to one gene with major effect or to more than one
gene? What do these genes do? The approach that is taken for the
genetic study is dependent on the dose–effect behaviors of the different
genotypes.

In order to use the concept of the norm of reaction in a practical
sense, dose–effect models for actual data must be considered. One of
these models is the probit dose–response model (Bliss, 1935a,b; Finney, 1971) which has been used to advantage in the genetic analysis of
the cortisone-induced cleft palate reaction (Biddle and Fraser, 1976;
Vekemans, 1982). One assumption of the model is that the underlying
teratogenic trait is dosage tolerance rather than the binomial one of
cleft palate (presence versus absence of cleft palate) and tolerance is
normally distributed on a log scale. Another assumption is that the
embryo is the responding unit to the teratogenic treatment, that is,
each embryo has an independent chance of responding with cleft palate
to the treatment.

The principle of the probit model is illustrated in Figs. 3 and 4. If
cleft palate is a typical biological response, a population of a single
genotype of mouse embryos (e.g., one strain of mice) will be that found
in Fig. 3a. At the median dose for the reaction (10 units in the example), half the population has responded, but half has not. In addition,
the distribution, plotted on a linear scale, is skewed to the right. A log

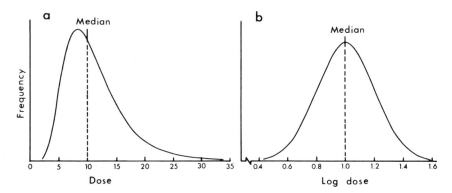

Fig. 3. A hypothetical distribution of the tolerance to cortisone-induced cleft palate in mouse embryos. (a) Frequency is plotted against linear dose. (b) Frequency is plotted against the logarithm of dose. (From Biddle, 1979.)

transformation of the dosage scale (Fig. 3b) may change the distribution of responding embryos to a normal distribution that is symmetrical about the median dosage for the reaction. If the frequencies of embryos that have responded by a specific dosage are accumulated across the dosage scale, a normal sigmoid response curve is obtained (Fig. 4a). The inflection point will coincide with the dosage at which 50% of the embryos have reacted. Instead of plotting the cumulative frequencies of affected embryos on a linear percent scale, the frequency can be plotted on a scale that is linear in probits (Fig. 4b), and the normal sigmoid response curve is transformed to a straight line.

A linear transformation of the frequency of response to different dosages provides a simple model to fit by standard regression analysis. Groups of embryos can be treated with single doses of teratogen above and below the median dose. If the frequency of responders (on a probit scale) can be fitted to linear regression on dosage (on a log scale), the mean dose for the response (median effective dose or ED_{50}) can be estimated. If this can be done, then the cleft palate response can be interpreted in terms of a tolerance model. The slope of the probit dose–effect relationship is a measure of the variance of the tolerance distribution. The probit dose–effect model represents nothing more and nothing less than a method of analysis. With the method, the effect of specific teratogens can be compared in different genotypes.

We can return to the concept of the norm of reaction, discussed in relation to Fig. 2, to ask whether the genetic differences between genotypes are differences in mean dosage tolerance (differences in ED_{50}), differences in slope of the dose–response relationship (suggesting an

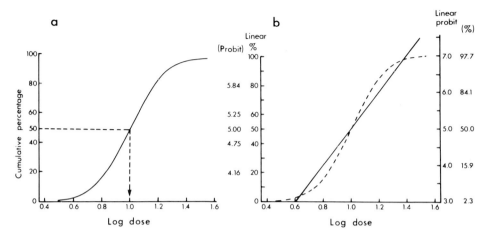

FIG. 4. (a) The cumulative frequency of embryos that have responded with cleft palate (from Fig. 3b) is plotted against log dose. The arrow indicates the median effective dose, the dose below which half the population has responded and above which half the population has not responded. (b) The cumulative frequency is transformed to a scale that is linear in probits. (From Biddle, 1979.)

interaction or differences in the underlying mechanism of response), or differences in both.

IV. Genetic Tools to Investigate the Homeostatic Process

There are a number of "genetic tools" that can be used in teratological genetics. A brief description of the tools is essential because they have a precise definition and, when they are brought into use in a genetic method, they are used as tools, not just as a group of mice. Extensive lists and characteristics of these tools can be found in a series of publications (e.g., Altman and Katz, 1979; Green, 1981; Heiniger and Dorey, 1981; Morse, 1978; Staats, 1980).

An inbred strain of mice is a single genotype. It is produced usually by strict sister–brother mating that starts with a single pair of mice, and one pair usually gives rise to the next generation of breeders. Through this inbreeding, genetic differences between the original pair are eliminated by chance, and the between-locus combination of genes that are compatible in the homozygous condition survive. By 20 generations of sister–brother inbreeding, the probability of heterozygosity at any one genetic locus is approximately 1.2% and the probability that any mating will be between two homozygotes is 98%. Most of the inbred strains in common usage today were started in the 1910s and 1920s, 200 or more generations have elapsed, and the probability of homozygosity is almost complete. Many new strains continue to be produced from crosses between different existing inbred strains and from wild-derived mice.

Congenic strains are inbred strains but they differ from an established strain in a selected genetic characteristic. Usually one mouse with a characteristic that is different from the inbred strain is crossed to the inbred strain and, in a series of backcrosses to the inbred partner, the characteristic of the other mouse is selected. Other genetic differences between this mouse and the established inbred strain are eliminated by the repeated backcrosses. For example, if a mouse with a genetic characteristic that is controlled by a single Mendelian factor (b/b) differs from the inbred strain (a/a), the F_1 generation will be heterozygous (a/b) for this characteristic as well as for any other differences between the starting mouse and the inbred strain. Continued backcrossing to the inbred strain will produce a/a homozygotes and a/b heterozygotes. The a/b heterozygotes are selected at each generation for breeding to the inbred strain. After eight generations, the probability of heterozygosity at other loci which are not closely linked to the genetic characteristic of interest (greater than 50% recombination units on the same chromosome) will be less than 1%. Hence, after 8–10 generations of backcrossing, the characteristic of interest (b/b) is selected from sister–brother inbreeding. The resulting congenic strain is illustrated in Fig. 5, but the important information in this figure is that the genetic material closely linked to the b allele comes from the original donor mouse.

An important concept with congenic lines is that the size of the

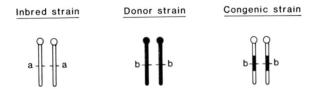

FIG. 5. The relationship between an inbred strain and its congenic partner is illustrated with a single pair of chromosomes. Allele b at a hypothetical genetic locus is transferred from a donor mouse by backcrossing to the inbred strain that has allele a. Allele b from the donor mouse is substituted for allele a in the chromosome of the inbred strain by crossing-over in a/b heterozygotes. The congenic strain differs from the inbred strain not only by the b allele but also by an indeterminant segment of chromosome from the donor strain (black in the figure).

differential segment of chromosome, which includes the specific locus of interest, can only be determined with other marker genes. For example, the *H-2* locus, for which several congenic strains have been used to investigate palate development, is approximately in the middle of chromosome 17 by translocation mapping but about one quarter of the distance from the centromere to the telomere by conventional recombination mapping. The size of the differential segment of chromosome 17 in some strains congenic for *H-2* has been estimated to be approximately 3–10 cM (centimorgans) but in others it appears to be the entire telomeric end of chromosome 17 that is distal to the *H-2* locus (Klein *et al.*, 1982).

Recombinant inbred (RI) strains are produced by crossing two existing inbred strains, raising the F_2 generation, and deriving a series of separate, independent inbred lines from F_2 pairs by full sister–brother matings (Bailey, 1971). The independent inbred lines are derived without selection. The inbreeding program is shown in Fig. 6; three independent Mendelian genetic characteristics (A, B, and C) that differ

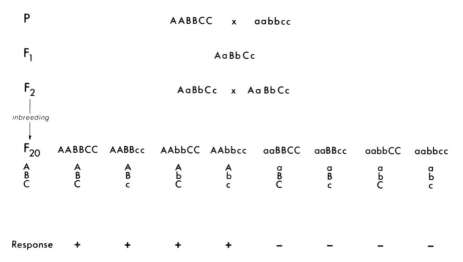

FIG. 6. The construction and use of recombinant inbred (RI) strains are illustrated with three independent Mendelian traits (A, B, and C). The two parental strains (P) have alternate alleles at the three loci. The three traits segregate and independently assort during the inbreeding process. If a teratogenic response differs between the parental strains (+ and −), the full set of RI strains can also be typed for the response. Segregation of the response trait in the RI strains can be used to estimate its genetic control, and association with the Mendelian traits can be tested. In the example, the response trait is associated with marker trait A. The value of RI strains is that this information is cumulative and can be used as a library.

between the two progenitor strains are used to illustrate the outcome of deriving this set of RI strains. The three characteristics that differed between the starting parental strains have recombined randomly and have been fixed in the homozygous condition in the finished set of RI strains.

Sublines of inbred strains are those that have been separated from the main inbreeding line of the strain for 20 or more generations, but they are still maintained by strict inbreeding. Twenty generations is taken as an arbitrary number. A chance mutation may have occurred and may be fixed in the subline, but unless the mutation results in an obvious visible effect, such as on the coat color or the skeletal system, it will not be seen. For example, a C57BL/6 mouse is genetically differ-ent from a C57BL/10 mouse [see matrix of allelic variants in the com-mon inbred strains in Heiniger and Dorey (1981)]. There is too little attention paid to the details of strain nomenclature in much of the teratology literature. A large difference in teratogenic reaction be-tween sublines of an inbred strain would suggest that one or a very few genetic factors control the difference in the reaction.

With a specific teratogen-induced malformation such as cleft pal-ate, other genetic tools could be considered [review in Table III of Juriloff (1980)]. There are strains with specific frequencies of spon-taneous cleft palate, single mutant gene-determined malformations or metabolic defects that have cleft palate associated with the syndrome of phenotypic effects, and chromosomal rearrangements with an asso-ciated cleft palate. The genetic basis for the liability to cleft palate in these other genetic resources has not been studied nor has any attempt been made to determine if there is a relationship between this liability and teratogen-induced cleft palate.

V. Methods of Genetic Analysis

The purpose of genetics is to describe the genetic architecture of a trait in terms of both the number of genes and the action of these genes. In our case of palate development and cortisone-induced cleft palate, do the genetic factors that control either the differences in development or the differences in the teratogenic reaction operate in the mother or the embryo or both? How many heritable factors are there? (Can they be counted, in the sense of number, in a segregation analysis?) If there are defined, separate genetic loci, how do the allelic differences at these loci act? (Is there additivity or a dominant–re-cessive relationship?) If there are several loci controlling the traits, what is the relationship among these loci? (Do the genes at the different loci act independently or is there some dependence or epistatic interaction between loci?)

With the tools that were outlined in Section IV, there are three basic "methods" of analysis from which genetic inferences can be drawn. The *strain distribution pattern* (SDP) requires that a large number of different strains (inbred strains, RI strains, congenic strains) be examined for both the cleft palate response to a specific teratogen and palate development. Can the strains be grouped into two or a few mutually exclusive categories or do they form a continuum with no two individuals being identical? A small number of mutually exclusive classes would suggest that there are relatively few major genetic factors controlling the traits. An association between the SDP for a teratogenic trait and the SDP of marker genes would lead directly to linkage studies and *gene mapping*.

When two different strains are mated (crossed with each other), it is the net genetic difference between the two individuals that is being examined. No attempt should be made to transfer this information universally to the species. Reciprocal crosses between the two strains will determine the action of this net difference and whether the action is maternal or embryonic. Gene counting is done by continued matings to look for *segregation*. This can involve either a standard breeding design of backcrossing with test matings, which has been extensively discussed elsewhere (Biddle and Fraser, 1977a; Biddle, 1979), or examination of a set of recombinant inbred (RI) strains that have been derived from a single pair of strains (Vekemans *et al.,* 1981). In both cases, the two parental classes are allowed to segregate. What is observed in the progeny, the same two classes or more than two classes? In the case of the RI strains, we can return to Fig. 6. If the two parental strains were defined with two different responses (+ versus −) and the RI strains could be classed as only these two types, this genetic evidence would suggest a single factor controls the difference in the trait between the two parental strains.

Congenic strains can be considered in the same way. Different "allelic" substitutions or regions of a specific chromosome are placed on a common genetic background. Is there a major change in palate development or in reaction to cortisone that is associated with the substitutions? The major limitation of the congenic strains is that they are restricted to substitutions on a single chromosome. They can, however, be used effectively in conjunction with segregation analysis.

The final major method is the *diallel analysis,* which is the set of crosses among *several* inbred strains. Comparisons are made between the inbred strains and their reciprocal F_1 hybrids; the major methods of diallel analysis with different genetic models are outlined elsewhere (Mather and Jinks, 1971). Little attention has been paid to this method in teratological genetics except by Francis (1971, 1973), but it has the advantage of defining relative degrees of maternal and embryonic effects across a number of different genotypes and, depending on whether generations beyond the F_1 are examined, interaction can be identified between genetic systems within the embryo or between embryonic and maternal systems.

VI. Results of Genetic Analysis

Using the tools for genetic analysis in the mouse and the methods for this analysis, what information has been obtained to date from genetic structure–function (number and gene action) studies of the mouse model for palate development?

A. CORTISONE-INDUCED CLEFT PALATE

1. Number of Genes

The cleft palate dose–response behaviors to cortisone of a number of different mouse strains (Table I) appear to have the same slope. Therefore, there is an additive relationship between genotype and teratogen in the expression of the cleft palate reaction (cf. Fig. 2b) and the genetic difference between the strains is in the median effective dose (ED_{50}) for cortisone. Since all strains of the mouse that have been tested to date with cortisone do react with cleft palate and they appear to do so with the same dose–response behavior, the genetic system or trait that is revealed is dosage tolerance.

TABLE I

STRAIN DISTRIBUTION PATTERN OF THE MEDIAN EFFECTIVE
DOSE FOR CORTISONE-INDUCED CLEFT PALATE

Strain	ED_{50} (mg/kg)	Reference
SW/Fr	50	Vekemans and Fraser (1978)
T1Wh	75	Vekemans et al. (1979)
A/J	115	Biddle and Fraser (1976)
SWV	122	Biddle and Fraser (1976)
DBA/2J	136	Vekemans (1982)
CL/Fr	180	Vekemans and Fraser (1978)
B10.BR	300	Vekemans et al. (1979)
C57BL/6J	687	Biddle and Fraser (1976)

The strain distribution pattern (SDP) of reactivities to cortisone (Table I) does not suggest any estimate of the number of genetic factors that controls the tolerance to cortisone. The log ED_{50} values (Table I) form a continuous unimodal distribution when analyzed by the method of ranked normal deviates or rankits (Sokal and Rohlf, 1969); there is no clustering that might suggest a few genetic factors regulate the trait. Any genetic inference from the SDP is premature because the number of strains so far tested is an insignificant sampling of the species. A continuous distribution of reactivities could be due to many separate genetic loci as well as to one locus or a few loci with multiple alleles at each locus.

Reciprocal crosses between strains have revealed maternal genetic effects as well as embryonic genetic effects on cortisone reactivity. The maternal effects that increase and decrease embryonic tolerance do not always follow the rank-order distribution of sensitivity of the parental inbred strains (see Table II). For example, the A strains are known to be more reactive than C3H (Section II,A), but the maternal effect of C3H to increase sensitivity to cortisone is greater relative to the maternal effect of the A strains. This fact argues that the genetic factors operating in the maternal system can be independent of those in the embryo. In some strain pairs there is an association between cortisone

TABLE II

SUMMARY OF MATERNAL AND EMBRYONIC GENETIC EFFECTS
ON CORTISONE-INDUCED CLEFT PALATE

Strain pair	Maternal effect to decrease tolerance and direction	Embryonic effect to increase tolerance and direction	Reference
Extensively studied			
A/J–C57BL/6J	A > B6	Overdominance → B6	Biddle and Fraser (1976)
DBA/2J–C57BL/6J	D2 > B6	Dominance → B6	Vekemans (1982)
Historical studies			
A/St–C3H	C3H > A	Dominance → C3H	Loevy (1963, 1968)
A/St–BALB/c	BALB > A	Dominance → BALB	Loevy (1963, 1968)
A/J–C3H	C3H > A	Dominance → C3H	Kalter (1965)
A/J–CBA	A > CBA	Dominance → CBA	Kalter (1965)
C3H–CBA	C3H > CBA	Additive	Kalter (1965)
Other			
B10.A–C57BL/10J	B10.A > B10	Additive	Vekemans and Fraser (1982)

reactivity and the major histocompatibility (*H-2*) locus on chromosome 17 (Bonner and Slavkin, 1975; Biddle and Fraser, 1977a). Further dissection of the *H-2* association with a series of congenic strains suggests that some "alleles" in the *H-2* region regulate both the maternal and embryonic effects while other "alleles" regulate only the embryonic response (Bonner and Tyan, 1983). No attempt has been made yet to estimate either the number or action of the genetic factors in the maternal system. There may be maternal genetic factors on other chromosomes but the strains of mice that have been examined so far have not revealed them.

When two strains are compared in a breeding study, a backcross test-mating scheme allows the embryonic system to be studied in a constant maternal environment. The principle of this breeding scheme has been discussed elsewhere (Biddle and Fraser, 1977a; Biddle, 1979). In the case of the A/J–C57BL/6J strain pair, a segregation analysis suggested that a minimum of two (or possibly three) gene loci control the embryonic reactivity to cortisone and one of these loci is linked to *H-2* on chromosome 17. Also, the separate loci appear to operate independently since there was no between-locus interaction or epistasis. These results may hold only for the A/J–C57BL/6J strain pair, but this can only be evaluated after more strain pairs have been examined in a similar type of breeding scheme and genetic analysis.

In contrast, the DBA/2J–C57BL/6J strain pair was studied with the BXD recombinant inbred (RI) strains (cf. Fig. 6) (Vekemans *et al.*, 1981). As a first approximation, the 14 BXD RI strains could be classified in two groups (sensitive like DBA/2J or resistant like C57BL/6J) and this suggested that a single major factor regulates cortisone reactivity in this strain pair. No association was found with the *H-2* locus; instead, there was an association of reactivity with the *Pgm-1* marker gene on chromosome 5.

From the limited genetic analysis that has been done to date, there are at least two or possibly three separate genetic loci that regulate the reactivity to cortisone of the mouse embryo. There is a locus on chromosome 17 and one on chromosome 5, and the response to cortisone of a series of strains congenic for chromosome 2 marker genes suggests there is another genetic locus on chromosome 2 (Gasser *et al.*, 1981). The number of alleles at each genetic locus and the magnitude and direction of their effects on cortisone cleft palate are unknown. In addition, some of the alleles at these loci act in both the mother and the conceptus, and others appear to be expressed only in the embryo. (For a further analysis of the alleles of the *H-2* locus involved in glucocorticoid teratogenesis, see the chapters by Bonner and by Goldman.)

2. Gene Action

The strain differences in reactivity to cortisone that have been studied so far have been found to be genetically determined by maternal and embryonic effects. For both the A/J × C57BL/6J (Biddle and Fraser, 1976) and DBA/2J × C57BL/6J (Vekemans, 1982) crosses there is a significant maternal effect (Fig. 7). When the reciprocal cross difference, that is, the maternal effect (in the broad sense) observed as a difference between the reciprocal F_1 generations, is subtracted from the median effective dose for the C57BL/6J strain, the remainder of the difference is due mainly to embryonic genes. Moreover, using the adjusted C57BL/6J median effective dose (C57BL/6', Fig. 7) it appears that for both crosses, one important component of the genetic basis for the embryonic difference in susceptibility is *dominance* in the direction of a higher tolerance to cortisone of the C57BL/6J embryo. Both the A.B6 F_1 and D2.B6 F_1 median effective doses are significantly higher than expected with an additive genetic model.

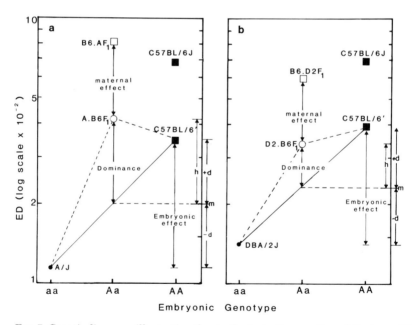

FIG. 7. Genetic diagrams illustrating the similarity in the genetic architecture of the differences in cortisone reactivity between (a) the A/J–C57BL/6J (data from Biddle and Fraser, 1976) and (b) the DBA/2J–C57BL/6J (data from Vekemans, 1982) strain pairs. The figure illustrates how gene substitution can be assessed in terms of phenotype (ED_{50}) and expressed in terms of genetic parameters on a linear scale.

The occurrence, direction, and degree of dominance may depend on the scale used in representing the degree of expression of the genetic character (Mather and Jinks, 1971). In our case, the genetic character is the median effective dose for cortisone cleft palate. It is helpful to make use of some scaling criteria and to express the nature, the magnitude, and the direction of the genetic components just described in terms of parameters. With respect to embryonic genes, one can envision that cortisone reactivity is determined by three genetic components whose magnitudes are m, d, and h (using the notation of Mather and Jinks). First, there is the effect of the gene or genes specifically concerned with the determination of the differences in cortisone reactivity. With a single gene model, this is the effect of substituting allele A for a in the a/a homozygotes and is represented by d. The capital letter (A) denotes the allele for increased tolerance. Second, there is the average effect of all other genes determining the phenotype of the zygote or the mean background effect and this effect is represented by m. Therefore, the effect of genes A and a is defined in terms of a deviation (hence d) about the average background effect, m, that is $m + d$ and $m - d$ for both the resistant and susceptible parental strains, respectively. Turning now to the F_1, in which all individuals are Aa, one might expect the genotype value to be equal to m, since the d's with opposite sign cancel out. But this assumes that the F_1 is exactly intermediate to the two parental inbred strains, that is, the character manifests no dominance. Clearly, this is not the case for both the A.B6 F_1 and the D2.B6 F_1 (Fig. 7), so that, allowing for dominance, one can write $F_1 = m + h$, where h measures dominance and can take the sign according to whether A is dominant to a ($+h$) or the other way around ($-h$).

Using some simple methods of matrix algebra with a model consisting of three parameters, at least three independent equations would allow a solution. Given three equations, this would be the exact solution; with four equations, however, the least-squares solution could be found and the adequacy of the model can be tested. If the fit of the model to the observations proves to be adequate, it would imply that no additional parameters, representing a more complex genetic situation, need to be fitted to the data. This biometric procedure provides a means of assessing whether the variation under study in one pair of inbred strains can be explained on an additive basis and whether interaction between genes is important.

By summarizing the genetic components into mathematical parameters and allowing predictions to be made from them, we have a useful tool and a general framework to evaluate cortisone susceptibility within the species. For the crosses of A/J × C57BL/6J and DBA/2J × C57BL/6J, one important component of the genetic model is dominance in the direction of higher tolerance to cortisone. Dominance has also been demonstrated in other crosses (Table II), suggesting that in the species, dominance is directional. Nevertheless, in the C3H × CBA crosses (Table II) an additive genetic model appears to be perfectly adequate.

In the biometric analysis just outlined, *apparent additivity does not exclude dominance*. Indeed, two inbred strains, raised in the same environment, may well have their mean phenotypes regulated by several different genes. The value d measures the *net* difference. The F_1 between the two strains will be uniformly heterozygous and it will differ from the average value of the strains (the mid-parent value) by $ha + hb = S(h)$, taking the signs of the various h's into account. Thus $S(h)$, the sum of all the h's, can be zero even though each h is not zero because of the opposing signs of the individual h's or, in genetic terms, because of the opposing dominances (ambidirectional dominance).

B. NORMAL PALATE DEVELOPMENT

Only a small number of studies have looked into the hypothesis that cleft palate in mice is determined by how late the palate closes normally with respect to a developmental threshold (see review in Fraser, 1980). It is clear that a correlation between reactivity to cortisone and stage of palate closure exists in the mass-inbred SW strain and the inbred SW/Fr strain (Vekemans and Fraser, 1979). SW/Fr not only has the greatest reactivity (lowest tolerance) to cortisone of any strain tested so far but also closes its palate late. SW/Fr has a 5% incidence of spontaneous cleft palate, as one would expect if the distribution of palate closure overlapped the threshold even in the absence of cortisone treatment. High sensitivity, late palate closure, and spontaneous cleft palate also occur in another strain, T1Wh (Miller and Atnip, 1977).

A reasonable amount of evidence supports the correlation of late palate closure with susceptibility to cleft palate, both spontaneous and induced, but the hypothesis has yet to be critically tested. For example, when the traits of cortisone-induced cleft palate (a discontinuous moiety) and time of palate closure (a continuous moiety) are allowed to segregate, it is critical to know whether low and high susceptibility and early and late time of palate closure, respectively, do cosegregate.

The question has been investigated first using the A/J and C57BL/6 strains (Walker and Fraser, 1956) and the reciprocal crosses between them (Trasler, 1965; Biddle, 1980). Thus in cortisone-sensitive A/J embryos, palatal shelf elevation usually occurs later during development than in more resistant embryos (A.B6 F_1, B6.A F_1, and C57BL/6) (Fig. 8). The reciprocal cross difference in stage of shelf movement also corresponds to the difference in cleft palate sensitivity to cortisone. Thus both embryonic and maternal genes are involved in the strain difference in palate closure and at least part of the embryonic and maternal effects on cleft palate susceptibility could be attributed to embryonic and maternal effects on palate closure. These two strains, A/J and C57BL/6, however, represent only a very small sample of the genetic variation under study in the species and the genetic basis for the difference in susceptibility might not be the same between two other strains of mice. Furthermore, the number of genes mediating the genetic variation under study is presumably too large to permit an understanding of their individual mechanisms of action. For example, in these two lines, the embryonic difference in susceptibility to cor-

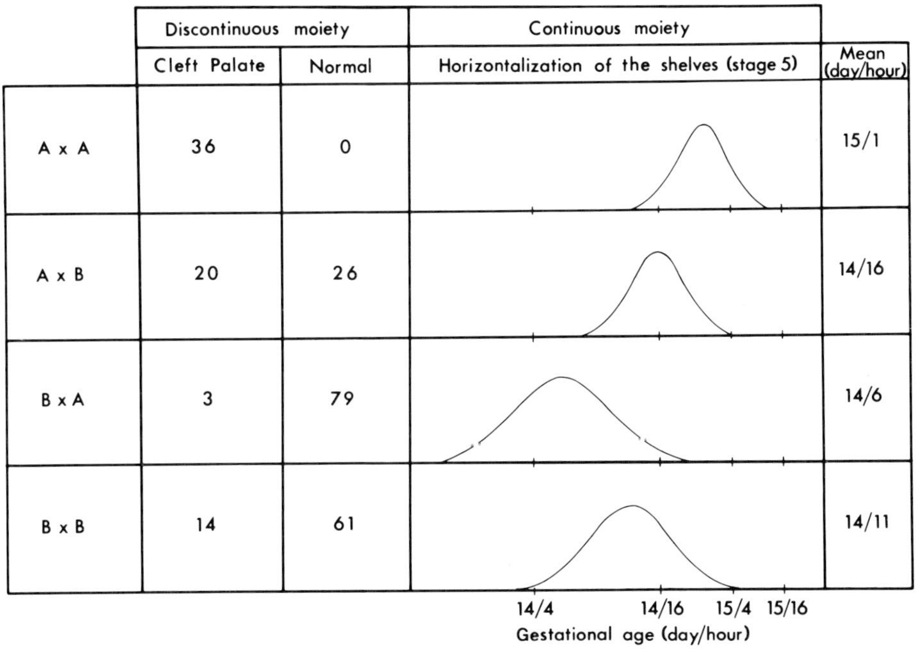

	Discontinuous moiety		Continuous moiety	Mean (day/hour)
	Cleft Palate	Normal	Horizontalization of the shelves (stage 5)	
A x A	36	0		15/1
A x B	20	26		14/16
B x A	3	79		14/6
B x B	14	61		14/11

14/4   14/16   15/4 15/16
Gestational age (day/hour)

FIG. 8. Diagram illustrating the close relationship between the stage of palate closure and the frequency of cleft palate in the A/J (A) and C57BL/6 (B) strains and their reciprocal crosses; $r = -0.890$ ($df = 2$). (Discontinuous moiety data from Kalter, 1954; continuous moiety data from Trasler, 1965.)

tisone-induced cleft palate is determined by at least two "major" gene loci, one of which appears to be linked to the major histocompatibility complex (*H-2*) on chromosome 17. It seems reasonable to speculate that differences in the *H-2* complex might alter the embryonic response to cortisone by altering the stage of normal palate development; however, since palate closure occurs at the same stage in the congenic mouse strains C57BL/10 and B10.A, this hypothesis had to be rejected (Vekemans and Fraser, 1982).

Recently, the difference in embryonic susceptibility to cortisone-induced cleft palate between C57BL/6 and another strain of mice, DBA/2J, has been shown to be relatively simple (Vekemans *et al.*, 1981). These two strains also differ in time of palate closure and the correlation between reactivity to cortisone and stage of palate closure extends to the reciprocal F_1 and backcross generations (Vekemans and Steinmetz, 1983). Therefore, for this particular strain pair, it appears that the genetic architecture of reactivity to cortisone matches very closely the genetic architecture of palate closure. Furthermore, the genetic architecture of palate closure shows to some extent the property of dominance (Fig. 9), as one would expect if the developmental difference in palate closure and the difference in susceptibility to cortisone were genetically associated. Such a correlation would arise if the genes that mediate the time of palate closure were themselves pleiotropic in action and were affecting susceptibility to cortisone-induced cleft palate in addition to their effect on time of palate closure. The use of the BXD set of recombinant inbred strains should provide an opportunity to investigate this hypothesis further.

VII. Discussion

It has been argued that one can infer from the genetic architecture of a trait the type of selection to which the trait has been exposed in the past (Mather, 1966). The impact of selection will vary from one character to another, not merely in its intensity but in its nature (Robertson, 1955). Directional selection on a quantitative trait will result in the trait manifesting directional dominance and duplicate epistasis (Breese and Mather, 1960; Kearsey and Kojima, 1966). On the other hand, stabilizing selection will result in either little dominance or, if present, ambidirectional dominance with epistasis, which can be weak or ambidirectional (Jinks and Broadhurst, 1963). With respect to cortisone reactivity, however, the data remain too fragmentary to describe with reasonable confidence the genetic architecture of the trait in the species. This is presumably because the studies concerned with

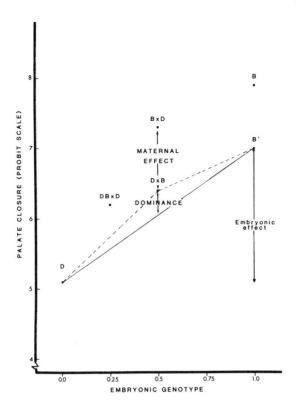

FIG. 9. Genetic diagram illustrating the genetic architecture of palate closure in the DBA/2J (D) and C57BL/6J (B) strain pair. The median time of palate closure is plotted against embryonic genotype as a frequency of B strain genes. (Data are from unpublished results of Vekemans.)

the genetics of the strain differences in susceptibility to cortisone-induced cleft palate have uncovered only a very truncated portion of the variation in the species. Furthermore, the information to be gained merely from a study of the means is very limited, and methods of analysis to identify changes in the components of variation, that is, a diallel analysis, should be undertaken in order to answer the question.

The gene action of the difference in embryonic reactivity between C3H and CBA appears to be additive and has been inadvertently overlooked. Any future diallel analysis with the well-described strains and untested strains should include C3H and CBA. An answer to whether some genes for cortisone tolerance exhibit true additivity or apparent additivity due to opposing dominance (Section VI,A,2) is critical to the further genetic analysis of the homeostatic model for palate development.

It is clear that dominance in the direction of higher tolerance to cortisone has been shown to be a property of the comparison between several strain pairs. Since it is unlikely that the mouse has been exposed to cortisone in its natural environment and at these massive doses (1000 times the LD_{50} for cells in culture), one may postulate that a trait correlated with cortisone-induced cleft palate has been exposed to natural selection. The multifactorial threshold model suggests that late palate closure is correlated with susceptibility to cleft palate. If this correlation is functional and not coincidental, it would indicate that palate closure is the character under natural selection.

Preliminary evidence does support the idea that the relationship between cortisone reactivity and palate closure is not coincidental. At least for one strain pair, DBA/2J–C57BL/6J, the genetic architecture of reactivity to cortisone matches very closely the genetic architecture of palate closure, as one would expect if both characters were genetically associated through pleiotropy or linkage (Vekemans, 1982; Vekemans and Steinmetz, 1983). The mechanism underlying the nature of this genetic architecture presumably has its origin in metabolic differences between the two parental strains (Kacser and Burns, 1980), even though at the present time the molecular basis remains unknown. This suggests that palate closure is a developmental process that can eventually be pieced together by the genetic analysis of several sets of pairs of inbred strains. For the DBA/2J–C57BL/6J strain pair, however, it remains to be shown whether the genetic traits of low and high susceptibility and early and late palate closure, respectively, do indeed cosegregate.

If the traits cosegregate, that is, if the genetic material regulating the difference in reactivity to cleft palate induced by cortisone also regulates the difference in palate closure in the absence of cortisone, we may have a handle on the genes that regulate normal palate development, provided those genes are assigned to specific chromosomal sites. Indeed, with the introduction of the most recent DNA technology in order to make inferences about the molecular changes in the chromosomal DNA, one may eventually elucidate the mechanisms by which the phenotypic variation originates even though no specific gene product has been identified.The study of the genetic difference in susceptibility to cortisone does not tell us anything about the mode of action of cortisone, but it may eventually elucidate how genes regulate normal palate development.

With respect to cortisone reactivity, a few countable genes have proved to mediate a large part of the genetic variation under study within a pair of strains. If these genes influence some aspect of palate closure, we would have a clue to how they predispose the embryo to cortisone-induced cleft palate. For example, if glucocorticoid receptor concentration did cosegregate with both cortisone reactivity and palate closure, we would know how they regulate normal palate development and how, doing so, they predispose the embryo to cortisone-induced cleft palate. However, the finding that different genes are involved in different pairs of inbred strains suggests that there is a continuous variation in gene expression. Therefore, with respect to the species, the demonstration of single-gene action does not mean that the identified gene is a major gene. For example, the haplotype at the major histocompatibility complex (*H-2*) may be seen as one identifiable gene among many other genes composing the genetic background that makes one individual strain likely to develop cleft palate.

Perhaps this segregating genetic variation of the continuous kind (reviewed in Thompson and Thoday, 1979) may result from modulation and/or evolution by molecular changes of families of repeated sequences of DNA, which indirectly affect gene control because of their affinities for regulatory molecules (Davidson and Britten, 1979). The fact that, in the mouse, cortisone susceptibility appears to be polygenetically (broad sense) controlled by loci that have different magnitudes of effect and that show pleiotropic effects on several characters is consistent with this hypothesis but does not yet prove it. Therefore, the middle or low copy-number repetitive sequences might be a good place to look because changes in these sequences might be relatively easy to detect. What we know of transposable genetic elements in other systems (Nevers and Saedler, 1977; Calos and Miller, 1980) suggests that those sequences are good candidates to be involved in the kinds of genomic rearrangements for which we are searching.

The genetic analysis of strain differences in the susceptibility to cortisone-induced cleft palate is an efficient approach to search for biological correlates of liability and for ways to influence them. Moreover, if one makes use of the conservation of syntenic groups of autosomal genes in mouse and man (Lalley *et al.*, 1978), we can envision moving from studies of the regulation of palate development in the mouse to palate development in man. In this way, the mouse model might provide some guidance for studies in man.

VIII. Summary

We are beginning to see a tantalizing picture by looking into the "genetic window" on the teratogenesis of cortisone-induced cleft palate and on normal palate development. We must continue to open this window. So far, all strains of mice that have been treated with cortisone do react with induced cleft palate and, from their dose–response behaviors, they appear to react in the same way. It is tempting to conclude that dosage tolerance is the only genetic variation in the reaction. We do not attach any significance to this because we must emphasize the fact that these different strains represent an insignificant sample of the hundreds of genetically different, recognized strains of the mouse.

We have emphasized previously that systematic strain surveys must become an active part of teratological genetics in order to obtain an approximation of how much genetic variation exists in a trait in the species (e.g., Biddle, 1981). Now, we need to go beyond strain surveys. Crosses between strains must become part of this activity. Dominance appears to be a property of the homeostatic model of palate development as far as the cortisone probe is concerned, but it may not be a universal property. The significance of dominance and the architecture of gene action can only be interpreted by exploring more strain pairs in the mouse. A study of two or three or four strains is simply inadequate.

From the crosses between a limited number of strains, major genetic factors in cortisone reactivity have been identified. These major genetic factors may regulate the homeostatic model of palate development, but we do not know this for a fact. The identification of major genetic factors has moved us to a new horizon; we can move now from a purely descriptive biology to a study of the functional biology of the process of palate development. This move will require not only the molecular probes with which to walk along the specific chromosomes to the major genetic factors but also a library of fully characterized strains of the mouse in which to use these probes. The library of strains that have been genetically characterized for the cleft palate reaction is missing.

ACKNOWLEDGMENTS

Our studies began with an additive framework but have progressed to a system with duplicate epistasis. The work discussed in this chapter was started under the guidance of Dr. F. Clarke Fraser with the support of both the Medical Research Council of Canada and the McGill University-Montreal Children's Hospital Research Institute. It continues in the authors' laboratories with the support of these agencies. F. G. B. is an Alberta Heritage Medical Research Scholar.

REFERENCES

Altman, P. L., and Katz, D. D., eds. (1979). "Inbred and Genetically Defined Strains of Laboratory Animals. Part 1. Mouse and Rat." Federation of American Societies for Experimental Biology, Bethesda, Maryland.

Bailey, D. W. (1971). *Transplantation* **11**, 325–327.

Baxter, H., and Fraser, F. C. (1950). *McGill Med. J.* **19**, 245–249.

Biddle, F. G. (1979). *In* "Advances in the Study of Birth Defects" (T. V. N. Persaud, ed.), Vol. 1, pp. 85–111. MTP Press, Lancaster.

Biddle, F. G. (1980). *Teratology* **22**, 239–246.

Biddle, F. G. (1981). *In* "Developmental Toxicology" (C. A. Kimmel and J. Buelke-Sam, eds.), pp. 55–82. Raven, New York.

Biddle, F. G., and Fraser, F. C. (1976). *Genetics* **84**, 743–754.

Biddle, F. G., and Fraser, F. C. (1977a). *Genetics* **85**, 289–302.

Biddle, F. G., and Fraser, F. C. (1977b). *In* "Handbook of Teratology" (J. G. Wilson and F. C. Fraser, eds.), Vol. 3, pp. 3–33. Plenum, New York.

Bliss, C. I. (1935a). *Ann. Appl. Biol.* **22**, 134–167.

Bliss, C. I. (1935b). *Ann. Appl. Biol.* **22**, 307–333.

Bonner, J. J., and Slavkin, H. C. (1975). *Immunogenetics* **2**, 213–218 .

Bonner, J. J., and Tyan, M. L. (1983). *Genetics* **103**, 263–273.

Breese, E. L., and Mather, K. (1960). *Heredity* **14**, 375–399.

Burdi, A., Feingold, M., Larsson, K. S., Leck, I., Zimmerman, E. F., and Fraser, F. C. (1972). *Teratology* **6**, 255–270.

Calos, M. P., and Miller, J. H. (1980). *Cell* **20**, 579–595.

Davidson, E. H., and Britten, R. J. (1979). *Science* **204**, 1052–1059.

Finney, D. J. (1971). "Probit Analysis," 3rd ed. Cambridge Univ. Press, London and New York.

Fitch, N. S. (1957). *J. Exp. Zool.* **136**, 329–357.

Francis, B. M. (1971). "Inheritance of Sensitivity to the Teratogenic and Embryocidal Effects of Cortisone in Four Strains of Mice." Ph.D. thesis, University of Michigan, Ann Arbor.

Francis, B. M. (1973). *Teratology* **7**, 119–126.

Fraser, F. C. (1976). *Teratology* **14**, 267–280.

Fraser, F. C. (1977). *In* "Handbook of Teratology" (J. G. Wilson and F. C. Fraser, eds.), Vol. 1, pp. 75–96. Plenum, New York.

Fraser, F. C. (1980). *In* "Etiology of Cleft Lip and Cleft Palate" (M. Melnick, D. Bixler, and E. D. Shields, eds.), pp. 1–23. Liss, New York.

Fraser, F. C., and Fainstat, T. D. (1951). *Pediatrics* **8**, 527–533.

Gasser, D. L., Mele, L., Lees, D. D., and Goldman, A. S. (1981). *Proc. Natl. Acad. Sci. U.S.A.* **78**, 3147–3150.

Green, M. C., ed. (1981). "Genetic Variants and Strains of the Laboratory Mouse." Fischer, Berlin.

Greene, R. M., and Pratt, R. M. (1976). *J. Embryol. Exp. Morphol.* **36**, 225–245.

Gruneberg, H., and Truslove, G. M. (1960). *Genet. Res.* **1**, 69–90.

Heiniger, H.-J., and Dorey, J. J., eds. (1981). "Handbook of Genetically Standardized JAX Mice." Jackson Laboratory, Bar Harbor, Maine.

Jinks, J. L., and Broadhurst, P. G. (1963). *Heredity* **18**, 319–336.

Juriloff, D. M. (1980). *In* "Etiology of Cleft Lip and Cleft Palate" (M. Melnick, D. Bixler, and E. D. Shields, eds.), pp. 39–71. Liss, New York.

Kacser, H., and Burns, J. A. (1980). *Genetics* **97**, 639–666.

Kalter, H. (1954). *Genetics* **39**, 185–196.

Kalter, H. (1965). *In* "Teratology: Principles and Techniques" (J. G. Wilson and J. Warkany, eds.), pp. 57–80. Univ. of Chicago Press, Chicago.

Kearsey, M. J., and Kojima, K. I. (1966). *Genetics* **56**, 23–37.

Klein, D., Tewarson, S., Figueroa, F., and Klein, J. (1982). *Immunogenetics* **16**, 319–328.

Lalley, P. A., Minna, J. D., and Francke, U. (1978). *Nature (London)* **274**, 160–162.

Loevy, H. (1963). *Anat. Rec.* **145**, 117–122.

Loevy, H. (1968). *Proc. Soc. Exp. Biol. Med.* **128**, 841–844.

Mather, K. (1966). *Proc. R. Soc., Ser. B* **164**, 328–340.

Mather, K., and Jinks, J. L. (1971). "Biometrical Genetics." Cornell Univ. Press, Ithaca, New York.

Miller, K. K., and Atnip, R. L. (1977). *Teratology* **16**, 41–46.

Morse, H. C., ed. (1978). "Origins of Inbred Mice." Academic Press, New York.

Nevers, P., and Saedler, H. (1977). *Nature (London)* **268**, 109–115.

Robertson, A. (1955). *Cold Spring Harbor Symp. Quant. Biol.* **20**, 225–229.

Seegmiller, R. E., and Fraser, F. C. (1977). *J. Embryol. Exp. Morphol.* **38**, 227–238.

Sokal, R. R., and Rohlf, F. J. (1969). "Biometry." Freeman, San Francisco.

Staats, J. (1980). *Cancer Res.* **40**, 2083–2128.

Thompson, J. N., and Thoday, J. M. (1979). "Quantitative Genetic Variation." Academic Press, New York.

Trasler, D. G. (1965). *In* "Teratology: Principles and Techniques" (J. G. Wilson and J. Warkany, eds.), pp. 38–55. Univ. of Chicago Press, Chicago.

Trasler, D. G., and Fraser, F. C. (1977). *In* "Handbook of Teratology" (J. G. Wilson and F. C. Fraser, eds.), Vol. 2, pp. 271–292. Plenum, New York.

Vekemans, M. (1982). *Can. J. Genet. Cytol.* **24**, 797–805.

Vekemans, M., and Fraser, F. C. (1978). *Teratology* **17**, 24A.

Vekemans, M., and Fraser, F. C. (1979). *Am. J. Med. Genet.* **4**, 95–102.

Vekemans, M., and Fraser, F. C. (1982). *Teratology* **25**, 267–270.

Vekemans, M., and Steinmetz, O. (1983). *Teratology* **27**, 82A.

Vekemans, M., Taylor, B. A., and Fraser, F. C. (1979). *Teratology* **19**, 51A–52A.

Vekemans, M., Taylor, B. A., and Fraser, F. C. (1981). *Genet. Res.* **38**, 327–331.

Waddington, C. H. (1942). *Nature (London)* **150**, 563–565.

Walker, B. E., and Fraser, F. C. (1956). *J. Embryol. Exp. Morphol.* **4**, 176–189.

Walker, B. E., and Fraser, F. C. (1957). *J. Embryol. Exp. Morphol.* **5**, 201–209.

CHAPTER 9

THE *H-2* GENETIC COMPLEX, DEXAMETHASONE-INDUCED CLEFT PALATE, AND OTHER CRANIOFACIAL ANOMALIES

Joseph J. Bonner

DENTAL RESEARCH INSTITUTE
CENTER FOR THE HEALTH SCIENCES
UNIVERSITY OF CALIFORNIA
LOS ANGELES, CALIFORNIA

I. Introduction

Results of recent experiments will expand the original observation that a gene associated with the major histocompatibility complex (*H-2*) influences susceptibility to glucocorticoid-induced cleft palate in the mouse (Bonner and Slavkin, 1975). The gene is *Dcp* (for dexametha-

193

CURRENT TOPICS IN
DEVELOPMENTAL BIOLOGY, VOL. 19

sone-induced cleft palate, DCP). The experiments were intended to demonstrate linkage with a backcross text and to map the chromosomal position of the gene. The gene products of *H-2* serve as the markers of subregions in chromosome 17.

The results show the following: (1) *H-2* and dexamethasone-induced cleft palate (*Dcp*) genes are linked. (2) Gene mapping analyses of *H-2* genotypes that are recombinants of $H-2^k$ and $H-2^d$ alleles show there are two *Dcp* loci, each controlling a different mechanism. (3) Mapping analyses with $H-2^a$ and $H-2^b$ recombinants can be interpreted to show two or three *Dcp* loci. (4) Whether there are two or three alleles of each locus remains obscure. (5) There appears to be a complexity of interactions between the loci and alleles in the form of epistasis and/or complementation. (6) There is an interaction with a sex-associated gene. (7) The expanded linkage analysis suggests that a factor of DCP susceptibility is transmitted horizontally from mother to female offspring.

Several unplanned observations come to light. First, genes associated with *H-2* modulate the spontaneous frequency of craniofacial anomalies. These birth defects are exencephaly, micrognathia, and microphthalmia. Second, the occurrence of these craniofacial defects is not due to the teratogenic action of dexamethasone. Third, *H-2*-associated genes modulate the frequency of dorsoventral vaginal septa, a birth defect of the female reproductive tract.

II. *H-2* and Chromosome 17—Background

A. THE NOBEL PRIZE

H-2 was discovered by George Snell, who won the Nobel Prize in 1981 for his discovery (Snell, 1981). *H-2* quickly gained a prominent position in biological research because most regulatory functions of the immune response and transplant rejection are linked to it. The genes in *H-2* seem to determine one's ability to fight off infectious diseases, to keep autoimmunity in check, and to destroy virally infected cancer cells (Snell *et al.*, 1976).

B. THE *H-2* GENE PRODUCTS

Three classes of molecules are encoded in *H-2*. Their detailed protein structure and gene structure are being described (Pease *et al.*, 1982; Steinmetz *et al.*, 1982; Klein *et al.* 1981), and the distribution of their polymorphic alleles throughout natural populations is being investigated (Nadeau *et al.*, 1982). These molecules now serve as definitive chromosomal markers in gene mapping, replacing the more subjective use of antigenic specificities.

Class I molecules (K, D, etc., see Fig. 1) are cell surface glycoproteins found on many cell types (Klein *et al.*, 1981). The quantity varies
among cell types (Klein, 1975). The gene and protein structures of
class I molecules are like that of an immunoglobulin (Pease *et al.*,
1982). Class II molecules, also immunoglobulin-like in structure, are
more restricted in their distribution, generally found on lymphoid cells
and selected epithelial cells (Steinmetz *et al.*, 1982). Class III molecules
are serum components of the complement system (Roos *et al*, 1978).
This system is activated by the antigen–antibody reactions.

The function of class I and class II molecules appears to be antigen
presentation and recognition by lymphocytes. Class I molecules are
believed to be the markers of self, protecting the cell from autoimmune
attack. The deviations from self expressed on the surfaces of virally
infected cells are recognized by lymphocytes that have the same class I
molecules as the infected cells. This is a characteristic called *H-2* re-

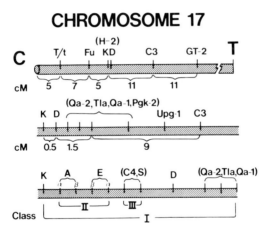

FIG. 1. Illustration of chromosome 17 in the mouse. Each bar represents increasing
detail of chromosomal structure from the centromere (C) to the telomere (T). Gene loci
are marked and the distance in centimorgans (cM) between them is shown. The gene loci
in the top bar are the tail-affecting loci (*T/t*), fused vertebrae and tail abnormalities (*Fu*),
H-2, component of complement (*C3*), and teratocarcinoma graft rejection (*Gt-2*). The
middle bar focuses on the region between *K* and *D*, the classical transplantation antigens. *Qa-1* and *Qa-2* are newly described transplantation antigens expressed on lymphocytes, *Tla* is thymus leukemia antigen in normal thymus cells and some leukemia cells,
Pgk-2 is phosphoglycerate kinase-2, and *Upg-1* is urinary pepsinogen-1. The bottom bar
focuses on the *H-2* complex and the genes for class I molecules (*K,D,Qa,Tla*), class II
molecules ($A_\alpha, A_\beta, E_\alpha, E_\beta$), and class III molecules *C4*, which is a component of complement, and *S*, which is the sex-limited serum protein whose function is unknown. The
parentheses indicate that the order of the genes is not definitive. (Data taken from D.
Klein *et al.*, 1982, and Steinmetz *et al.*, 1982.)

striction (Zinkernagel and Doherty, 1975; J. Klein *et al.*, 1982).

Several investigators have proposed that the class I molecules, in addition to their role in the immune recognition system, play a role in intercellular recognition in embryonic development (Bennet *et al.*, 1972; Boyse and Cantor, 1978; Bonner, 1979; Snell, 1980). As attractive as this hypothesis may be, there is no direct evidence that supports it. Nevertheless, the *T* complex, which affects the occurrence of early embryonic defects and tailless mice (Bennett, 1980; Artzt *et al.*, 1982), and the *H-2* complex, which affects the occurrence of craniofacial defects (see Section V), and the linkage between these two large gene complexes in chromosome 17 present an exciting research problem in mammalian genetics. Understanding their relationship will deepen our knowledge of regulatory mechanisms in intercellular communication and embryonic development.

C. CONGENIC STRAINS OF MICE

We can benefit now from the use of the exceptionally refined gene mapping of chromosome 17 made possible by the formation of *H-2* congenic strains of mice by Snell, Stimpfling, Shreffler, Klein, and Boyse. These inbred mice were selectively bred to have genetic differences restricted to only chromosome 17. The rest of the mouse genome is identical in every way among the strains in a congenic line.

The mice used in our investigations are listed in Table I. All strains have the C57BL/10 genomic background and each has a different *H-2* haplotype. The haplotype is the sequence of alleles of linked loci in the *H-2* complex. For example, $H-2^b$ has mostly *b* alleles that are linked.

TABLE I

LIST OF CONGENIC STRAINS OF MICE
AND THE *H-2* HAPLOTYPE

Strain	*H-2* haplotype
C57BL/10ScSn	*b*
B10.A/SgSn	*a*
B10.BR/SgSn	*k*
B10.D2/nSn	*d*
B10.A(2R)/SgSn	*h2*
B10.A(4R)/Sg	*h4*
B10.A(5R)/SgSn	*i5*
B10.A(18R)/Sg	*i18*

H-2ᵃ, on the other hand, is a recombinant haplotype of two different linked alleles, *k* and *d* (see Table II).

In many cases the genetic difference between congenic strains extends beyond the traditionally defined *H-2* complex from *K* to *D* (see Fig. 1). More often, large chromosomal segments are different between the strains and in some cases the whole chromosome may be different (D. Klein *et al.*, 1982). The minimum genetic difference between strains C57BL/10-*H-2ᵇ* and B10.A-*H-2ᵃ*, for example, is *K* to *Qa-1*; the maximum possible genetic difference may be from the centromere to *Pgk-2*. A gene for a phenotypic difference between these two strains probably maps in this subregion of the chromosome. A mutation elsewhere in the genome that may have occurred since the formation of the strains can cause the phenotypic difference too. Therefore linkage should always be confirmed with a backcross test, that is, in our case, a cross between DCP-resistant and -susceptible strains, then backcrossing the progeny with one of the parents, and finally, monitoring both the frequency of DCP and the *H-2* haplotypes in the backcross progeny.

TABLE II

LIST OF ALLELES FOR EACH OF THE *H-2* HAPLOTYPES[a]

H-2 haplotype	Alleles												
	C	K	A	E_β	E_α	S	D	Qa-2	Tla	Qa-1	Pgk-2	Upg-2	T
h4	a or b	k	k	k/b	b	b	b	a	b	b	a	s	b
h2	a or b	k	k	k	k	d	b	a	b	b	a	s	b
a	a or b	k	k	k	k	d	d	a	a	a	a	s	b
i5	b	b	b	b/k	k	d	d	a	a	a	a	s	b
i18	b	b	b	b	b	b	d	a	a	a	a	s	b
b	b	b	b	b	b	b	b	a	b	b	a	s	b
d	d or b	d	d	d	d	d	d	a	c	b	a	s	b
k	k or b	k	k	k	k	k	k	b	a	a	a	s	k or b

[a]Horizontal bars highlight allelic differences between adjacent *H-2* haplotypes. Broken bars signify regions that may be different. The sequence of alleles in *i18* is extrapolated from the data of D. Klein *et al.* (1982). C represents the centromere and T represents the telomere.

III. Linkage Analysis

A. *H-2* AND *Dcp* ARE LINKED

F_1 hybrids of C57BL/10 and B10.A were backcrossed to C57BL/10 (Bonner and Tyan, 1982, 1983b). The backcross progeny were H-$2^{a/b}$ or H-$2^{b/b}$. Forty-four pregnant females were given a dose of dexamethasone (a synthetic, high-potency glucocorticoid) on day 12 of pregnancy. On day 18 each fetus was scored for the presence or absence of cleft palate and then for its *H-2* haplotype. The haplotype was determined with the immunofluorescent technique and monoclonal antibodies reactive to H-2K^k. Results of this backcross test are shown in Table III. The frequency of DCP in the H-$2^{a/b}$ fetuses was 36%, and in H-$2^{b/b}$ fetuses, 23%. The statistical test for independence (the G statistic of Sokol and Rohlf, 1981) shows that *H-2* and DCP susceptibility do not segregate independently ($G = 5.47, p < 0.025$).

This experiment settles the issue of linkage. The difference in DCP susceptibility between C57BL/10 and B10.A originates not from a gene elsewhere in the genome but from a gene linked to *H-2*. Not settled are the questions of the evolutionary origin of the genetic difference between the strains and the mechanism through which the gene is expressed.

B. SURVIVAL ADVANTAGE FOR *H-2* HETEROZYGOTES

The rules for the Mendelian segregation of alleles predict that H-$2^{a/b}$ and H-$2^{b/b}$ fetuses occur in the backcross progeny in a 50:50 ratio. A significant deviation from this indicates a survival advantage for one of the two types.

Table III does not contain an even number of homozygotes and heterozygotes. The ratio is 41:59 ($p < 0.005$), heterozygotes pre-

TABLE III

THE 2 × 2 TABLE FOR THE BACKCROSS TEST OF INDEPENDENT
SEGREGATION OF *H-2* AND *Dcp*

H-2 haplotype	DCP+	DCP−	Σ	Percentage DCP
ab	62	111	173	35.8
bb	28	93	121	23.1
Σ	90	204	294	

dominating. There are two possible explanations. One is that *H-2* heterozygotes have the survival advantage. This is not the first time an *H-2* heterozygotic advantage has been reported, but it is not a consistent finding (Stimpfling and Richardson, 1965; Palm, 1974). The second explanation is that subjective bias favors positive fluorescence when scoring the fetal spleen cells in the immunofluorescence assay.

C. Maternal and Embryonic Factors

How does the gene exert its influence? Maternal and embryonic factors are indicated.

The *H-2*-linked *Dcp* gene exerts itself in both ways. In Table IV is the DCP frequency of reciprocal crosses between B10.A (identified as A) and C57BL/10 (B) (Bonner and Tyan, 1983b). The difference between the two hybrids, the reciprocal crosses A ♀ × B ♂ F_1 and B ♀ × A ♂ F_1, indicates that a maternal factor modulates the DCP frequency (see also the discussion by Vekemans and Biddle, this volume). The fetuses are genetically identical F_1 individuals, at least for chromosomal inheritance. Factors that could cause the differences are the maternal intrauterine environment and matriclinous inheritance.

TABLE IV

DCP Frequency at 160 mg/kg Given as the
Arcsine of the Percentage of Fetuses
with Cleft Palate in the Reciprocal
Crosses and Backcrosses between B10.A
and C57BL/1Q

Cross[a] ♀ × ♂	DCP arcsine (SE)[b]
A × A	53.1 (2.2)
A × B	54.3 (4.5)
B × A	44.2 (4.0)
B × B	37.6 (0.3)
B × (B/A)[c]	42.6 (4.4)
B × (A/B)	44.6 (5.3)
(B/A) × B	41.6 (3.8)
(A/B) × B	51.5 (2.8)

[a] A, B10.A; B, C57BL/10.
[b] SE, Standard error of the mean.
[c] B/A, C57BL/10 ♀ × B10.A ♂ F_1; A/B, B10.A ♀ × C57BL/10 ♂ F_1.

The difference in DCP frequency between the parental strain, B × B, and the cross, B × A, indicates that there is an embryonic factor as well, because the mothers in this comparison are the same genotype. Only the embryonic genotypes differ. This property of maternal and embryonic factors of DCP genetics has been observed by many investigators (Kalter, 1965; Bonner and Slavkin, 1975; Biddle and Fraser, 1976; Melnick *et al.*, 1981).

D. The Grandmother Effect

The DCP frequencies of the backcrosses are listed also in Table IV. The *H-2* genotypes of the dams in the backcrosses were interchanged between F_1 hybrid and homozygotic females. Additional variation in the F_1 hybrids was added so that dams and sires were either A × B F_1 or B × A F_1. When the dam was B and the sire was A × B F_1 or B × A F_1 there was no significant difference between the DCP frequencies in the backcross progeny. When the sire was B and the dam was either A × B F_1 or B × A F_1 there was a significant difference in the DCP frequencies in the backcross progeny ($p < 0.05$) (Bonner and Tyan, 1983b). The experiment was done with two doses of dexamethasone and in each case the A × B F_1 dam's progeny had a higher frequency of DCP. This maternal effect was imposed alike on $H-2^{a/b}$ and $H-2^{b/b}$ fetuses. The difference between the A × B F_1 and B × A F_1 dams caused a reduction in the DCP frequency in both $H-2^{a/b}$ and $H-2^{b/b}$ fetuses.

What causes this difference? What is different between the A × B F_1 and B × A F_1 dams? It is not somatic or sex-linked genes, because the dams are genetically identical F_1 mice and they are congenic, with the same X chromosomes. It is not specific cytoplasmic inheritance, like that of mitochondria, because the breeding method to produce the congenic strains removes any possibility of matriclinous or patriclinous dissimilarity in the vertical transmission of inheritance (unless the A strain acquired it since the strain was made). A possibility that comes to mind is pre- or postnatal horizontal transmission of inheritance. A factor in the maternal intrauterine environment or in the sucklings' environment could be altering the F_1 dams. When the F_1 females became pregnant adults in the backcross test, whatever it was that altered them pre- or postnatally manifested itself by causing the difference in DCP susceptibility in their backcross progeny. In relation to the backcross progeny the difference is thus a "grandmother effect." Fetuses with $H-2^a$ grandmothers are more susceptible to DCP than fetuses with $H-2^b$ grandmothers.

IV. Gene Mapping Analyses

A. THE STRATEGY

Now that linkage between *H-2* and *Dcp* is established firmly, the next useful information is the location of the gene in chromosome 17. How many centimorgans from *H-2* is it? The traditional method to measure the recombination frequency between two linked loci such as *H-2* and *Dcp* is not appropriate, because DCP is a quantitative trait and to measure the shift in frequency resulting from recombination in backcrosses would be experimentally impractical. Instead, the known *H-2* recombinant haplotypes can be used to subdivide chromosome 17 into subregions and measure the effect of each chromosomal subregion on DCP susceptibility. The best we can hope to do is to find which *H-2* gene loci lie closest to *Dcp*. This must suffice until a gene product for DCP is discovered.

Only DCP susceptibility differences between strains give useful information. No difference means no information, but DCP susceptibility similarities do not mean that two strains have the same gene in regions of genetic similarity. Only physical properties of a gene or its product show that two strains have the same gene.

B. DOSE–RESPONSE ANALYSIS

An experimental method for measuring DCP susceptibility with a sensitive ability to detect strain differences is dose–response analysis. Several measurements are made simultaneously; each can be used to detect strain differences. The measurements are (1) the slope of the line (the regression coefficient); (2) the *y* intercept or some other point on the *y* axis that corresponds to a dose on the *x* axis; and (3) the variance, which is a measure of the amount of variation in the dose response of DCP.

Different slopes of DCP dose–response lines indicate that there are different mechanisms through which dexamethasone induces the cleft palate. Differences between the *y* intercepts or *y* coordinates at specified doses indicate that the strains differ in sensitivity to dexamethasone. When the strains differ in variance, one strain has a larger range of responses to dexamethasone than the other. Results are summarized in Table V and Figs. 2 and 3.

C. THE *k/d* RECOMBINANTS—TWO *Dcp* LOCI

The first strain comparisons ascertain the effect of two *H-2* subregions. The strains are B10.A-*H-2^a*, B10.D2-*H-2^d*, and B10.BR-*H-2^k*.

TABLE V

RESULTS OF THE DOSE–RESPONSE ANALYSIS OF SEVEN CONGENIC STRAINS
WITH DIFFERENT *H-2* HAPLOTYPES

H-2 haplotype	Regression coefficient (SE)[a]	Estimated arcsine at 160 mg/kg	Variance
b	37.5 (1.4)	37.6	406
i5	45.3 (4.8)	36.9	332
a	45.3 (4.1)	53.1	283
h2	51.9 (5.5)	54.5	295
i18	54.5 (6.0)	39.7	283
k	67.3 (10.8)	33.1	273
d	70.5 (9.7)	25.0	344

[a]SE, Standard error of the mean.

The *H-2*^{a} haplotype is a recombinant of both *k* and *d* alleles (see Table II). The minimal genetic difference between *H-2*^{a} and *H-2*^{d} is K–E_α and Tla–Qa-1. The minimal genetic difference between *H-2*^{a} and *H-2*^{k} is S–Qa-2. These strains differ in DCP susceptibility ($p < 0.001$) (Bonner and Tyan, 1983a). They also differ in regression coefficients ($p < 0.05$). The difference in DCP susceptibility can be seen in Table V by comparing the estimated cleft palate arcsine at 160 mg/kg. *H-2*^{a} is the

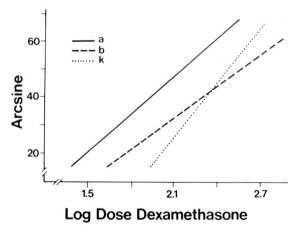

FIG. 2. Dexamethasone-induced cleft palate dose–response analyses of three *H-2* congenic strains of mice. On the *y* axis is the arcsine, which represents the frequency of cleft palate. An arcsine of 45 is equivalent to 50% cleft palate. The *x* axis is the log of the doses of dexamethasone given to pregnant mice on day 12 of pregnancy (log 2.2 is equivalent to 160 mg/kg dexamethasone). The results are of strains B10.A/SgSn (a), C57BL/10Sn (b), and B10.BR/SgSn (k).

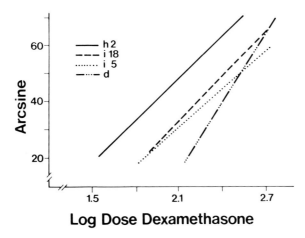

FIG. 3. Dexamethasone-induced cleft palate dose–response analyses of four additional *H-2* congenic strains. The strains are B10.A(2R)/SgSn (h2), B10.A(18R)/Sg (i18), B10.A(5R)/SgSn (i5), and B10.D2/nSn (d).

susceptible haplotype, and *H-2^k* and *H-2^d* are resistant. *H-2^a* has a regression coefficient that is less than either *H-2^k* or *H-2^d*.

The difference in the regression coefficients suggests that there are two different mechanisms through which dexamethasone induces cleft palate. To substantiate the two mechanisms, a cross of the strains in all possible combinations detected maternal and embryonic effects. The data are shown in Table VI and Fig. 4 (Bonner and Tyan, 1983a). Reciprocal crosses between *H-2^a* and *H-2^k* show only an embryonic effect. On the other hand, crosses between *H-2^a* and *H-2^d* show both maternal and embryonic effects. *H-2^k* and *H-2^d* crosses show no differences except that *H-2^k* is slightly more susceptible than *H-2^d*.

The *k/d* recombinant haplotypes analyses suggest two *Dcp* loci, each with a different mechanism. The *K–E$_\alpha$* and/or *Tla–Qa-1* chromosomal subregion affect both maternal and embryonic factors. The *S–Qa-2* subregion affects only an embryonic factor. I carefully choose the word "suggest" because there is some doubt. Uncharted chromosomal regions could be different between these strains (D. Klein *et al.*, 1982). The centromeric and telomeric regions in particular could be *k* or *b* for *H-2^a*, *d* or *b* for *H-2^d*, and *k* or *b* for *H-2^k* (see Table II). These uncharted chromosomal regions leave an element of doubt and uncertainty in mapping studies.

D. THE *a/b* RECOMBINANTS—THREE *Dcp* LOCI

The *a/b* recombinants are more suitable for mapping studies because doubt from uncharted chromosomal regions is mostly elimi-

TABLE VI

DCP Frequency Given as the Arcsine of the
Percentage of Fetuses with Cleft Palate
in the Reciprocal Crosses between
B10.A, B10.D2, and B10.BR

Dose (mg/kg)	Cross[a] ♀ × ♂	DCP arcsine (SE)[b]
160	A × A	53.1 (2.2)
160	A × K	47.4 (3.1)
160	K × A	51.7 (4.3)
160	K × K	33.1 (2.3)
160	A × A	53.1 (2.2)
160	A × D	39.8 (5.4)
160	D × A	29.7 (3.8)
160	D × D	25.0 (2.7)
226	K × K	43.4 (2.3)
226	K × D	36.1 (5.0)
226	D × K	38.1 (6.2)
226	D × D	35.6 (1.8)

[a]A, B10.A; D, B10.D2; K, B10.BR.
[b]SE, Standard error of the mean.

nated. For example, $H\text{-}2^{h4}$, $H\text{-}2^{h2}$, and $H\text{-}2^a$ have the same chromosomal region from the centromere to K, whether it is a or b. Likewise, $H\text{-}2^{i5}$, $H\text{-}2^{i18}$, and $H\text{-}2^b$ have the same region from the centromere to K, which is b. All a/b recombinant congenic strains have the same chromosomal region from $Pgk\text{-}2$ to the telomere.

1. Dcp-1 in C–E_β

The significant difference in DCP susceptibility between $H\text{-}2^a$ and $H\text{-}2^{i5}$ ($p < 0.001$) can be seen by comparing the cleft palate arcsine at 160 mg/kg in Table V (Bonner and Tyan, 1983b). It indicates a Dcp locus somewhere between the centromere (C) and E_β, a chromosomal distance of approximately 15 cM (D. Klein et al., 1982). The end point of this region is in the structural gene for E_β, a class II molecule. The point of recombination in E_β was identified by Steinmetz et al. (1982). A more precise chromosomal position (less than 15 cM) of this locus, tentatively designated $Dcp\text{-}1$, cannot be identified with these congenic strains until markers between C and K are found.

2. Dcp-2 in E_β–S

The second locus, $Dcp\text{-}2$, is in a 0.2-cM chromosomal distance marked by E_β and S. The effect of this locus can be seen in two ways by

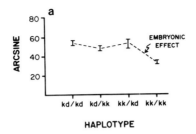

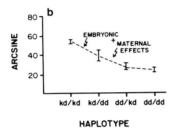

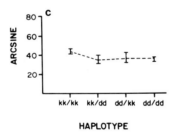

FIG. 4. A graphic representation of the results of the reciprocal cross test with the cleft palate frequency expressed as an arcsine on the y axis and the *H-2* haplotype of the cross on the x axis. The length of the bar is ± standard error of the mean. Crosses are (a) B10.A (kd) and B10.BR (kk): (b) B10.A (kd) and B10.D2 (dd); (c) b10.BR (kk) and B10.D2 (dd). (Reprinted with permission from Bonner and Tyan, 1983a.)

incorporating the data presented here with data from a report by Gasser *et al.* (1981) (see also discussion by Goldman in this volume). The comparison between H-2^{i5} and H-2^{i18} shows a *Dcp* locus with a weak effect on susceptibility in E_β–S. The effect on susceptibility was 36.9–39.7 ($p < 0.05$) cleft palate arcsine at 160 mg/kg. The allelic change was E_β^k–S^d to E_β^b–S^b. In Gasser's report a single dose of cortisone was used to induce cleft palate. A first approximation of susceptibility is possible with this technique. They reported the same pattern of susceptibility that we saw with the dose–response analyses. That is, H-2^a and H-2^{h2} are susceptible; H-2^b, H-2^{i5}, H-2^k, and H-2^d are resistant. The additional allele of interest that they tested was H-2^{h4}. It was found that H-2^{h4} was indistinguishable from H-2^b. The sample size was 10 litters, so a dose–response analysis should confirm the finding. A safe assumption is that the magnitude of the difference between H-2^{h2} and H-2^{h4} is comparable to what we saw between H-2^a and H-2^{i5}. The genetic difference between H-2^{h4} and H-2^{h2} is E_β–S. The allelic change is E_β^k–S^d to E_β^b–S^b, and it had a strong effect on DCP susceptibility.

Why in one case does the allelic change in the E_β–S subregion have a weak effect (that is, the $i5$ and $i18$ comparison) and in another a strong effect (the $h2$ and $h4$ comparison)? There are several possibilities. First, the point of recombination in $i5$ and $h4$ is separated by approximately 5000 nucleotide bases (Steinmetz et al., 1982). A possibility is that the structural difference between the two E_β genes caused by recombination caused different magnitudes of change in DCP susceptibility. This possibility directly implicates E_β as the Dcp gene. Second, if Dcp-1 is not E_β and the point of recombination between $h2$ and $i18$ in the subregion between S and D is the same, the data then suggest an epistatic interaction between Dcp-1 in C–E_β and Dcp-2 in E_β–S. The k allele of C–E_β allows expression of the allelic change at E_β–S, but the b allele of C–E_β suppresses the expression of the allelic change of E_β–S. Third, assuming that the point of recombination between S and D of haplotypes $h2$ and $i18$ is not the same, the point of recombination in $h2$ may be closer to D and it may include a third Dcp locus. In this case the comparison between $h2$ and $h4$ shows the additive effect of allelic changes in Dcp-2 and Dcp-3, but the $i5$ and $i18$ comparison shows the effect of an allelic change at Dcp-2.

3. Dcp-3 in D–Qa-1

The arguments for epistatic interactions and different points of recombination between $h2$ and $i18$ apply to the proposal for a third Dcp locus in the D–Qa-1 subregion. It is a chromosomal distance of 1.7 cM. Evidence for Dcp-3 lies in the comparison between H-2^b and H-2^{i18}. There is a difference between the strains' susceptibility and variance in this comparison (see Table V). The allelic change is D^b–Qa-1^b to D^d–Qa-1^a. Again we have a paradox; this allelic change is the same as in the H-2^a and H-2^{h2} comparison. There is no phenotypic difference between H-2^a and H-2^{h2} ($p > 0.25$) (Bonner and Tyan, 1983b). If points of recombination between $h2$ and $i18$ are the same, then epistasis applies. But if the crossover of $h2$ is different from that of $i18$, then

H-2^a and H-2^{h2} may have the same allele at *Dcp-3* and H-2^b and H-2^{i18} may have different *Dcp-3* alleles. These arguments will be resolved only with the nucleotide sequences of the *S* and *D* subregions that show the points of recombination.

4. Summary

One interpretation of the mapping analyses of the genes linked to *H-2* that affect dexamethasone-induced cleft palate is that there are three loci. The loci are tentatively designated *Dcp*. *Dcp-1* is in the chromosomal region marked by C–E_β; *Dcp-2* is in the region E_β–S; *Dcp-3* is in the subregion D–Qa-1 (see Fig. 5).

Three alleles, H-2^b, H-2^k, and H-2^d, were observed, but the overlap between the recombinants and the uncharted chromosomal subregions precludes distinguishing between the two or three alleles of each *Dcp* locus.

Another interpretation of the data on *a/b* recombinants is that there are two *Dcp* loci. Implicit in this interpretation is that the *Dcp* genes are in the regions of overlap in the analysis of the *a/b* recombinants. The *Dcp-1* locus is gene E_β. *Dcp-2* is in the region between *S* and *D* (see Fig. 5). This conclusion yields a refined map indeed.

E. SEX-ASSOCIATED GENE

Francis (1973) reported that sex-linked genes modify susceptibility to glucocorticoid-induced cleft palate in the mouse. In some inbred

CHROMOSOME 17

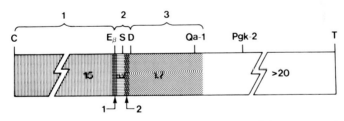

FIG. 5. Graphic representation of the two interpretations of the gene mapping data of the *H-2*-linked dexamethasone-induced cleft palate susceptibility genes (*Dcp* in the text). Across the top are (1) *Dcp-1* in the 15-cM chromosomal segment from the centromere (*C*) to E_β; (2) *Dcp-2* in the 0.2-cM segment from E_β to *D*; and (3) *Dcp-3* in the 1.7-cM segment from *D* to *Qa-1*. The alternative interpretation is that genes are in the regions of chromosomal overlap when comparing the *a/b* recombinant haplotypes. Overlap is marked by the 1 and 2 and the arrows on the bottom of the illustration; in this case *Dcp-1* is the structural gene for E_β and *Dcp-2* is in the chromosomal segment between *S* and *D*.

strains the females have a higher frequency of cortisone-induced cleft palate than males. However, surveys of inbred and congenic strains indicated that expression of high female sensitivity is variable (Loevy, 1972, Biddle and Fraser, 1976; Tyan and Miller, 1978).

The sex of many fetuses in our investigations was determined by internal examination of the gonads. The sex distribution in the fetuses and the results of the G test (Sokol and Rohlf, 1981) for the independent occurrence of sex and cleft palate are shown in Table VII. The only strain with a statistically significant association between sex and DCP was B10.A(18R). Next was B10.A(5R) but the level of confidence was less than 90%.

This observation suggests there is an interaction between the Dcp loci linked to H-2 and a gene associated with sex. The combination of alleles in the H-2^{i18} haplotype allows expression of the sex-associated effect. All others, except H-2^{i5}, hide its expression. The interaction may be epistasis.

V. *H-2* and Craniofacial Anomalies

During experiments to map the Dcp genes linked to H-2, the frequency of other gross craniofacial anomalies was recorded. Two unplanned observations are notable. First, genes associated with H-2 haplotypes influence the frequency of occurrence of exencephaly (EX, incomplete anterior neural tube formation), micrognathia (MG, incomplete jaw formation), and microphthalmia (MI, incomplete eye formation). The second notable observation was that dexamethasone's

TABLE VII

DCP FREQUENCY IN MALES AND FEMALES
OF SIX CONGENIC STRAINS OF MICE

H-2 haplotype	Percentage DCP in females	Percentage DCP in males	G statistic
i18	49	40	6.4, $p < 0.05$
h5	41	34	3.0, $p < 0.1$
b	50	47	0.2, ns[a]
a	33	32	0.1, ns
k	45	46	0.1, ns
h2	42	44	0.3, ns

[a]ns, Not significant.

teratogenic action had no effect on the frequency of these craniofacial birth defects.

An analysis of the *a/b* recombinant haplotypes shows the subregion of chromosome 17 that contains genes affecting the frequency of each anomaly. The frequency of EX is influenced by *C–S*, MG by *C–S* and *D–Qa-1*, and MI by E_β–*Qa-1*. There also seem to be chromosomal interactions between subregions. Other subregions are implicated by the comparisons of the *k/d* recombinant haplotypes, but the uncertainty of the chromosomal differences between these strains preclude serious discussion of the mapping possibilities.

A. DEXAMETHASONE HAS NO EFFECT ON EX, MG, AND MI

Table VIII shows the comparison between increasing doses of dexamethasone and the frequency of occurrence on MI, MG, and EX in strain C57BL/10. There is a considerable amount of variation in the arcsine percent (%) frequency of MI and MG. This number is the number of litters with defective fetuses (the litter is the responding unit) in proportion to the total number of litters in the group. In one group (280 mg/kg) no fetus had MI out of 11 litters, while in another group 6 litters out of 31 had a fetus with MI. A regression analysis was done with a single value of *y* for each value of *x* (Sokol and Rohlf, 1981)

TABLE VIII

DOSE–RESPONSE ANALYSIS: DEXAMETHASONE AND THE
FREQUENCY OF MICROPHTHALMIA, MICROGNATHIA,
AND EXENCEPHALY

Dose (mg/kg)	Total litters	Number of litters with defective fetuses[a]		
		MI	MG	EX
0	20	1 (15.3)	1 (15.3)	0
80	15	3 (27.8)	1 (17.6)	0
120	11	1 (21.0)	5 (42.6)	0
155	31	6 (26.8)	4 (24.5)	1
217	30	5 (24.9)	4 (22.4)	1
280	11	0 (8.4)	1 (20.4)	0
340	18	3 (25.4)	1 (21.2)	0
Total	136	19	17	2

[a]Arcsine values in parentheses. For MI, F (1,4) = 0.83, $p > 0.25$. For MG, F (1,4) = 0.27, $p > 0.5$.

and the results are shown at the bottom of Table VIII. There was no significant regression of the MI or MG frequency on the dose of dexamethasone ($p > 0.25$ and $p > 0.5$). EX was too infrequent to be analyzed, but when one considers all strains and all doses there was no significant regression. This same pattern was seen for seven congenic strains (Bonner *et al.*, 1983). It can be stated with a high degree of confidence that dexamethasone does not influence the frequency of MI, MG, and EX and that our observation is the spontaneous occurrence of these anomalies. At times the anomalies appeared to cluster in incidence in time, but the experiments were not planned with time in mind and a planned observation should be made.

B. EX IN *C–S*

EX occurred the least number of times (see Table IX). Only one fetus per litter ever had the anomaly. The frequency of occurrence among the congenic strains with different *H-2* haplotypes ranged from 0.5% for *H-2^{i18}* to 5.5% for *H-2^a*. There is significant heterogeneity among the frequencies for the strains ($p < 0.025$). The results of the unplanned tests of the homogeneity of replicates tested for goodness of fit using the *G* statistic (Sokol and Rohlf, 1981) are shown at the bottom of Table IX.

Comparisons of the *a/b* recombinant haplotypes indicate the chromosomal subregions that are affecting the frequency of EX. Comparing the *H-2^a* frequency and *H-2^{i18}* frequency, the difference between

TABLE IX

THE FREQUENCY OF OCCURRENCE OF EXENCEPHALY, MICROGNATHIA, AND
MICROPHTHALMIA IN SEVEN *H-2* CONGENIC STRAINS OF MICE

H-2 haplotype	Total litters	Number of litters with defective fetuses[a]		
		MI	MG	EX
k	122	31 (25.4)	10 (8.2)	1 (0.8)
i5	112	29 (24.0)	6 (5.4)	3 (2.7)
a	181	39 (21.5)	13 (7.2)	10 (5.5)
i18	215	36 (16.7)	5 (2.3)	1 (0.5)
h2	128	20 (15.6)	8 (6.3)	2 (1.6)
b	136	19 (14.0)	17 (12.5)	2 (1.5)
d	84	1 (1.2)	1 (1.2)	3 (3.6)

[a]Percentage values in parentheses. For MI, *G* (6) = 37.8, $p < 0.001$. For MG, *G* (6) = 21.0, $p < 0.005$. For EX, *G* (6) = 13.8, $p < 0.025$.

0.5 and 5.5% is significant ($p < 0.005$). The maximal genetic difference between these haplotypes is from the centromere to the S subregion of H-2. There appears to be an epistatic interaction between two loci because the genetic difference between H-2^b and H-2^{h2} is the same chromosomal region, but there is no difference of EX frequency between them.

C. MG in $C-S$ and $D-Qa-1$

MG occurred in frequencies that ranged from 1.2% of H-2^d litters to 12.5% of H-2^b litters. There is significant heterogeneity among the frequencies among the strains ($p < 0.005$) (see Table IX).

There are two strain comparisons that are appropriate for the gene mapping analysis. They are H-2^b compared to H-2^{i18}, and H-2^a compared to H-2^{i18}. The genetic difference between H-2^b and H-2^{i18} is the $D-Qa-1$ subregion and the difference between 12.5 and 2.3% is significant ($p < 0.001$). The maximal genetic difference between H-2^a and H-2^{i18} is $C-S$, and the difference between 2.3 and 7.2% is significant ($p < 0.025$). There is no overlap between the two chromosomal subregions, so a conclusion is that two genes affect the MG frequency. Epistasis applies to the frequency of MG because there is a difference between H-2^b and H-2^{i18} but no difference between H-2^a and H-2^{h2}. Both comparisons, however, have the same genetic difference.

D. MI in $E_\beta-Qa-1$

MI is the most frequently occurring anomaly in these congenic strains of mice. Often it occurs twice in the same litter (Bonner *et al.*, 1983). Approximately 26% of H-2^k litters had the anomaly and only 1.2% of H-2^d litters did. There are strain-associated differences in the frequencies ($p < 0.001$).

The only a/b recombinant comparison with a statistically significant difference is H 2^{i5} and H-2^b, 24 and 14 %, respectively ($p < 0.025$). The genetic difference between them is the $E_\beta-Qa-1$ subregion.

E. Common Features of EX, MG, and MI

These craniofacial anomalies have common features. First, they usually occur in females. Second, sometimes two of the defects will occur together in the same fetus, MI and MG in particular. Third, the birth defects are in organs that are components, extensions, or induced derivatives of the anterior neural tube. Fourth, they occur in a wide range of severity and sometimes border on normality. Fifth, each results from incomplete morphogenesis and growth. Sixth, they do not breed true, at least for MI, and this is probably the case for MG and EX too. EX and usually MG are lethal; neonates die, so a test of inheritance is impossible. Mice with MI usually survive and if they breed, the frequency of MI in their progeny is no different from the inbred strain (Dagg, 1966). MI mice are phenodeviants described in the C57BL/6 and C57BL/10 strains and the occurrence of MI is probably induced by an environmental factor (Dagg, 1966).

One impression is that EX, MG, and MI do not result from mutant genes but are the products of normal genes. The normal genes control morphogenesis, size, and shape of the developing organs and the environment causes variations in the expression of these genes. Mice with these birth defects probably are in the extreme end of a probability distribution graph of variation in size and shape. The genes associated with the H-2 haplotypes cause fluctuations in the shape of the curve so that one strain rarely has a fetus in the MG portion of the graph, for example, while another strain often has one in the "small jaw" end of the graph.

F. A PUZZLING FEATURE

At first glance one would think that these three birth defects are actually varying degrees of severity of the same defect, EX as the most severe case and MI as the least severe. If that were the situation, one would predict that the rank order of the strains would be the same for the defects. In fact the rank order of the strains is not the same for each. MI and MG rarely occur in H-2^d litters, yet H-2^d ranks second in the frequency of EX. Another example is H-2^b. It has the highest frequency of MG but it ranks close to the bottom of the rank for both MI and EX. Even the observation that the defects sometimes occur together in the same fetus should not mislead us because the occurrence of multiple defects may be a function of fetal liability and susceptibility and not a common genetic mechanism for the three birth defects.

It must be stressed that these data demonstrate an association between H-2 haplotypes and the frequency of EX, MG, and MI. The data do not demonstrate linkage. A backcross test must be done to demonstrate that. Without the confirming backcross test, one possible interpretation of the data is that a significant amount of genetic and evolutionary divergence has occurred since these congenic strains were formed. The differences in phenotypes reported here may be the result of random mutations at many points in the genome. And if genetic drift occurs at such a rapid rate, the genetic foundation upon which the concept of congenic strains of mice is built ought to be reevaluated.

VI. *H-2* and Dorsoventral Vaginal Septa

While probing a countless number of females for vaginal plugs for inclusion in the study on birth defects, we noticed that the frequency of dorsoventral vaginal septa (DVS) varied among the *H-2* congenic strains. The data are shown in Table X (Bonner, 1981; Bonner and Tyan, 1983c). DVS occurred most frequently in females with $H\text{-}2^{i5}$ haplotype and least frequently in $H\text{-}2^{a}$ females. Here, too, there are strain-associated differences in the frequencies ($p < 0.001$).

The mapping analysis with the a/b recombinant haplotypes show that two subregions of *H-2* affect the DVS frequency. The maximal genetic difference between $H\text{-}2^{a}$ and $H\text{-}2^{i5}$ is $C\text{-}E_{\beta}$ and the difference in frequency of DVS is significant ($p < 0.001$). The maximal genetic difference between $H\text{-}2^{h2}$ and $H\text{-}2^{a}$ is $D\text{-}Qa\text{-}1$ and the DVS frequency difference is significant ($p < 0.001$). The concept of epistasis applies because the genetic difference between $H\text{-}2^{b}$ and $H\text{-}2^{i18}$ is the same as for $H\text{-}2^{a}$ and $H\text{-}2^{h2}$, yet there is no difference between the DVS frequencies of $H\text{-}2^{b}$ and $H\text{-}2^{i18}$.

The frequency of DVS was also observed in the F_1 females of a cross between B10.A and C57BL/10. There was no difference between the reciprocal crosses (Bonner, 1981), which indicated that there was no maternal effect as in the DCP frequency.

TABLE X

THE FREQUENCY OF DORSOVENTRAL VAGINAL SEPTA
IN SEVEN CONGENIC STRAINS OF MICE[a]

H-2 haplotype	Total females	DVS females	Percentage
i5	166	41	25
h2	182	36	20
b	265	52	20
d	109	20	18
i18	201	34	17
k	161	22	14
a	287	18	6

[a]G (6) = 38.9, $p < 0.001$.

VII. Concluding Remark

Is the link between *H-2* and birth defects coincidental or functional? This is a question of fundamental interest. Functional is the more interesting answer. With this answer a theoretical framework could be built that would describe molecular processes used by the cell to sense and respond to its environment. The theory adapts the immunoglobulin-like molecules of *H-2* to roles as sensors on the cell surface. When the Ig-like molecules sense and bind to arrangements of extracellular molecules or molecules on the surfaces of adjacent cells, the cells respond by differentiating. This process is analogous to the process of antigen recognition by cell interactions in the immune response and lymphocyte differentiation, a glucocorticoid-sensitive process. It is not too far-fetched to believe that "Mother Nature" would use the molecular process of self-recognition of development as the molecular process for nonself recognition in the immune response.

ACKNOWLEDGMENTS

I thank William Harris for editing and the UCLA Word Processing Center for manuscript preparation. The research was supported by Grant DE-05165 from the National Institute for Dental Research.

REFERENCES

Artzt, K., Shin, H. S., and Bennett, D. (1982). *Cell* **28**, 471–476.
Bennett, D. (1980). *Harvey Lect.* **74**, 1–21.
Bennett, D., Boyse, E. A., and Old, L. J. (1972). *In* "Cell Interactions" (L. G. Silvestri, ed.), pp. 247–263. American Elsevier, New York.
Biddle, F. G., and Fraser, F. C. (1976). *Genetics* **84**, 743–754.
Bonner, J. J. (1979). *Birth Defects: Orig. Article Ser.* **15**, 55–88.
Bonner, J. J. (1981), *J. Immunogenet.* **8**, 455–458.
Bonner, J. J., and Slavkin, H. C. (1975). *Immunogenetics* **2**, 214–218.
Bonner, J. J., and Tyan, M. L. (1982). *Teratology* **26**, 213–216.
Bonner, J. J., and Tyan, M. L. (1983a). *Genetics* **103**, 263–276.
Bonner, J. J., and Tyan, M. L. (1983b). In preparation.
Bonner, J.J., and Tyan, M. L. (1983c). *J. Immunogenet.* (in press).
Bonner, J. J., Dixon, A. D., Baumann, A., Riviere, G. R., and Tyan, M. L., (1983). In preparation.
Boyse, E. A., and Cantor, H. (1978). *Birth Defects: Orig. Article Ser.* **14**, 249–269.
Dagg, C. P. (1966). *In* "Biology of the Laboratory Mouse" (E. L. Green ed.), pp. 309–328. McGraw-Hill, New York.
Gasser, D. L., Mele, D., Lees, D. D., and Goldman, A. S. (1981). *Proc. Natl. Acad. Sci. U.S.A.* **78**, 3147–3150.
Francis, B. M. (1973). *Teratology* **7**, 119–126.
Kalter, H. (1965). *In* "Teratology: Principles and Techniques" (J.G. Wilson and J. Warkany, eds.), pp. 57–79. Univ. of Chicago Press, Chicago.

Klein, J. (1975). "Biology of the Mouse Histocompatibility-2 Complex." Springer-Verlag, Berlin and New York.

Klein, J., Juretic, A., Baxevanis, C. N., and Nagy, Z. A. (1981). *Nature (London)* **291**, 455–460.

Klein, J., Mursic, M., and Nagy, Z. A. (1982). *Transplant. Proc.* **16**, 581–582.

Klein, D., Tewarson, S. Figueroa, F., and Klein, J. (1982). *Immunogenetics* **16**, 319–328.

Loevy, H. T. (1972). *J. Dent. Res.* **51**, 1010–1014.

Melnick, M., Jaskoll, T., and Slavkin, H. C. (1981). *Immunogenetics* **13**, 443–449.

Nadeau, J., Collins, R. L., and Klein, J. (1982). *Genetics* **102**, 583–596.

Palm, J. (1974). *Cancer Res.* **34**, 2061–2063.

Pease, L. R., Nathenson, S. G., and Leinwand, L. A. (1982). *Nature (London)* **298**, 382–385.

Roos, M. H., Atkinson, J. P., and Shreffler, D. C. (1978). *J. Immunol.* **121**, 1106–1115.

Snell, G. D. (1980). *Harvey Lect.* **74**, 49–80.

Snell, G. D. (1981). *Science* **213**, 172–178.

Snell, G. D., Dausset, J., and Nathenson, S. (1976). "Histocompatibility." Academic Press, New York.

Sokol, R. R., and Rohlf, F. J. (1981). "Biometry." Freeman, San Francisco.

Steinmetz, M., Minard, K., Horvath, S., McNicholas, J., Frelinger, J., Wake, C., Long, E., Mach, B., and Hood, L. (1982). *Nature (London)* **300**, 3b/42.

Stimpfling, J. H., and Richardson, A. (1965). *Genetics* **51**, 831–846.

Tyan, M. L., and Miller, K. K. (1978). *Proc. Soc. Exp. Biol. Med.* **158**, 618–621.

Zinernagel, R. M., and Doherty, P. C. (1975). *J. Exp. Med.* **141**, 1427–1436.

CHAPTER 10

BIOCHEMICAL MECHANISM OF GLUCOCORTICOID- AND PHENYTOIN-INDUCED CLEFT PALATE

Allen S. Goldman

SECTION OF TERATOLOGY
DIVISION OF CHILD DEVELOPMENT AND REHABILITATION
THE CHILDREN'S HOSPITAL OF PHILADELPHIA, AND DEPARTMENT OF PEDIATRICS
UNIVERSITY OF PENNSYLVANIA SCHOOL OF MEDICINE
PHILADELPHIA, PENNSYLVANIA

I. Introduction

The process of mammalian development can be considered as a series of genetically preprogrammed instructions carried in the structure of the DNA of the zygote. These instructions regulate all the biochemical transformations necessary to obtain the chemical diversity of the adult at specified critical periods. The complexity of the human developmental program is extraordinary; the fertilized human egg contains 100 billion bits of information, calculated on the basis of the diversity of H, C, O, and N atoms in a cubic millimeter of the zygote (Dancoff and Quastler, 1953) and on the basis of the diversity of the nucleotide pairs in the DNA in the human chromosomes (Britten and

CURRENT TOPICS IN DEVELOPMENTAL BIOLOGY, VOL. 19

ISBN 0-12-153119-8

Davidson, 1969). A single letter of the alphabet is defined as 6 bits (binary digits). The information content of a single page is 10,000 bits. Thus, the complexity of the program of human differentiation is equivalent to 10 million printed pages, or the contents of a huge library. The Viking landers that arrived on the surface of Mars in 1976 had preprogrammed instructions of a few million bits, or an information content between that of a bacterium and an alga. If the errors of programming are added to the errors caused by nongenetic miscues or external insults, due to drugs for example, the complexity of development appears infinite. Considering this enormous complexity, it is astonishing that errors in the developmental program are so few, amounting at most to 7% of live births.

How do teratogens interfere with the developmental program? They most probably disrupt the preprogrammed instructions contained in the human zygote at the critical periods of development. They probably do this by producing an abnormal amount (high or low) of a substance which is required for, or which can interfere with, the developmental program. Martians interested in learning how the Viking landers work might try to disrupt the preprogrammed instructions. If they did so with a sledge hammer, they would not learn as much as they would if they stopped the program at the level of certain transistors in a very sophisticated manner, such as with an antigen–antibody reaction. Unfortunately, almost all of our understanding of agents known to affect human differentiation is of the sledge hammer type.

II. Androgens and Sexual Differentiation

It was a mistake of nature, congenital adrenal hyperplasia, a human genetic deficiency of one of several steroid-synthesizing enzymes, which contributed to the unraveling of the first molecular mechanism of human differentiation, that of sexual differention. The search to create an animal model to duplicate the genital defects of this disease with specific enzyme inhibitors led to the development of the kind of specific probes of embryonic differentiation mentioned above. Space does not allow the tracing of the details of the unraveling of this developmental program, which I have described elsewhere (Goldman, 1977), but suffice it to say that this developmental program involves the hormonal control of human sexual differentiation. The understanding of this control has been advanced by studies using specific natural and experimental fetal hormone-depriving agents as "antibody-to-transistor" type probes (Goldman, 1977).

These studies indicated that the program of male differentiation appears to be directed by fetal testosterone through the same chain of molecular events by which testosterone produces its hormonal action in the adult, with the exception that in the embryo the events are irreversible. The chain of events is initiated genetically at different critical periods. Gonadotropically stimulated testicular synthesis of testosterone makes a complex of androgen–receptor protein in the cytosol of various target organ cells. After incorporation into target organ nuclei, the androgen–receptor complexes cause DNA- and RNA directed synthesis of male-specific proteins. Interference with this program at any of the variety of sites involving embryonic testosterone, in either the synthesis, circulation, or its uptake or action in the target organs, allows the inborn female program to be expressed. This interference can be effected by antibodies to gonadotropins, selective inhibitors of certain testosterone biosynthetic enzymes, antibodies to testosterone, or antihormone blockers of receptor protein, as well as genetic deficiencies of testosterone biosynthetic enzymes (congenital adrenal hyperplasia) or of androgen receptor proteins (testicular feminization). In this developmental program, androgen is required for normal masculine differentiation, and interference with androgen synthesis or with the androgen–receptor complex or its nuclear uptake blocks the induction of the masculine program, thereby allowing readout of the inborn female program. These studies made several interesting suggestions that possibly may be applied to other developmental systems: (1) Interference with hormonal receptor proteins in target organs can lead to malformations. (2) Specific probes can be found which are able to "turn off" or "turn on" hormonal functions in differentiation. (3) The teratogenic action can be reversed by bypassing the blocked biosynthetic pathway and replacing the missing hormonal precursor or product at the next step.

III. Glucocorticoids and Cleft Palate

The experimental production of cleft palate by glucocorticoids in sensitive and resistant inbred mouse strains is one of the most intensively studied animal models of congenital malformations since its discovery over 35 years ago (Greene and Kochhar, 1975). This model appeared to be a very promising developmental error for unraveling the molecular mechanism as suggested above. Glucocorticoids are hormones, and induction of *de novo* protein synthesis appears to be a common mechanism of action of corticoids in a variety of tissues and physiologic processes (Baxter *et al.,* 1971; Baxter and Forsham, 1972).

This induction is initiated by a specific cytoplasmic corticoid–receptor system in target tissues (Baxter and Forsham, 1972). The hormone–receptor complex then interacts with the genome, resulting in activation or depression of transcription (Dahmus and Bonner, 1965; Beato *et al.,* 1969; Baxter and Funder, 1979). Thus, it appears that corticosteriods have a molecular basis involved in their action in adult tissues that is similar to that of androgens.

A. Glucocorticoids, Inflammation, and Cleft Palate

Glucocorticoids with anti-inflammatory activity prevent the release of the precursor acid, arachidonic acid, whereas cyclooxygenase inhibitors, such as aspirin, inhibit the transformation of this acid into prostaglandins and thromboxanes (Fig. 1). The steroid-induced inhibition of arachidonic acid release, proposed to be due to formation of peptide inhibitors (phospholipase-inhibitory proteins) of phospholipase A_2, prevent formation of not only prostaglandins and thromboxanes but also leukotrienes and other oxygenated derivatives (Blackwell *et al.,* 1980; Hirata *et al.,* 1980). Since the cleft palate teratogenicity of glucocorticoids is known to be correlated with their anti-inflammatory potency (Pinsky and DiGeorge, 1965; Walker, 1971) and since the degree of inhibition of the arachidonic acid pathway by glucocorticoids is directly related to their anti-inflammatory potency (Tam *et al.,* 1977),

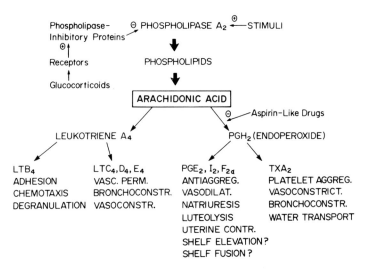

Fig. 1. Arachidonic acid: schematic depicting its metabolic derivation, end products, and their physiological effects. Inhibitors and promoters affecting the pathway are marked as − and +, respectively.

the possibility should be considered that the teratogenic and anti-inflammatory effects of glucocorticoids could involve some of the same biochemical reactions, although other pathways may be involved as well.

Thus, if one followed these glucocorticoid-mediated pathways, one would have an idea of which compounds may "reverse" teratogenicity and which may again "turn off" the developmental program. If inhibition of the arachidonic acid pathway by glucocorticoids is involved in their teratogenic action, it is reasonable to assume that the reaction would correspond to susceptibility, i.e., one may expect a greater response of this pathway in sensitive strains and a lesser or absent response in resistant strains. This type of approach should lead to an understanding of at least one pathway of the basic molecular mechanisms underlying the process of palatogenesis and teratogenicity of palatal formation. This pathway, then, in our hypothesis should include glucocorticoid receptors and the anti-inflammatory biochemical pathway. Moreover, cortexolone, an 11β-dehydroxy analog of the rodent glucocorticoid corticosterone is an antiglucocorticoid which acts at the level of the receptor *in vitro* and prevents glucocorticoid action *in vitro* (Kaiser *et al.*, 1972; Turnell *et al.*, 1974). Inhibitors of protein synthesis, such as cycloheximide, inhibit glucocorticoid anti-inflammatory action (Blackwell *et al.*, 1980). Thus, the teratogenic action should be blocked by cycloheximide and by cortexolone, if the teratogenic action is receptor mediated and involves protein synthesis.

B. Genetics of Cleft Palate Susceptibility

1. *H-2 on Chromosome 17*

Most examples of cleft palate have been explained by the interaction of several genes and several environmental factors. Biddle and Fraser (1977) also concluded from their genetic studies that at least two or three loci, possibly with independent effects, appear to explain the differences in the phenotype of susceptibility to glucocorticoid-induced cleft palate. Nongenetic factors such as the type of food used (Miller, 1977) or the amount of stress the mothers receive (Hemm *et al.*, 1977) are known to influence this trait, but in spite of these effects, there is general agreement among investigators concerning the relative susceptibilities of various inbred strains. A major breakthrough in identifying genetic influences on susceptibility was the discovery by Bonner and Slavkin (1975) of a role of the *H-2* histocompatibility complex on the mouse chromosome 17. This complex is a group of genes controlling transplantation antigens and several other functions (Gasser and Goldman, 1983). Thus, the B10.A congenic strain, which has the same *H-2* haplotype as the highly susceptible A/J strain but the background of the C57BL/10 (or B10) strain, is significantly more susceptible than the B10 strain. These findings have been confirmed in several laboratories (Biddle and Fraser, 1977; Tyan and Miller, 1978; Gasser *et al.*, 1980, 1981; Melnick *et al.*, 1981; see the discussions by Vekemans and Biddle, and by Bonner, this volume).

2. *H-3 on Chromosome 2*

Another gene involved in determining susceptibility is closely linked to the *H-3* locus on the second chromosome (Gasser *et al.*, 1980, 1981). This was shown by the demonstration that two congenic strains, B10.LP and B10.LP-*H-3^b*, are significantly more susceptible than their inbred partner strain, B10. These congenic strains have the same genetic background as B10, but have a short chromosomal segment from LP/J which includes the *H-3* histocompatibility locus and the *Ir-2* immune response gene, and the allele for susceptibility is *H-3^b* (B10.LP and B10.LP-*H-3^b*) and that for resistance is *H-3^a* (B10). The gene for β_2-microglobulin, which is associated on the cell surface with a number of *H-2*-linked antigens, is also linked to *H-3* (Michaelson, 1981).

3. *Other Genes*

The importance of non-*H-2*-linked genes is illustrated by the observation that the susceptibility of strain C3H (*H-2^k, H-3^b*) is much greater than that of CBA (*H-2^k, H-3$^{not\ a\ or\ b}$*) (Kalter, 1965), and that of ABY (*H-2^b, H-3$^{not\ a\ or\ b}$*) is much greater than that of B10 (*H-2^b, H-3^a*) (Gasser and Goldman, 1983). It is possible that the increased susceptibility of C3H is due to its *H-3^b* allele, but the results with ABY and B10 indicate that there is still at least one other genetic system affecting susceptibility. Using recombinant inbred strains derived from the cross of strains DBA/2J (*H-2^d, H-3^b*) and C57BL/6J (*H-2^b, H-3^a*) and various chromosomal markers, Vekemans and co-workers suggested involvement of a gene in cortisone-induced cleft palate at one time on chromosome 9 (Vekemans *et al.*, 1978), at another on chromosome 2 (Vekemans and Fraser, 1980), and still at another time on chromosome 5 (Vekemans *et al.*, 1981). The difference in susceptibility between these two strains may also be explained at least in part by the fact that the susceptible strain has a resistant *H-2* allele but a susceptible *H-3* allele on chromosome 2 compared to the C57BL/6J. In any case the number of genes that affect this trait could be quite large.

4. Mapping Susceptibility within the H-2 Complex

We have used congenic strains of mice with the genetic background of the A/J or B10 mice in order to determine which part of the H-2 region may be involved in susceptibility to glucocorticoid-induced cleft palate (Gasser *et al.*, 1980, 1981; Gasser and Goldman, 1983). Table I shows a map of the mouse H-2 and H-3 regions and genotypes of the various congenic strains. These experiments demonstrated that the rank of susceptibility of congenic strains, which have genetic differences only at H-2, is B10.A (H-2^a) = B10.Q (H-2^q) = B10.S (H-2^s) > B10.BR (H-2^k) > B10 (H-2^b) > B10.D2 (H-2^d) (Gasser *et al.*, 1980, 1981).

The H-2^a haplotype of the highly susceptible A/J strain (Kalter, 1954) originated in the AWySn strain, which is one of the many A substrains. The haplotype probably is a recombinant between a strain bearing H-2^k and H-2^d. The subregion H-$2K$ to H-$2E$ has the k allele and I-C to H-$2D$ has the d allele (Table I). The best interpretation of our data supports the conclusion of Tyan and Miller (1978) that at least two H-2-linked loci are involved in controlling susceptibility (Gasser and Goldman, 1983). One of these genes appears to map in the H-$2B$ region, since B10.A(4R) and B10.A(5R) have low susceptibilities,

TABLE I

H-2 AND *H-3* REGIONS

Strain	*H-2* Alleles								*H-3* Alleles			
	K	A	B	J	E	C	S	D	*H-3*	*Ir-2*	*H-13*	A
B10	b	b	b	b	b	b	b	b	a	a	a	a
B10.A	k	k	k	k	k	d	d	d	a	a	a	a
B10.BR	k	k	k	k	k	k	k	k	a	a	a	a
B10.D2	d	d	d	d	d	d	d	d	a	a	a	a
B10.A(2R)	k	k	k	k	k	d	d	b	a	a	a	a
B10.A(5R)	b	b	k	k	k	d	d	d	a	a	a	a
B10.A(4R)	k	k	b	b	b	b	b	b	a	a	a	a
B10.A(18R)	b	b	b	b	b	b	b	d	a	a	a	a
A/J	k	k	k	k	k	d	d	d		not *a* or *b*		
AWY	k	k	k	k	k	d	d	d		not *a* or *b*		
ABY	b	b	b	b	b	b	b	b		not *a* or *b*		
B10	b	b	b	b	b	b	b·	b	a	a	a	a
B10.LP	b	b	b	b	b	b	b	b	b	b	b	A^w
B10.LP-*H-3^b*	b	b	b	b	b	b	b	b	b	b	a	a

whereas B10.A and B10.A(2R) have high susceptibility levels. If the *B* locus does not exist, as appears likely (Gasser and Goldman, 1983), our results can only be explained by complementary effects of at least two genes. High susceptibility would be determined by a *k* gene in the *K/A* region in combination with a *d* gene in the *C/S/D* region. Even if the *B* locus does exist, our comparison of the B10, B10.BR, B10.D2, and B10.A strains can only be explained by the action of two complementary genes, one to the left of *C* and the other to the right of *E*. In a recent study Bonner and Tyan (1982) mapped susceptibility of cleft palate produced by a single dose of dexamethasone (160 mg/kg on day 12 of gestation) rather than the four daily doses of cortisone (100 mg/kg on days 11/14 of gestation) used in the other studies. They also used the B10.A(18R) strain, which has the *b* allele in the *K–S* region and the *d* allele in the *D* region. Since the degree of clefting produced by dexamethasone in this strain was significantly higher than that in the B10 strain, these authors concluded that one of the genes is in the *D* region. However, since they found a significant difference between the susceptibility of B10.A(5R) and B10 unlike any found in the studies using cortisone (Tyan and Miller, 1978; Gasser *et al.*, 1980, 1981), this observation needs to be confirmed.

At any rate susceptibility to cortisone-induced cleft palate seems to be determined by *H-2*-linked genes which act by complementation, a characteristic that is well documented for the antigen-coding genes in the central regions of *H-2*. The simplest explanation for the results obtained so far would seem to be that the antigen-coding genes themselves are responsible for the effect on susceptibility to glucocorticoid-induced cleft palate. Whether this results from an effect of these antigens on hormone binding (Svejgaard and Ryder, 1976) or perhaps derives from the concept that the ancestral function of MHC gene products is the regulation of cell interactions (Snell, 1981) has not been determined.

The general conclusion emerging from a variety of studies is that both the *H-2* and *H-3* regions include a number of genes which control lymphocyte antigens and immunologic responsiveness. The fact that both regions also include genes for susceptibility to glucocorticoid induced cleft palate could be coincidental, or it could have biological significance. Which of these alternatives is correct can only be determined by future investigations. The mechanism by which immune responses are controlled by *H-3*-linked *Ir* genes has not been fully elucidated, but we find it most interesting that susceptibility to cortisone-induced cleft palate should be controlled by genes closely linked to *Ir* genes in both chromosomes 17 and 2.

5. H-2 and Hormonal Functions

Genes linked to *H-2* are known to affect some androgen-dependent traits (Ivanyi, 1978). The B10.A strain has higher testis, thymus, and lymph gland weights but lower seminal vesicular weights. A gene controlling the androgen-dependent trait was localized to the left of the *S* region in the vicinity of the *K* region of the *H-2* complex. The plasma concentration of testosterone, testosterone-binding capacity, and responses to testosterone have also been shown to be dependent upon the *H-2* haplotype (Ivanyi, 1978). In these studies B10.A has a higher concentration of plasma testosterone, a higher capacity to bind testosterone, and a higher response to injected testosterone than does B10.

It has recently been shown that there are *H-2* dependent differences in the proportion of cortisone-sensitive lymphoid cells and these differences are determined by *H-2*-linked genes (Pla *et al.*, 1976; Tyan, 1979). A similar situation occurs in humans, and lymphocytes from HLA-B12 persons require less prednisolone to inhibit PHA-induced transformation than lymphocytes of other persons (Becker *et al.*, 1976). The levels of cyclic AMP in the liver are influenced by *H-2* (Meruelo and Edidin, 1975), and this is now known to be the result of an *H-2*-linked effect on glucagon receptors (Lafuse and Edidin, 1980). An effect of *H-2* on the quantity of estrogen receptors in the uterus (Palumbo and Vladutiu, 1979) and on insulin receptor levels (Lafuse, 1978) has also been reported. It has been suggested that histocompatibility antigens could mimic hormone receptors and could interfere with hormone binding (Svejgaard and Ryder, 1976). The only direct evidence in favor of this hypothesis so far is the report that binding of both insulin and glucagon could be inhibited by anti-*H-2* sera (Meruelo and Edidin, 1980).

It is difficult to conceive of the mechanism by which these effects could result from the modifications in the immune response that the *H-2* region is known to control, but it has now been shown that the levels of cyclic AMP and presumably glucagon receptors (Lafuse and Edidin, 1980) and glucocorticoid-induced thymolytic activity (Pla *et al.*, 1976; Tyan, 1979), as well as susceptibility to cortisone-induced cleft palate, are controlled by genes that map within the *I* region and involve genetic complementation. Because the only gene products that have been identified so far as having these properties are Ia antigens, the possibility should be considered that Ia antigens might be involved in the structure or regulation of hormone receptors (Meruelo and Edidin, 1980). If this is not correct, then there seem to be other genes within the *I* region that play this role.

C. Glucocorticoid Receptors and Clefting

Before returning to our hypothesis that the teratogenic action of glucocorticoids may be receptor mediated, it should be pointed out that genetic differences in fetal or maternal glucocorticoids are not apparently involved in susceptibility. Endogenous concentrations in maternal plasma or embryos of corticosterone, the major glucocorticoid in the mouse, did not differ significantly between the A/J and C57BL/6J (genetically equivalent to B10) strains (Salomon *et al.*, 1978).

However, there is evidence that genetic differences in susceptibility to glucocorticoid-induced cleft palate may be related to differences in the quantity of glucocorticoid receptors. The first indication of genetic differences in cortisone binding was reported about 15 years ago when it was shown that after administration of [^{14}C]cortisone to mice on day 11 of gestation there was a significantly higher total fetal retention of label in the cleft palate-susceptible A/J strain than in the insensitive CBA strain (Levine *et al.*, 1968). These observations were extended some 5 years later by experiments showing that 30 minutes after injection of [^{14}C]cortisol on day 12.5 methanol-insoluble (tightly bound) label was significantly higher in A/J fetuses than in C57BL fetuses, while there were no significant differences in methanol and water-soluble (conjugated) label (Reminga and Avery, 1972). Based on these findings, these investigators suggested that differences in the binding of corticosteroids to fetal tissue proteins (possibly directly in the palatal primordium) rather than in corticosteroid metabolism may explain in part the differential teratogenic sensitivity to corticosteroids of different mouse strains. Furthermore, synthetic corticoids are recovered in the unmetabolized state from embryonic A/J tissues (Zimmerman and Bowen, 1972) and inhibit embryonic RNA and protein synthesis at the critical period of cleft palate production (Zimmerman *et al.*, 1970). A/J embryos are more sensitive to an inhibition of RNA synthesis than are those of the C3H/HeJ strain (Andrew *et al.*, 1973) and the effect is not due to a difference in metabolism of the steroid by A/J and C3H/HeJ strains (Zimmerman and Bowen, 1972). These observations led to experiments by Goldman *et al.* (1976, 1977), who measured the amounts of cytosolic [1,2,6,7-^{3}H]cortisol-binding proteins in embryonic palatal tissues of various strains by gel filtration and isoelectric focusing, taking into account that differences in glucocorticoid hormonal responses have been explained in other tissues as being due to variations in receptor levels (Baxter and Funder, 1979; Baxter *et al.*, 1971). The sensitive A/J palatal cytosol had a higher receptor level than the resistant CBA strain had (Goldman *et al.*, 1976). The A/J and DBA/1J strains, which are highly susceptible to cortisone-induced cleft palate, had a prominent peak of cortisol-binding protein at a p*I* of approximately 6.9–7.0 (Goldman *et al.*, 1977). Other strains which are less susceptible had significantly lower amounts of activity at this peak. Since the B10.A congenic strain had approximately twice the amount of material in this peak as the parental B10 strain had, it was suggested that the cortisol-binding protein observed either was coded by a gene closely linked to *H-2*, or was coded elsewhere in the genome but was affected in some way by an *H-2*-linked gene. It was subsequently shown that the locus for the major glucocorticoid receptor is on chromosome 18 (Francke and Gehring, 1980). Therefore, the *H-2*-linked gene on chromosome 17 either codes for a different receptor or, what is more likely, has an indirect effect on the major receptor to increase its level.

Recently, we have mapped within the *H-2* complex receptor level using [³H]dexamethasone (Katsumata *et al.*, 1981a). Compared to cortisol, dexamethasone is more tightly bound to the receptor, binds poorly to ligandin (Litwack *et al.*, 1973), does not bind to transcortin (Rousseau *et al.*, 1972), and stabilizes the receptor (Schmid *et al.*, 1976). In these experiments, cytosols were incubated with various concentrations of [³H]dexamethasone in the presence or absence of 20 μ*M* nonradioactive dexamethasone in a classical Scatchard analysis of receptor level. The observations are summarized as follows: (1) [³H]dexamethasone binding is significantly greater in embryonic jaw cytosols from B10.A and 2R mice than from B10 and 5R strains, respectively; (2) no significant differences were observed in cytosols from adult liver; and (3) primary cell cultures were prepared from palates and maxillary processes of B10.A and B10 fetuses. The amount of dexamethasone binding was significantly greater in the cytosols from B10.A cells than from B10 cells. The amount of [³H]dexamethasone measured in the nuclei of these cells was also significantly greater in the B10.A than B10 strains. The absence of the difference in the liver was in agreement with the observations of Butley *et al.* (1978). The p*I* 7.0 protein bound to dexamethasone is a candidate for the receptor, inasmuch as it was bound to DNA cellulose, and the level of this receptor was significantly higher in the embryonic palates of B10.A mice than in those of B10 mice (Katsumata *et al.*, 1981a).

Evidence in agreement with our findings was reported independently by Salomon and Pratt (1976) to the effect that embryonic A/J facial mesenchymal cells contain about twice the amount of saturable dexamethasone receptors as those of C57BL/6J obtained either directly or in primary culture. These investigators have extended these findings and have shown that specific binding of [³H]dexamethasone to embryonic maxillary cytosol is correlated with susceptibility in several inbred strains (Salomon and Pratt, 1979) in confirmation of our findings (Goldman *et al.*, 1977), but they did not investigate the role of *H-2*. It is not possible at this point to conclude unequivocally that the high susceptibility of A/J and B10.A can be attributed excusively to their relatively high levels of glucocorticoid receptors, but enough data have been accumulated to accept the correlation of palatal glucocorticoid receptor levels in several strains of mice with the degree of cortisone-induced cleft palate and the fact that genes controlling embryonic palatal glucocorticoid receptor levels map in the same portion of the *H-2* chromosome as do those controlling susceptibility to cortisone-induced cleft palate.

Some results with triamcinolone acetonide have not been in agreement with our findings. Although Zimmerman and Bowen (1972) showed that embryos of the CBA strain retained unmetabolized [³H]triamcinolone acetonide to about 60% of the level of the more sensitive strains C3H and A/J, Hackney (1980) reported that receptor binding of [³H]triamcinolone acetonide in mouse embryo heads was lower in the A/J strain than in C3H and CBA. Hackney also showed that the dose–response curves for triamcinolone acetonide-induced cleft palate were not parallel in these strains as they were for cortisone, suggesting that cleft palate induction by triamcinolone acetonide may involve slightly different mechanisms than those involved in cortisone-induced cleft palate.

It is not clear at this point how important the receptor level is in determining the *H-2*-linked susceptibility difference, but it is interesting that the same two sets of genes in *H-2* seem to be involved in both of these traits. It may also be relevant that other hormone receptors are apparently influenced by the *H-2* region, such as the level of insulin and glucagon receptors (Lafuse and Edidin, 1980) and several other hormone-associated phenomena (Ivanyi, 1978). Even if the high susceptibility of A/J and B10.A mice is related to a higher level of glucocorticoid receptor than that which is present in less sensitive strains, this clearly is not the only mechanism involved in the genetic determination of susceptibility. Mice that are homozygous for the brachymorph (*bm*) mutation are as susceptible to cortisone-induced cleft palate as A/J mice are, but the level of glucocorticoid receptor in the *bm/bm* palate on day 14 was the same as the low level found in the C57BL6 (B6) palate (Pratt *et al.*, 1980). In this case the increased susceptibility to cortisone-induced cleft palate that the *bm/bm* gene imparts to the C57 mouse may be related to a defect in sulfation of cartilage proteoglycans due to deficient 3′-phosphoadenosine 5′-phosphosulfate synthesis secondary to deficient adenosine 5-phosphosulfate kinase and ATP sulfurylase (Sugahara and Schwartz, 1981a, b). Moreover, a variety of other genes having no histocompatibility function may have an effect on the number of hormone receptors but not be the genes coding for the receptors themselves. For example, the quantity of insulin receptor sites per cell is affected by genes closely linked to the albino locus in mice, although the insulin receptor itself does not seem to map in this region (Goldfeld et al., 1981). It is interesting that one of the radiation-induced lethal deletions of these genes near the albino locus on chromosome 7 produces a severe deficiency of insulin receptors and insulin responses as well as a severe deficiency of glucocorticoid receptors and glucocorticoid responses (Goldfeld et al., 1981).

Tissue Distribution of H-2 Influence on Receptor Level

Initial studies indicated general agreement by different methods and different ligands for receptor measurements that there was a correlation of receptor level in embryonic palatal tissues or maxillary cell cytosols with susceptibility (Goldman et al., 1976, 1977; Goldman and Katsumata, 1980; Salomon and Pratt, 1977, 1979; Salomon et al., 1978; Katsumata et al., 1981a). There was an H-2 influence on maternal palatal receptor level (Goldman et al., 1977), but no receptor level difference could be shown in forepaws between A/J (H-2^a) embryos and B6 (H-2^b) embryos (Salomon and Pratt, 1979). The next tissue to be examined by Salomon et al. (1978) was the liver. They showed a significant difference in receptor level (50–100 fmol/mg protein) in maternal livers between A/J and B6 on day 12 but not on days 13 or 14 using a dilution ratio of 2–3× buffer to liver in preparation of the cytosol. Butley et al. (1978), using a dilution ratio of 10 to 1, found a much higher hepatic receptor level (1200 fmol/mg protein) and a significantly higher level in males of the A/J (H-2^a) and ABY (H-2^b) than in males of the B10.A (H-2^a) and B10 (H-2^b) but not between H-2^a or H-2^b with either genetic background. When we used a high dilution ratio of 8 to 1 (Goldman and Katsumata, 1980), we obtained significantly higher hepatic receptor levels (~1000 fmol/mg protein) in A/J (H-2^a) females and in B10.A (H-2^a) females than in B10 (H-2^b) females. However, when we used a much lower dilution ratio of 2 to 1, we found much lower hepatic receptor levels (~300 fmol/mg protein) and no significant effect of H-2 (Katsumata et al., 1981a,b).

These discrepant results concerning hepatic receptor level and H-2 effects appeared to us to be possibly due to differences in dilution of the cytosol and suggested studies to determine whether the liver may have an *H-2*-dependent endogenous modifier of receptor binding. Evidence that such is the case was obtained from studies using a mathematical analysis, partial removal of the modifier(s) by gel filtration, and mixing of cytosols of the two types of strains [B10.A and B10.A(2R) versus (B10 and B10.A(5R)] (Katsumata *et al.*, 1981b). The results indicated that the nonsusceptible strains [B10 and B10.A(5R)] contained more of the modifier which increased the degree of hepatic binding than the susceptible strains [B10.A and B10.A(2R)], thus making it difficult to determine whether hepatic receptor level is influenced by *H-2*. This modifier is heat-labile (Goldman, to be reported) and not the *H-2*-independent, heat-stable glucocorticoid receptor stabilizing factor (Leach *et al.*, 1982).

The recent reports of Pla *et al.* (1976) and Tyan (1979) demonstrate that *H-2* regulates the thymolytic action of glucocorticoids in mice, and susceptibility to this action of glucocorticoids also appears to result from a complementation of the same genes in *H-2* as are involved in cleft palate susceptibility (Tyan, 1979). These observations led us to determine whether *H-2* influences receptor levels in thymocytes as well as the degree of inhibition of radioimmunoassayable prostaglandins and thromboxanes produced by glucocorticoids (Gupta and Goldman, 1982). The thymocytes and lungs of the B10.A strain of mice have significantly higher glucocorticoid receptor levels and a significantly greater degree of inhibition of production of three prostaglandins (6-keto-prostaglandin $F_{1\alpha}$, the stable metabolite of prostacyclin; prostaglandin E_2; and prostaglandin $F_{2\alpha}$) and thromboxane B_2 (the stable metabolite of thromboxane A_2) than those of the B10 strain. Thus, the anti-inflammatory hormonal response correlated to hormone receptor level in these two other tissues, and both degree of response and receptor level in these tissues are influenced by the *H-2* complex.

D. ARACHIDONIC ACID CASCADE AND CLEFTING

If glucocorticoids inhibit the release of arachidonic acid and subsequent prostaglandin production in their teratogenic action, one may expect that coadministration of arachidonic acid with glucocorticoid may reverse the teratogenic action of glucocorticoids. Evidence supporting the hypothesis that glucocorticoids induce palatal clefting by blocking the release of arachidonic acid is given in the experiments of Tzortzatou *et al.* (1981). Exogenous arachidonic acid given at the same time as dexamethasone produced a significant reduction in the percentage of rats fetuses with cleft palate. The effect of exogenous arachidonic acid on dexamethasone-induced cleft palate was reversed by treatment with indomethacin. Since this drug is an inhibitor of cyclooxygenase (Vane, 1971; Flower *et al.*, 1973), this observation supports the proposal that reduction in the quantities of prostaglandins and/or thromboxanes (rather than leukotrienes, see Fig. 1) is teratogenic in the palate. Finally, dexamethasone was also shown to inhibit the release of labeled free arachidonic acid from the precipitable fraction of rat embryonic jaws, suggesting that there was less arachidonic acid available to the microsomal cyclooxygenase in the supernatant fraction. These experiments were all done in rats, but it has also been shown that arachidonic acid reduces the clefting action of cortisone in sensitive strains of mice (Piddington *et al.*, 1983).

The hypothesis that the clefting action of glucocorticoids involves a reduction in the production of prostaglandins and/or thromboxanes makes one wonder whether these agents may be involved in normal palatal differentiation. Primary cultures of mouse embryo palatal mesenchymal cells can be stimulated to produce several prostaglandins from labeled arachidonic acid *in vitro* (Chepenik and Greene, 1981). If prostaglandins or thromboxanes are involved in normal palatal differentiation, one would expect palatal clefting to be produced by indomethacin and other nonsteroidal anti-inflammatory inhibitors of cyclooxygenase, such as aspirin and phenylbutazone (Vane, 1971; Flower *et al.*, 1973). Indomethacin does not produce cleft palate in mice *in vivo* (Kalter, 1973) but only blocks the corrective action of arachidonic acid on dexamethasone-induced clefting (Tzortzatou *et al.*, 1981), probably due to its limited passage across the placenta (Scott and Klein, 1981). Aspirin and phenylbutazone, two other inhibitors of cyclooxygenase, do produce cleft palate in rodents (Trasler, 1965; Montenegro *et al.*, 1976), and aspirin also increases the frequency of clefting induced by cortisone (Fritz, 1976). Thus, it is quite possible that prostaglandins do participate in normal palatal development, and that indomethacin produces an inhibition of embryonic cyclooxygenase sufficient to block the effects of exogenous arachidonic acid, but not sufficient to produce cleft palate by itself.

E. GLUCOCORTICOIDS, SHELF ELEVATION, AND PROGRAMMED CELL DEATH

Glucocorticoids induce a delay in the elevation of palatal shelves (Walker and Fraser, 1957; Walker and Patterson, 1978; Gasser and Goldman, 1983), and they affect programmed cell death (Greene and Kochhar, 1973; Herold and Futran, 1980; Goldman *et al.*, 1981). It was once thought that the delay in shelf elevation was sufficient to explain cortisone induction of cleft palate, since it was assumed that when the palatal shelves finally do become horizontal, they are too far apart to meet in the midline and fuse. However, an *in vivo* study by Greene and Kochhar (1973) using frozen, cryostat-sectioned fetal heads from glucocorticoid-treated ICR mice showed that, in addition to showing a delay in elevation, palatal shelves made contact but then failed to undergo epithelial breakdown and fusion. This is consistent with studies showing that epithelial cell death can occur in the absence of shelf contact (Smiley and Koch, 1972; Tyler and Koch, 1974; Goldman *et al.*, 1981). Thus, the cells of the normal palatal epithelium are programmed to die and this is independent of the contact between the palatal shelves, but both of these events can be influenced by glucocorticoids.

In a recent report by Walker and Patterson (1978), fetuses from cortisone-treated CD-1 mice were released from the uterus and amnion and chorion and allowed to develop for 8 hours in a fluid medium with the umbilical cord left intact. Removal of these tissues permits shelves from glucocorticoid-treated fetuses as well as controls to move with delay to the horizontal and fuse, indicating that fetal membranes and tongue are major obstacles to shelf elevation in glucocorticoid-treated mice. However, even under these conditions, shelves exposed to glucocorticoids appeared to fuse less readily than controls. The *in vivo* studies of frozen cryostat sections were extended to include the highly sensitive strain A/J and the less sensitive strain B10 (Goldman *et al.*, 1981). Shelf contact occurred in A/J subsequent to a steroid-promoted delay in shelf elevation; the percentage of cortisone-treated fetal heads showing lysosomal activity was virtually unaffected. In an *in vitro* culture model the actions of cortisol on medial edge epithelium have been examined in the highly sensitive strains A/J, CD-1, and ICR and in the more resistant strains B6 and B10 (Herold and Futran, 1980; Goldman *et al.*, 1981). In this culture model, cortisol prevented the programmed breakdown of the medial edge epithelium and inhibited in this epithelial population the synthesis and/or release of various lysosomal enzymes, such as acid phosphatase or trimetaphosphatase (Goldman *et al.*, 1981; Ads *et al.*, 1983). These changes were produced by cortisol only in shelves of the susceptible strains which have high levels of glucocorticoid receptors, suggesting that cortisol–receptor interactions may be involved in the steroid inhibition of programmed cell death in this palatal epithelium.

These results provide further evidence for the hypothesis that inhibition of programmed cell death is also important in glucocorticoid-promoted clefting. The inhibition of programmed cell death, like the delay of shelf elevation, is related to genetic differences in susceptibility to steroid-induced cleft palate.

Receptors, Protein Synthesis, and Programmed Cell Death

The *in vitro* model may be useful in helping to examine the biochemical mechanisms underlying the teratogenic action of glucocorticoids in inhibiting programmed cell death in the absence of the mother. This method has been used to compare the effect of exogenous arachidonic acid on programmed cell death *in vitro* and *in vivo* in sensitive and resistant mouse strains (Piddington *et al.*, 1983). Exogenous arachidonic acid significantly reduced the frequency of palatal clefting in both A/J and CD-1 strains treated with cortisone *in vivo*. Arachidonic acid in vitro (1 ng to 1 µg/ml) reversed the inhibition of medial edge epithelial breakdown by cortisol in palatal shelves of CD-1 and A/J mice and the reversal was inhibited by indomethacin (100 ng/ml). Thus, arachidonic acid reversed the teratogenic effect of glucocorticoids both in the embryo and in organ cultures, and indomethacin prevented the corrective action of arachidonic acid *in vivo* and *in vitro*. Indomethacin alone also inhibits programmed cell death *in vitro* (Piddington *et al.*, 1983; Montenegro *et al.*, 1984).

The inhibition of programmed cell death of the palatal midline epithelium in this *in vitro* model by cortisol is virtually completely blocked by the antiglucocorticoid cortexolone, which only blocks by competitive binding of the glucocorticoid receptor site (Goldman *et al.*, 1983a). This inhibition produced by cortisol is also prevented by the protein synthesis blocker cycloheximide (Goldman *et al.*, 1983c). Thus, blockade of programmed cell death by glucocorticoids involves the glucocorticoid receptor site and requires protein synthesis.

IV. Phenytoin and Cleft Palate

A. COMMON MECHANISM WITH GLUCOCORTICOIDS?

Both phenytoin and glucocorticoids have many aspects of teratogenicity in common. Zimmerman *et al.* (1970) have shown that glucocorticoid exposure during the critical embryonic period causes inhibition of RNA and protein synthesis in mouse fetal palates. Phenytoin also significantly and persistently depresses embryonic palatal RNA and protein synthesis in the cleft palate-sensitive A/J strain as compared to the resistant B6 strain of mice (Sonawane and Goldman, 1981). Both phenytoin and glucocorticoids induce general developmental retardation and diminution of the embryonic muscular movements at an early embryonic stage, indicating interference with palatal shelf rotation (Walker, 1979). Mandibular differentiation can also be adversely affected by cortisone and phenytoin (Goldman *et al.*, 1983a).

When phenytoin is given in conjunction with cortisone, it does not alter the frequency of isolated cleft palate induced by the latter, suggesting a common pathway (Fritz, 1976). Recently, in a study of the comparative teratogenicity of cortisone and phenytoin in mice a probit analysis indicated that both agents may have an identical mechanism (McDevitt *et al.*, 1981).

B. Genetics of Susceptibility

As in the case with glucocorticoids, susceptibility to cleft palate produced by phenytoin is affected in part by genes within the *H-2* region of chromosome 17 (Gasser *et al.*, 1980; Goldman *et al.*, 1982, 1983a,b) and within the *H-3* region of chromosome 2 (Goldman *et al.*, 1983b). Other genes are involved. Mapping studies indicate that susceptibility to phenytoin is influenced by the same two genes within the *H-2* as susceptibility to cortisone (Goldman, *et al.*, 1983b). Furthermore, susceptibility to phenytoin-induced cleft lip with or without cleft palate is also influenced by *H-2* in mice of the A/J background (Goldman *et al.*, 1983a).

C. Metabolic Differences

Martz *et al.* (1977) proposed an interesting theory that phenytoin-induced palatal clefting may be due to an arene oxide (epoxide) metabolite. They proposed this theory on the finding of "covalent" binding of [^{14}C]phenytoin to embryonic tissues after maternal injection and that embryonic toxicity and the teratogenicity of phenytoin were increased with TCPO, an inhibitor of the epoxide hydratase. However, two recent findings from different approaches tend to cast doubt on the validity of this theory. Atlas *et al.* (1981) have shown that phenytoin-induced clefting does not correlate with inbred strains having arene oxide metabolic capability as compared with those that do not. Moreover, Wells *et al.* (1982) have shown that embryonic toxicity was produced by L-nirvanol, a metabolite of the hydantoin mephenytoin, but not by its D isomer, D-nirvanol. Only L-nirvanol, the isomer producing less arene oxide, demonstrated embryonic toxicity, thus raising doubt concerning the arene oxide as the putative hydantoin teratogen.

D. Phenytoin Receptors

The observation that the same genes in *H-2* and *H-3* appear to influence susceptibility to phenytoin as well as to glucocorticoids suggested to us that phenytoin may have the same teratogenic biochemical pathway as glucocorticoids (Goldman and Katsumata, 1980).

In our first study of the association between phenytoin teratogenicity and the glucocorticoid receptor, we demonstrated the blocking of [³H]dexamethasone incorporation into human embryonic palatal cells by 0.5 μM phenytoin (Goldman *et al.*, 1978). Salomon and Pratt (1979), however, were unable to demonstrate direct blocking of [³H]dexamethasone binding to the receptor of embryonic maxillary cytosol of Swiss Webster mice by 10 μM phenytoin. Although the method for solubilizing phenytoin was not given in their report, their negative results may be due to the limited solubility of phenytoin. Burnham *et al.* (1981) also reported saturable binding of phenytoin to distinct sites on the membrane fraction of rat brain when they used an alkaline buffer consisting of NaOH, Tris, and EDTA for solubilizing phenytoin. Recently, solubilizing phenytoin with Na_2CO_3, we have presented evidence that phenytoin is an alternative ligand of a glucocorticoid receptor affecting prostaglandin generation in A/J mice (Katsumata *et al.*, 1982). Binding of 5,5-diphenylhydantoin (phenytoin) and glucocorticoids to a common receptor was demonstrated for pulmonary and hepatic cytosols and thymocytes of A/J female mice. The phenytoin–protein complex is adsorbed by DNA cellulose and is incorporated into nuclei. Phenytoin, like glucocorticoids, inhibits the production of radioimmunassayable prostaglandins and thromboxanes in thymocytes. Thus, a common receptor is probably responsible for the inhibitory and teratogenic effects of these drugs.

Usually, ligands that bind to a receptor have similar chemical structures. Although phenytoin seems to behave as an alternative ligand of the glucocorticoid receptor affecting prostaglandin production, the chemical structure of the drug is quite different from that of glucocorticoids. Similar phenomena, however, have been reported for the estrogen receptor, which binds with diethylstilbestrol, *o,p'*-DDT, and chlordecone, an insecticide (Hammond *et al.*, 1979). These compounds have estrogenic properties, but have vastly different chemical structures from estrogen, especially in the case of chlordecone. Thus, it is possible that the drugs of different chemical structure can bind to a hormone receptor and effect a hormone-like response.

With respect to glucocorticoids, it recently has been demonstrated that certain calmodulin inhibitors may act as glucocorticoid receptor binders and antagonists, not via calmodulin inhibition, but through a direct interaction with the glucocorticoid receptor (Van Bohemen and Rousseau, 1982).

E. PHENYTOIN AND ARACHIDONIC ACID CASCADE

Phenytoin, as mentioned above, inhibits the production of 6-keto-prostaglandin $F_{1\alpha}$, the stable metabolite of prostacyclin, and thromboxane B_2, the stable metabolite of thromboxane A_2, in thymocytes of A/J mice in parallel to dexamethasone (Katsumata *et al.*, 1982). This observation suggests that it is possible that the teratogenic pathway of phenytoin may involve inhibition of arachidonic acid release, as does that of glucocorticoids.

F. PHENYTOIN AND PROGRAMMED CELL DEATH

Phenytoin inhibits breakdown of medial edge epithelium in embryonic shelves of sensitive mouse strains *in vitro* (Goldman *et al.*, 1983a). Moreover, this teratogenic action *in vitro* is blocked by cortexolone, the antiglucocorticoid, and cycloheximide. Thus, it appears that this site of teratogenic action of phenytoin is mediated by the glucocorticoid receptor and requires protein synthesis just as glucocorticoids do.

V. Summary

The production of cleft palate by glucocorticoids and phenytoin is a complicated interference in a complex developmental program involving many genetic and biochemical processes. The *H-2* histocompatibility region includes genes which affect (1) susceptibility to glucocorticoid- and phenytoin-induced cleft palate; (2) glucocorticoid receptor level in a variety of tissues including maternal and embryonic palates, adult thymuses, and lungs; and (3) the degree of inhibition of prostaglandin and thromboxane production by glucocorticoids and phenytoin in thymocytes. A gene linked to a minor histocompatibility locus (*H-3*) on the second chromosome also influences susceptibility to glucocorticoid- and phenytoin-induced cleft palate. Phenytoin is an alternate ligand for the glucocorticoid receptor affecting prostaglandin and/or thromboxane production.

The capacity of glucocorticoids to induce cleft palate is correlated with their anti-inflammatory potency. At least some of the anti-inflammatory effects of glucocorticoids can be explained by the inhibition of prostaglandin and/or thromboxane release, which in turn could be caused by inhibition of arachidonic acid release from phospholipids. Similar mechanisms may be involved in cleft palate induction, as exogenous arachidonic acid injected into pregnant rats and mice at the same time as glucocorticoids reduces the teratogenic potency of the steroids, and indomethacin, an inhibitor of cyclooxygenase, blocks the corrective action of arachidonic acid. Glucocorticoids and phenytoin cause a delay in shelf elevation, and this delay is promoted by fetal membranes and the tongue. However, the cells of the medial edge epithelium are programmed to die whether contact is made with the apposing shelf or not. Glucocorticoids and phenytoin interfere with this programmed cell death, and this interference by both drugs seems to be glucocorticoid receptor mediated, to require protein synthesis, and to be related to arachidonic acid release.

ACKNOWLEDGMENTS

The author is grateful for the enlightened participation of his collaborators, Drs. Gasser, Piddington, and Herold, and his colleagues, Drs. Katsumata and Gupta. This research was supported in part by Grants DE-4622 and DE-5041 from the National Institutes of Health.

REFERENCES

Ads, A. H., Piddington, R., Goldman, A. S., and Herold, R. (1983). *Arch. Oral Biol.* **28,** 1115–1119.

Andrew, F. D., Bowen, D., and Zimmerman, E. F. (1973). *Teratology* **7,** 167–176.

Atlas, S. A., Zweier, J. L., and Nebert, D. W. (1981). *Dev. Pharmacol. Ther.* **26,** 1–19.

Baxter, J., and Forsham, P. J. (1972). *Am. J. Med.* **53,** 573.

Baxter, J. D., and Funder, J. W. (1979). *New Eng. J. Med.* **301,** 1149.

Baxter, J. D., Harris, A. W., Tomkins, G. M., and Cohn, M. (1971). *Science* **171,** 189.

Beato, M., Homoki, J., and Sekeris, C. E. (1969). *Exp. Cell Res.* **55,** 107–117.

Becker, B., Shin, D. H., Palmerg, P. F., and Waltman, S. R. (1976). *Science* **194,** 1427–1428.

Biddle, F. G., and Fraser, F. C. (1977). *Genetics* **85,** 289–302.

Blackwell, C. J., Carnuccio, R., DiRosa, M., Flower, R. J. Parente, L., and Persico, P. (1980). *Nature (London)* **287,** 147–149.

Bonner, J. J., and Slavkin, H. C. (1975). *Immunogenetics* **2,** 213–218.

Bonner, J. J., and Tyan, M. L. (1982). *Immunogenetics* **9,** 243–248.

Britten, R. J., and Davidson, E. H. (1969). *Science* **165,** 349–351.

Burnham, W. M., Spero, L., Okasaki, M. M., and Madras, B. K. (1981). *Can. J. Pharmacol.* **59,** 402–404.

Butley, M. S., Erickson, R. P., and Pratt, W. B. (1978). *Nature (London)* **275,** 136–138.

Chepenik, K. P., and Greene, R. M. (1981). *Biochem. Biophys. Res. Commun.* **100,** 951–958.

Dahmus, M. E., and Bonner, J. (1965). *Proc. Natl. Acad. Sci. U.S.A.* **54,** 1370.

Dancoff, S. M., and Quastler, H. (1953). *In* "Essays on Information Theory in Biology" (H. Quastler, ed.). Univ. of Illinois Press, Urbana, Illinois.

Flower, R. J., Cheung, H.S., and Cushman, D. W. (1973). *Prostaglandins* **4,** 325–341.

Francke, U., and Gehring, U. (1980). *Cell* **22,** 657–664.

Fritz, H. (1976). *Experientia* **32,** 721–722.

Gasser, D. L., and A. S. Goldman. (1983). *In* "Biochemical Actions of Hormones" (G. Litwack, ed.), Vol. 10, pp. 357–382. Academic Press, New York.

Gasser, D. L., Mele, L., and Goldman, A. S. (1980). *Int. Convoc. Immunol., 7th, Niagara Falls,* pp. 320–328.

Gasser, D. L., Mele, L., Lees, D. D., and Goldman, A. S. (1981). *Proc. Natl. Acad. Sci. U.S.A.* **78,** 3147–3150.

Goldfeld, A. E., Rubin, C. S., Siegel, T. W., Shaw, P. A., Schiffer, S. G., and Waelsch, S. G. (1981). *Proc. Natl. Acad. Sci. U.S.A.* **78,** 6359–6361.

Goldman, A. S. (1977). *Handb. Teratol.,* **2,** 391–420.

Goldman, A. S., and M. Katsumata (1980). *In* "Etiology of Cleft Lip and Cleft Palate" (M. Melnick *et al.,* eds.), pp. 91–120. Liss, New York.

Goldman, A. S., Katsumata, M., Yaffe, S., and Shapiro, B. H. (1976). *Teratology* **13**, A22.

Goldman, A. S., Katsumata, M., Yaffe, S. J., and Gasser, D. L. (1977). *Nature (London)* **265**, 643–645.

Goldman, A. S., Shapiro, B. H., and Katsumata, M. (1978). *Nature (London)* **272**, 464–466.

Goldman, A. S., Herold, R. C., and Piddington, R. (1981). *Proc. Soc. Exp. Biol. Med.* **166**, 418–424.

Goldman, A. S., Baker, M. K., Tomassini, N., and Hummeler, K. (1982). *J. Craniofac. Genet. Dev. Biol.* **2**, 277–284.

Goldman, A. S., Fishman, C. L., and Baker, M. K. (1983a). *Proc. Soc. Exp. Biol. Med.* **173**, 82–86.

Goldman, A. S., Baker, M. K., and Gasser, D. L. (1983b). *Immunogenetics* **18**, 17–22.

Goldman, A. S., Baker, M. K., Piddington, R., and Herold, R. (1983c). *Proc. Soc. Exp. Biol. Med.* **174**, 239–243.

Greene, R. M., and Kochhar, D. M. (1973). *Teratology* **8**, 153–166.

Greene, R. M., and Kochhar, D. M. (1975). *Teratology* **11**, 47–56.

Gupta, C., and Goldman, A. S. (1982). *Science* **216**, 994–996.

Hackney, J. F. (1980). *Teratology* **21**, 39–70.

Hammond, B., Katzenellenbogen, B. S., Krauthammer, N., and McConnel, J. (1979). *Proc. Natl. Acad. Sci. U.S.A.* **76**, 6641–6643.

Hemm, R. D., Arslanoglou, L., and Pollock, J. J. (1977). *Teratology* **15**, 243–248.

Herold, R. C., and Futran, N. (1980). *Arch. Oral Bio.* **25**, 423–429.

Hirata, F., Schiffman, E., Venkatsubramanian, K., Salomon, D., and Axelrod, J. (1980). *Proc. Natl. Acad. Sci. U.S.A.* **77**, 2533–2536.

Ivanyi, P. (1978). *Proc. R. Soc. London Ser. B.* **202**, 117–158.

Kaiser, N., Milholland, R. J., Turnell, R. W., and Rosen, F. (1972). *Biochem. Biophys. Res. Commun.* **49**, 516–521.

Kalter, H. (1954). *Genetics* **39**, 185–196.

Kalter, H. (1965). *In* "Teratology: Principles and Techniques" (J. B. Wilson and J. Warkeny, eds.), pp. 57–80. Univ. of Chicago Press, Chicago, Illinois.

Kalter, H. (1973). *Teratology* **7**, A19.

Katsumata, M., Baker, M. K., Goldman, A. S., and Gasser, D. L. (1981a). *Immunogenetics* **13**, 319–325.

Katsumata, M., Baker, M. K., and Goldman, A. S. (1981b). *Biochim. Biophys. Acta* **676**, 245–256.

Katsumata, M., Gupta, C., Baker, M. K., Sussdorf, C. E., and Goldman, A. S. (1982). *Science* **218**, 1313–1314.

Lafuse, W. (1978). Ph.D. thesis, Johns Hopkins University, Baltimore.

Lafuse, W., and Edidin, M. (1980). *Biochemistry* **19**, 49–54.

Leach, K. L., Erickson, R. P., and Pratt, W. B. (1982). *J. Steroid Biochem.* **17**, 121–127.

Levine, A., Yaffe, S. J., and Back, N. (1968). *Proc. Soc. Exp. Biol. Med.* **129**, 86–88.

Litwack, G., Filler, R., Rosenfield, S. A., Lichtash, N., Wishman, C. A., and Singer, S. (1973). *J. Biol. Chem.* **248**, 7481–7486.

Martz, F., Failinger, C., III, and Blake, D. A. (1977). *J. Pharmacol. Exp. Ther.* **203**, 231–239.

McDevitt, J. M., Gautieri, R. F., and Mann, D. C. Jr. (1981). *J. Pharm. Sci.* **70**, 631–634.

Melnick, M., Jaskall, T., and Slavkin, H. C. (1981). *Immunogenetics* **13**, 443–449.

Meruelo, D., and Edidin, M. (1975). *Proc. Natl. Acad. Sci. U.S.A.* **72**, 2644–2648.

Meruelo, D., and Edidin, M. (1980). *Contemp. Top. Mol. Immunol.* **9**, 231–233.

Michaelson, J. (1981). *Immunogenetics* **13**, 167–171.

Miller, K. K. (1977). *Teratology* **15**, 249–252.

Montenegro, M. A., Cubrillo, P., and Palomino, H. (1976). *Rev. Med. Chile* **104**, 606–609.

Montenegro, M. A., Demus, D., Buenzalida, M., Illanes, J., and Mery, C. (1984). *IRCS Med. Sci.* **12**, 45.

Palumbo, D. A., and Vladutiu, A. O. (1979). *Experientia* **35**, 1103–1104.

Piddington, R. L., Herold, R. C., and Goldman, A. S. (1983). *Proc. Soc. Exp. Biol. Med.* **174**, 336–342.

Pinsky, L., and Di George, A. M. (1965). *Science* **147**, 402–403.

Pla, M., Zakany, J., and Fachet, J. (1976). *Folia Biol. (Prague)* **22**, 49–50.

Pratt, R. M., Salomon, D. S., Diewert, V. M., Erickson, R. P., Burns, R., and Brown, K. S. (1980). *Teratogen. Carcinogen. Mutagen.* **I**, 15–23.

Reminga, T., and Avery, J. K. (1972). *J. Dent. Res.* **51**, 1426–1430.

Rousseau, G. G., Baxter, J. D., and Tomkins, G. M. (1972). *J. Mol. Biol.* **67**, 99–115.

Salomon, D. S., and Pratt, R. M. (1976). *Nature (London)* **264**, 174–177.

Salomon, D. S., and Pratt, R. M. (1979). *Differentiation* **13**, 141–154.

Salomon, D. S., Zubairi, Y., and Thompson, E. B. (1978). *J. Steroid Biochem.* **9**, 95–107.

Schmid, W., Grote, H., and Sekeris, C. E. (1976). *Mol. Cell. Endocrinol.* **5**, 223–241.

Scott, W. J., and Klein, K. L. (1981). *In* "Culture Techniques" (D. Neubert and H. J. Merker, eds.), pp. 227–293. De Gruyter, Berlin.

Smiley, G. R., and Koch, W. E. (1972). *Anat. Rec.* **173**, 405–416.

Snell, G. D. (1981). *Science* **213**, 172–178.

Sonawane, B. R., and Goldman, A. S. (1981). *Proc. Soc. Exp. Biol. Med.* **168**, 175–179.

Sugahara, K., and Schwartz, N. B. (1981a). *Arch. Biochem. Biophys.* **214**, 589–601.

Sugahara, K., and Schwartz, N. B. (1981b). *Arch. Biochem. Biophys.* **214**, 602–609.

Svejgaard, A., and Ryder, L. P. (1976). *Lancet* **2**, 547–549.

Tam, S., Hong, S.-C., and Levine, L. (1977). *J. Pharmacol. Exp. Ther.* **203**, 162–168.

Trasler, D. G. (1965). *Lancet* **1**, 606–607.

Turnell, R. W., Kaiser, N., Milholland, R. J., and Rosen, F. (1974). *J. Biol. Chem.* **149**, 1133–1138.

Tyan, M. L. (1979). *Immunogenetics* **8**, 177–181.

Tyan, M. L., and Miller, K. K. (1978). *Proc. Soc. Exp. Biol. Med.* **158**, 618–621.

Tyler, M. S., and Koch, W. E. (1974). *J. Dent. Res.* **53**, A64.

Tzortzatou, G. G., Goldman, A. S., and Boutwell, W. C. (1981). *Proc. Soc. Exp. Biol. Med.* **166**, 321–324.

Van Bohemen, C. G., and Rousseau, G. G. (1981). *FEBS Lett.* **143**, 21–24.

Vane, J. R. (1971). *Nature (London) New Biol.* **231**, 232–235.

Vekemans, M., and Fraser, F. C. (1980). *Teratology* **21**, A73.

Vekemans, M., Taylor, B. A., and Fraser, F. C. (1978). *Am. J. Hum. Gen.* **30**, A105.

Vekemans, M., Taylor, B. A., and Fraser, F. C. (1981). *Genet. Res.* **38**, 320–331.

Walker, B. E. (1971). *Teratology* **4**, 39–42.

Walker, B. E. (1979). *J. Dent. Res.* **58**, 1740–1747.

Walker, B. E., and Fraser, F. C. (1957). *J. Embryol. Exp. Morphol.* **5**, 201–209.

Walker, B. E., and Patterson, A. (1978). *Teratology* **17**, 51–56.

Wells, P., Kupfey, A., Lawson, J. A., and Harbison, R. D. (1982). *J. Pharmacol. Exp. Ther.* **221**, 228–234.

Zimmerman, E. F., and Bowen, D. (1972). *Teratology* **5**, 335–344.

Zimmerman, E. F., Andrew, F., and Kalter, H. (1970). *Proc. Natl. Acad. Sci. U.S.A.* **67**, 779–785.

INDEX

A

Alcohol, 41
Androgens and sexual differentiation, 218
Anticonvulsant agents, 41
Arachidonic acid cascade and cleft palate, 91, 230

B

Basal lamina
characterization at oral active segment, 30
Bromodeoxyuridine, 123

C

Catecholamines in palate development
adenylate cyclase, 55, 72
β-adrenergic receptor, 73–77
dopamine concentration, 55
propranol, 72
(^{3}H) dihydroalprenolol, 73
Collagen
distribution, 21
Congenic strains, 175, 196, 221
Cyclic AMP on palate differentiation, 66
developmental change, 68, 96
epidermal growth factor, 96
glycosaminoglycans, 69
serotonin, 51

D

Diallel analysis, 178
Diazepam on palate
genetic effects, 56
shelf reorientation, 56

E

Ectomesenchymal phenotypes, *see* Mesenchymal phenotypes
Epidermal growth factor
on epithelial differentiation, 94
on epithelial growth, 94
medial palatal epithelium, 94
receptor, 97
Epithelial involvement during shelf reorientation, 27–28, 42
Epithelial–mesenchymal interaction of palate
chick–hamster recombinants, 113
interspecies recombinants, of alligator, chick, mouse, 150
mandible, with, 143
medial edges coincident, 150
mesenchyme specificity, 6, 113, 137–162
production of noncleft in chick, 156
Epithelial phenotypes, 4
medial edge, 4, 95
nasal, 4, 95
oral, 4, 95
oral active, 28
oral inactive, 28
Evolution of palate, 108
Extracellular matrix
chondroitin sulfate, 19
collagen, 19
fibronectin, 19
hyaluronate, 19, 54

F

5-Fluorouracil, 123

241

CONTENTS OF PREVIOUS VOLUMES

245